BRU

north african

cookery

arto der haroutunian

GRUB STREET | LONDON

Published in 2009 by
Grub Street
4 Rainham Close
London
SW11 6SS
Email: food@grubstreet.co.uk
Web: www.grubstreet.co.uk

First Published in Great Britain in 1985 by Century Publishing Co. Ltd

A CIP record for this title is available from the British Library

ISBN 978-1-906502-34-8

Printed and bound in Great Britain by MPG, Bodmin, Cornwall
This book is printed on FSC (Forest Stewardship Council) paper

Acknowledgements
Many thanks are due to all the authors and publishers from whose works I have quoted (see Bibliography), and apologies to those who unintentionally may have been overlooked.
   All works from Arabic and French have been edited and translated by myself.
   I must also thank all the kind people of North Africa who helped in many a small way in the shaping and writing of this book. Special thanks as well to Odile Thivillier and Rina Srabonian.

contents

introduction
history and people of the meghrib

'The only conceivable geographical unity in the Meghrib can be described as a repetitive pattern of mountains, plains, steppes and desert, and a related pattern of economic activity.'

Africa — A Geographical Study

'The Berber tribes in the West are innumerable, they are all Bedouins, members of groups and tribes. When one tribe is destroyed another takes its place and is as refractory and rebellious as the former one had been. It has taken the Arabs a long time to establish their dynasty in the land of Ifrigiyah[1] and the Meghrib.'

The Mugaddimah

The Meghrib ('the land of sunset' in Arabic)[2] extends over a coastal strip of about 4,200 kilometres along the southern shores of the Mediterranean. The Meghrib consists of four modern states — Morocco, Algeria, Tunisia and Libya.

Climatically there are three parallel east-west regions: the first is the Mediterranean coast, which represents one-fifth of the total area of Morocco, Algeria and Tunisia. In Libya, predominantly a desert land, this region exists only in a very narrow strip. The second is the intermediate, which incorporates the Atlas system of mountains in Morocco which extends towards Algeria and western Tunisia. The third and last is the Sahara desert in the south. The vegetation of the Meghrib, as with the rainfall, diminishes progressively from north to south. It is vital to appreciate the geography of the region since the entire history of its people has been shaped by these topographical divisions.

Early History

When the Meghrib first came into the light of history after the arrival of the Phoenicians (who built trading posts on its coastline in the first millennium BC), it was already inhabited by groupings of people who are today called Berbers.[3] The Phoenicians were merchant adventurers par excellence, thus were not particularly interested in the lands and people with whom they traded. As a result, the Carthaginians, who were related to the Phoenicians, gradually established their rule not only over the Phoenician trading settlements, but, in time, over most of the Meghribian coastline.

1   Ifrigiyah (the origin of the name Africa) was the Greek-Roman name for modern Libya and Tunisia.
2   I have used the Arab name Meghrib in my introduction as opposed to 'North Africa' since geographically the latter includes Egypt, which is out of context in this essay. In other chapters (for ease of description) I sometimes refer to the region as North Africa.
3   the Berbers call themselves Imazighen — free men.

The city of Carthage had been founded (near the modern Tunis) at the end of the ninth century BC by emigrants from Tyre (southern Lebanon). They cultivated commerical and blood relationships with the Berber tribes by intermarriage. They also dealt with the Negroes of western Africa by means of caravans that crossed the Sahara. The political structure of Carthage survived unaltered until she was conquered and destroyed by Rome. Throughout her long period of domination, Carthage remained strictly a commercial power, though during the fifth century BC, and more so during the last century of her existence, much more emphasis was put on agriculture — large areas of Northern Tunisia and the Sahil were planted with fruit, olive trees and cereals.

The Carthaginians, besides being excellent traders, were also known for their intense religiosity and superstitiousness, characteristics which survived their physical extinction, and which were passed onto and spread amongst the indigenous people (Berbers) of the Meghrib, causing havoc and great social unrest in post-Islamic Meghrib, particularly between the eighth and fifteenth centuries.

After two centuries of bloody confrontation Carthage finally fell to the might of Rome. The outstanding personality of the period was Hannibal, whose crossing of the Pyrenees in the spring of 218 BC with 40,000 men and elephants on the way to Rome has become a legend of inspiration and determination. Much was made of this epoch of Meghribian history by Algerians, Moroccans and Tunisians during the 'Wars of Liberation' of the twentieth century. Carthage resisted for three years, but was finally destroyed in 146 BC, fires raging for five days after her surrender.

'What remained after the destruction of this most important of the Liby-Phoenician cities, was the impact of her civilisation which spread widely among the Berbers — and the Punic language.'

A History of the Meghrib

In the early period Rome ruled only the Meghribi coastline (excepting Tunisia), but wanted a more definite frontier to enclose her territories. The Fossa regia (royal ditch) was begun by Scipio Africanus, and later 'limes' (Roman fortifications) were also constructed. The region was divided up into four provinces, and security was provided by the third Augustan legion. The legionaries were Roman citizens and a fair percentage were of Berber origin. By the middle of the second century AD 'it was the Africans who ensured order in Africa on behalf of Rome' (*L'Afrique Romaine*).

Economically Roman Africa was an agricultural domain. Wheat, olive oil, wine, marble, wood and mules were all exported to Rome, and large agricultural estates appeared in the Meghrib. Many towns were built with all the necessary social conveniences such as forums adorned with honorific monuments, market places and temples. The lack of water did not stand in the way of the Roman rulers. If water was not available or close at hand they brought it from afar. The great aqueducts striding across the desolated plains and mountain ranges remain as impressive monuments to the genius of Rome. 'These dams and cisterns made possible the building of the dead cities which astonish us today. That these works are now in ruins is not due to the failure of the rainfall and the springs. It is sometimes due to earth movements, but more usually to the hand of Man. For nearly 2,000 years the people of the country have been using Roman monuments as stone quarries for the building of houses and mosques. But wilful destruction by invaders also played havoc with the magnificent buildings the Romans left behind them' (*The Golden Trade of the Moors*). These 'wilful destroyers' were the Vandals, followed centuries later by the nomadic Arabs and Ottoman Turks. 'The civilised life which the Romans developed in the Meghrib during four centuries suffered an unmistakable setback in one century of Vandal rule' (*A History of the Meghrib*).

The Vandals, following attacks by the Visigoths, left Spain and entered the Meghrib in the expectation of finding in it both security and abundant food. Led by King Gaiseric they occupied — through pillage, war and marauding expeditions into Roman and Berber territories — most of the Meghrib. For a time they even possessed Sicily, Corsica and Sardinia. But their suzerainty withered away under persistent Byzantine attacks. The Vandal period is noted for the virulent conflicts between Arianism[4] and the Catholic Church; an important social element for it helped to ease, a century or so later, the advancement of Islam in the region and the total effacement of Christianity from some of its strongest outposts.

The Vandals were thrown out of the Meghrib by Byzantines in 533 AD primarily because Emperor Justinian wished to restore the Roman Empire to her former glory and, so it is said, because a certain Greek Orthodox bishop had confirmed a vision in which the Lord marched in front of the Emperor's troops to make Africa his! Vandal royalty and nobility were taken to Constantinople and the rest were in time absorbed into the indigenous Berber population.

Resistance to the Byzantines in the Meghrib from the Berber tribes lasted for well over 100 years. Belisarius (the first commander) was replaced by Solomon 'the Armenian', then his nephew Sergius, and thus followed a succession of Byzantine leaders who attempted to control and subdue the independent spirit of the Berber tribes. The Arabs, to their cost, were to experience similar rebellions a century or so later.

During the rule of Heraclius (610–641 AD) a semblance of peace and prosperity was achieved which, however, was tragically destroyed by the arrival of the Arabs. The history of the Meghrib then changed dramatically, for while during the Roman period the Berbers showed themselves ready to adopt Roman civilisation, the Latin language and the Christian religion — which had already penetrated deep into the desert — all these achievements were wiped out under the hooves of the invading Arab horses. For the Arabs brought with them a new dynamic egalitarian religion, a new unifying language of the 'Holy Book' and a primitive yet adaptable culture.[5]

Islam had arrived. It entered the Meghrib as a region of a new unstoppable force led by nomadic southern Arabian tribes, and augmented by converts from their newly conquered territories.

---

4 A Christian heresy started by Arius of Alexandria (fourth century AD) who instigated the doctrine that Christ was not truly divine.

5 Christianity disappeared completely from the Meghrib in a very short time. Only a few regions (Volubilis and Tangiers in Morocco) retained some Christian sanctuaries up to the ninth century.

'The common people follow the religion of the ruler'

Moorish saying

It is a great fallacy to call the North African Arab. There is in fact very little 'Arab' blood in a Meghrib — the majority of people being of Berber stock with a certain amount of Negro (from Sudan, Ghana and West Africa) and Arab (from southern Arabia) influence.

The Berbers are a composite race 'formed of dissimilar ethnological elements within which the Mediterranean type dominates'. Briefly, they emerged as a result of the intermingling of an eastern people, the Libou (hence Libya) who emigrated during the third to second millennium BC, with its prehistoric inhabitants who, in turn, originated from southern Spain. Berber tradition claims the race originated in Canaan (Palestine) with the biblical Goliath as their ancestor. The Persian historian al-Hamadani, in *Description du Maghreb et de l'Europe*, has this to say about Berber ancestry:

'The Berbers are the Hawwara, Zanata, Darisa, Maghila and Warfajjowa, and there are many other ... the Berbers originated in Palestine. They moved to Meghrib when their king, Goliath, was killed by David. They settled in the nearest Sus behind Tangier and in the furthest Sus some 2,050 miles from Qamuniya which is the place where al-Quyrawan starts today. The Berbers disdained to settle in towns. They prefer mountains and sandy deserts ... they are heedless and dull-witted, the prophet has said "the women among the Berber are of greater worth than the men".'[6]

A true Berber is of Caucasoid origin with fair skin, light hair, a short straight nose and fine thin lips much like all Mediterranean people. The 'semitic' characteristics (hooked nose, brown skin) are scarce outside historically Arab regions such as Fez, Kairwan etc; but what is evident in abundance is the admixture of negro blood (from African slaves). Indeed, as one travels further south throughout the entire region the negro element increases accordingly. The Berbers in the Moroccan Rif or the Algerian Kabylia regions are 'white' — a substantial proportion of them with blue eyes. The Tuareg and those living near Mauritania are black, although all speak one or other of the Berber dialects.

These Berber races are widespread throughout North Africa and the Sahara. Their language differs greatly in their sound systems, but very little in grammar and vocabulary. Today there are still ten to fifteen million people who speak a Berber 'language'[7] which has been enriched over the centuries by many Arabic, Latin and Punic words. There is little written literature, but a rich folk tradition, much of which is still not collected.

6   The fact that the prophet had never heard of Berbers or of the Meghrib did not stop bigoted persons (historians!) from passing on to posterity their racialist and sacrilegious opinions.
7   The language belongs to the 'Hamito-Semitic' family. Some of the dialects are Tuareg, Shawia, Tamazigt. All except the Tuareg use Arabic script. The latter use one derived from an original Berber alphabet.

The Arabs on the other hand are relative newcomers to the region, though some historians do claim that nomadic Arabian tribes have traversed the Sahara from time immemorial. This claim cannot be satisfactorily substantiated. The camel only arrived in the Sahara about the beginning of the Christian era, previous to which man had travelled with oxen, on horseback or in horse-drawn chariots. There were also no practical (or economic) reasons for the pre-Islamic Arabian tribes to penetrate the Meghrib. It was Islam and the desire to 'internationalise' it that drove the Bedouin of southern Arabia to the Atlantic coast and later into Spain.[8]

In 642 AD, after the fall of Alexandria (Egypt), the Arab army under the leadership of Amr b.al-As started the penetration of the Meghrib. Initially (as was the custom with Bedouin tribes) these raids were for slaves and booty, but after 667 AD a systematic war or conquest was initiated. When the Arab armies entered the Meghrib for the first time to stay, they met resistance, not, as they expected, from the Byzantine army, but from the strong Berber tribes.

The African Christians and the Berber tribes formed an alliance, but their forces were defeated by the Arabs near Tahirt, and the Arabs marched all the way to Tangier. These forces were led by a great commander — Ugba — who also laid the foundation of Kairwan (Tunisia) which he intended to use as a military and cultural base for spreading Islam amongst the Berbers. In time the Byzantines left the region, leaving the Berbers to fend for themselves; which they did successfully for a short period under the leadership of such formidable personalities as Kusaila and al-Kahina (the priestess). The former led the Christian Berbers of the Algerian Auras, the latter the Jarawa Jewish tribe, again from the Auras.

'The Islamization of the Berbers went further than their Arabization, and in many ways the latter process was the product of the former — a great inducement to Islamization was enlistment in the Arab army and being treated (at least during the period of conquest) on an equal footing with the Arabs in the distribution of booty. The Arab conquest of Spain in the eighth century especially contributed towards the Islamization of the Berbers since it opened to their warriors a new field for fighting and gain.'

A History of the Meghrib

However, the Berbers' innate love of freedom and a democratically based social structure, so well illustrated in their fierce resistance throughout the centuries against Spaniards, Turks and, in our own times, the French, was equally, if not more forcefully, applied against the Arabs. For generations, the Arabs were able to control only certain towns and cantonments outside of which — as with Carthage, Rome, Byzantium and Ottoman Turkey before them — the countryside belonged to the Berbers.

Thus throughout the centuries (with sporadic exceptions) the whole of North Africa was controlled by one or other of the Berber tribes — religious groupings — culminating with two truly outstanding dynasties, the Almoravids and the Almohads.

---

8   It is estimated that the initial Arab thrust into the Meghrib consisted of only 20,000 warriors; that the large migration of Banu Hilal and Banu Sulaim tribes consisted of 50,000 warriors and their families — many of the wives already of non-Arab origin.

During 800 years of Arab rule four dynasties of importance succeeded one another in the Meghrib. The first of these tribo-religious groupings was the Kharijites, a religious political movement which harassed the ruling Umayyad dynasty between 660–675 AD. In Tahirt (Tunisia) a Persian, Abdul-Rahman-b.Rustam, founded the theocratic Rustamid state which was an offshoot of Kharijism. In 800 AD, Ibrahim-b.Agleb became the governor of Tunisia and founded the Aghlabid dynasty which lasted till 909 AD. The Aghlabid rulers were great constructors. They rebuilt the magnificent mosques of Kairwan and Zaituna (Tunisia); also the *ribat* of Susa (a monastery for the education of warriors for the holy war against the Christians of Sicily — the conquest of which island commenced in 827 AD). The Aghlabids also lavished money and attention on agriculture, especially the building of hydraulic works on Roman foundations.

They were followed, in Morocco, by the Idrisids, father and son, who built their capital Fez where Arab refugees from Spain and Tunisia settled — the latter in their district quarter Adwat al Kairawan, while those from Spain were in Adwat al Andalus. These two groups brought new blood into the Meghrib and although for many generations they held aloof from each other, from these two communities sprang all that is uniquely Moroccan in culture, learning and civilisation. Both Idrisids, father and son, are now the most worshipped saints in Morocco, and their tombs are places of pilgrimage. These two outstanding leaders were the first to attempt to organise the country and introduce Moslim civilisation. After their deaths Morocco was divided between their descendants which soon made her the object of rivalry between the Fatimides (also known as Ismailis),[9] the Umayyads of Spain and several ambitious Berber chieftains.

It was not surprising that many Arabs and Berbers were induced to emigrate to Spain where there was peace and prosperity.[10] The Arabs of course retained the best lands while the Berbers were left with the mountainous parts — their homelands even today in Morocco and Algeria.

In the middle of the eleventh century a new religio-political force, sweeping northwards from the Sahara, conquered the whole of Morocco and Algeria. These were the Almoravids — the Spanish name for the al-Murabitun (people of the monastery fortress) — a fierce religious confederation of Sanhaja Berbers led by two extraordinary leaders, Abu Bakr and Yusuf b.Tashufin. The latter built Marrakech, enlarged Fez and conquered most of Muslim Spain. But his descendants — having found themselves surrounded by an ancient and refined civilisation which they (once hardy, simple nomads) found very pleasant — wholeheartedly threw themselves into exploiting the fruits of their conquests. They began to amass wealth, surround themselves with luxury and soon 'became incapable of continuing their military exploits — quickly became sunk in bigotry and narrowness of spirit, going as far as to burn in the public square in Cordova the masterpiece of eastern theologian and mystic al-Ghazali, because they considered it to be heterodox' (*Cambridge History of Islam*).

9   An extremist group who failed to secure Morocco or Algeria, moved on to Tunisia and finally settled in Egypt where they founded a powerful dynasty which lasted until destroyed by Saladin in 1171 AD.
10   Under Abdul Rahman III (912-61), one of the truly outstanding Arab leaders of all time, who forged differing ethnic groups in Andalus into one nation, and who avidly encouraged the arts, sciences and was the instigator of the remarkable Hispano-Moorish culture.

The Almoravids were quickly replaced by the Almohads — Spanish name for the *al-Muwahidun* (those who proclaim the unity of God) — who, under the brilliant leadership of Abd-al-Mumin (a Berber from the region of Tlemcen), conquered the whole of North Africa and Southern Spain.

The empire of the Almohads marks the apogee of Berber power in the history of the Meghrib. Al-Mumin was perhaps the first Meghribi leader who deliberately set out to create a unified Muslim community. He developed a professional administration — *Makhzin* — to levy taxes on agriculture and trade to raise money for the sustenance of the armed forces. His reign brought prosperity: commerce flourished, and foreign merchants from city states such as Pisa, Marseilles and Genoa opened *funduks* (warehouses) all along the Mediterranean coastline. Urban life prospered. Marrakech was enlarged and endowed with monuments such as the al-Kutabiya mosque. Algiers, Tunis, Rabat and other towns were enlarged. At the same time, with the help of Spanish Muslims,[11] notable achievements in architecture, music, medicine, poetry and philosophy were attained. The writings of Ibn Rushd (Averróes), who had an appointment at the Almohad court, were one of the principal means of introducing the philosophy of Aristotle to Europe — just awaking from her centuies' long sleep.

Yet the Almohad empire, with all its achievements, crumbled and, within forty years, all had vanished. There were several causes for this cataclysm. *A History of Africa* says: 'Like the Abbasid empire or that of the Charlemagne, the Almohad empire was too large for the resources of its time.' There was also no national unity in the empire of the type that was then beginning to emerge for some European peoples such as the Portuguese, French and English. 'The very concept was difficult for the Berbers of this time to grasp. Their basic loyalty was to their own tribes and they could not readily contemplate larger or other units' (*A History of Africa*). Other contributory factors were Christians who, for long on the defensive, were now beginning to make encroachments into Muslim territories in Spain and North Africa; simultaneously Arab Bedouin tribes were steadily eroding the resources and the power of the government in the plateau and steppe lands.

The collapse of the Almohad state brought the political unity of the Meghrib to an end. It was henceforth divided into three regions — between the Hafsids, Abd-al-Wadids and the Marinids — a pattern that was firmly established during Ottoman rule in the sixteenth century, and which was to endure into modern times.

The Sixteenth Century Onwards

At the beginning of the sixteenth century the Meghrib was in complete political decay, a situation which helped both the Christians (in Portugal and Spain) and the Ottomans to penetrate with intent to stay. The Christians, after some initial success, withdrew because of the discovery of both the New World and the route to India via the Cape of Good Hope. The political and economic potential that these discoveries implied soon attracted the notice of the Spanish, Portuguese and English governments. But the Ottomans, who had founded small military governments based on privateering,

---

11   Not all Spanish Muslims were of Arab or Berber origin. Indeed most were converts of either Spanish, Visigoth or Vandal blood. There was a lot of intermarriage. Arabized children were called *Mozarabs*.

stayed and expanded.

The architects of Ottoman rule in the Meghrib were the Barbarossa brothers who came from the Greek island of Mytilene (ancient Lesbos). They were sea-rovers operating from Goulelta (Tunisia). The eldest brother, Aruj, had gained great prestige and, with covert help from the Hafsid Sultan (who had shares in his booty), he had succeeded in extending his authority throughout north-west Algeria. He was slain while fleeing from the Spaniards who, with the Ottomans, were carving up the Meghrib. Aruj's work was carried on by his brother Khayr al-Din who was to become the founder of the *ojak* (home, hearth) of Algiers, better known as the Regency of Algiers.

From 1525 Algiers became the principal centre of Ottoman authority in the Maghrib, whence they carried out their expansionist plans against their chief rival in Africa — Spain. For a century or more governors were directly appointed or removed by Istanbul, but in time the regencies (Algiers, Tunis and Tripoli) acquired a considerable degree of independence although they always recognised the suzerainty of the Sultan in the Sublime Porte, and were obliged to contribute naval and military assistance when called upon to do so. The *ojak* of Algiers was the most powerful, and the ships at her disposal the most numerous — the primary use of these being privateering. The ports of Tripoli, Tunis and Algiers as well as being centres for trade (wheat, olive oil etc) were also bases from which the corsairs operated. The majority of these were renegades (from Corsica, Sicily or Calabria) or Europeans converted to Islam. The Barbarossa brothers were Greek, the four Ottoman governors of Algiers between 1574-1586 were Sardinian, Albanian, Hungarian and Venetian in turn. Those operating from Moroccan bases were Muslims of Spanish origin. The Ottoman soldiery (Janissaries) too were of non-Turkish stock. They were primarily drawn from Greece, Georgia and Armenia and were converted to Islam at an early age and brought up in a disciplined military way of life. There were constant disagreements between the corsairs and the military who wished to share in the former's booty of plunder and slaves (negroes and Christians).

The countryside, however, was little affected by the Ottoman administration. 'Tribalism continued to be the most important feature of social organisation and the Turks contributed towards its entrenchment by using tribal chiefs for keeping their respective areas under control' (*A History of the Meghrib*).

Algeria became an oligarchic republic with the ruler or *dey*[12] elected for life like the Doge of Venice. This form of government lasted till 1830. In Tunisia and Tripolitania, similar Ottoman institutions were installed, and both lands profited from the sea-faring trade of privateering. The slaves were consigned to *bagnios* where life was harsh, but no worse than for their counterparts in European vessels. Unlike Algiers, however, hereditary dynasties were developed in time in Tunisia and Tripoli and these, although they did still pay lip service to the Sultan in Istanbul, were for all practical purposes independent 'corsair' states.

The great days of those states were during the sixteenth and seventeenth centuries. By the eighteenth, the growing technical superiority of the European fleets was already reducing profits from the captures. Algiers, which had a population of

12 From Turkish *dayi* (uncle). Elected by the Diwan, principle officers of state.

over 100,000 in the sixteenth century of which one-third were slaves, could claim only a mere hundred or so slaves by the time of the French attacks in 1830. Slavery was a profitable trade and charitable missions[13] were created to look after their welfare.

'European historians have usually taken a very unfavourable view of the North African or as they call them the "Barbary" states during this period. It was in fact a time of slow decay for Islam, in the west just as in the east; and it can not be said that the Barbary states in the Turkish period made any particular contribution to civilisation. Still the same could be said of many other countries — the bad reputation of the North African was primarily a reaction to the privateering; which was "legal", as was Elizabethan English [privateering].'

North West Africa

In Tunisia a Cretan Muslim, Husain Bey, created a dynasty which lasted from 1705–1957 when the last Bey Amin was deposed on the proclamation of the Tunisian Republic; while in Tripolitania, in 1711, Ahmad Qaramanli founded a dynasty which lasted over 120 years. Tunisia had a less anarchic and troubled political life than both Algeria and Morocco which, though ruled by several local dynasties, went through much pain. The Ottomans were never able to control Morocco, though a great deal of time and effort was spent with that intent. The Saidits (1553–1654) wasted their reign fighting off the Portuguese and Spanish. The outstanding leader of this period was Ahmad al-Mansour who took power after the 'Battle of the Three Kings' (1578). He founded an army on the Ottoman model — incorporating renegades from Andalusia, Turks, negroes and Spaniards — and did a thriving trade with England and France.

Another outstanding personality was Moulay Ismail (1672–1727) who was proclaimed Sultan on the death of his brother. He struggled for several years to bring the country to submission. Law and order were established by brutal means. Piracy became a state enterprise with the Sultan owning half of the vessels operating from Moroccan ports. His descendants tried hard to keep control over the country, but with little success. Morocco, more than any of her Meghribi neighbours, was a backward-looking, tribal society with little political infra-structure, no technology or social cohesion.

The beginning of the nineteenth century saw the collapse of the British, French and Spanish American colonies which, one after the other, acquired local independence. It also heralded the end of the Napoleonic wars in Europe, the further weakening of the Ottoman empire and a new phenomenon — colonisation of that vast yet uncharted continent of Africa.

The French, who had not made much impact in the Americas, had several footholds in West Africa and were the first to make a move. They needed a pretext, and it arrived in the shape of a fly swatter. On April 29 1827 the Dey of Algiers, Husain, struck the French consul with a swatter. This insult to a representative of the French government started a crisis which grew out of hand and, due to internal party politics and commercial pressures, King Charles X was forced to announce his decision to invade Algiers. There was no heart in the French assault, but it was nevertheless an opportune

---

13   The 'Trinitarians' and 'Notre Dame de la Merci' as well as the 'Lazarists'.

moment for the French who took advantage of an internal crisis in the Dey's affairs. In May 1830 an army of 37,000 men sailed from Toulon, landed at Sidi Ferruch and immediately entered Algiers. The Dey capitulated and left for Naples. The French had won an easy victory — but not for long.

The Berber tribes, as ever, rose up in arms. They were led by an outstanding leader called Abd al-Qadir who raised the countryside in a holy war against the Christian infidels. French propaganda, claiming that they had come to liberate the people from their Turkish tyrants, received the rebuff it deserved. The age however was 'the age of imperialism and after months and years of indecision it was decided to conquer and colonise the whole country in the high Roman style' (*North West Africa*).[14] The effects of the conquest were two fold. Firstly there was destruction, loss of lives and money, and indeed the population of the country fell from 3 million in 1830 to 2,100,000 some forty years later. The military victories were then followed by colonisation with Italians, Maltese and French (particularly after the Franco-Prussian war) settling on the most fertile lands and pushing the natives further south towards the desert. Mosques were converted to churches, Muslim feast days ceased to be legal holidays and large portions of tribal lands were confiscated. In 1841 General Bugeaud told his soldiers, 'You have often beaten the Arabs. You will beat them again, but to rout them is a small thing. They must be subdued . . . the Arabs must be reduced to submission so that only the French flag stands upon the African soil' (*Life in Africa*).

Once French rule was established in Algeria it was only a matter of time and diplomacy before France extended her control to the other Meghribi lands. In 1881 Tunisia lost her independence. The country was not conquered, but became a protectorate, retaining its monarchy and something of her former state and nationhood — although in practice all form of authority was soon in the hands of French officials. There are those who claim that the best thing that ever happened to the Meghrib was the arrival of the French. In *The Arab Revival*, Francesco Gabrieli said: 'Whatever has happened since, the French expedition to Algiers in 1830 must be regarded as a service to civilisation more important then any question of nationality. . . . Opinions about this war will vary, according to whether or not one recognises the right of a superior civilisation to impose itself on primitive peoples, to give them the benefits of technical progress and to take in exchange the riches which they themselves cannot appreciate, beginning with their land.' This, of course, from a writer whose countrymen so savagely conquered Ethiopia and Libya (in 1911), and found themselves involved in a long and bitter struggle with the Arabs, particularly in Cyrenaica! Finally, in 1912, Morocco was made a French protectorate. The Moroccans however, led by Abd al-Karim, fought for independence until 1934.

If the nineteenth century was the age of colonialism, the twentieth was that of nationalism, and after the Second World War all the countries of the Meghrib acquired their independence. After two years of terrorism and lengthy negotiations, Morocco was granted independence. Several years of civil disturbances, with killings on both sides, resulted in Tunisia being declared an independent state with Habib Bourguiba forming the first government. In 1949 the UN General Assembly voted that Libya

14   In 1848 northern Algeria was proclaimed an integral part of France, then in 1919 the whole of Algeria was made part of metropolitan France.

should become an independent state with Mohammad Idris as king. Algeria, the first victim of colonisation, was also to be the last to free herself. The French came with blood and left with blood. General Charles de Gaulle offered self-determination, and independence was formally proclaimed in 1962.

For the first time since the days of Carthage and Rome the four nations of the Meghrib are truly independent of foreign domination, but as the Stevens's put it so succinctly in *Algeria and Sahara*, they are searching for an identity: 'A country without history may be blessed. Countries burdened with two thousand years of history documented beyond denial may at times ask to be relieved of the burden, but a country which has just won its independence not only wants to have a history but wants that history to be its own property, not a footnote to that of Spain, France, Morocco or Turkey.'

Time however is on their side and gradually they will resurrect their past and build their future in freedom and peace — two commodities of which the Meghrib has had very little for generations.

Social and Religious Influences

'Better a handful of dry dates, and contentment, than to own the gate of peacocks and to be kicked in the eye by a broody camel'

Libyan proverb

Islam is the religion of the Meghrib. The *Koran* contains the very words that God put in the mouth of the Prophet Mohammad; it contains the truth and defines the veracity of all previous revelations and the righteousness of all the prophets. The *Koran*, coupled with the *Hadith* (the record of how the Prophet and the early Muslims had behaved), is a way of life for all people. The teachings of those two books more than anything else have created the Meghribi society as it was and still is today.

Using modern terminology we could say that the Meghrib is part of the 'third world'. This connotation suggests a backward agriculture and economy, little industrialisation and lack of the sort of social-welfare amenities to which most Europeans are accustomed. And indeed the poverty prevalent throughout the region is one that has been created over the centuries, one that cannot be eliminated overnight. Governments are trying hard to eradicate this misery and better the lot of their people — some using socialist ideas and methods, others keeping in line with general Islamic concepts. The land is being cultivated at a faster rate than ever; housing, health and education are given top priority. Time and wise leadership are all that is needed. Some people see all the guidance and all the answers to their problems in the *Koran*, others believe modern society — or 'western' society — with materialist and technological solutions, is the answer.

The *Koran* — apart from dealing with religio-philosophical dicta such as the concept of God, man and the universe, life after death etc — also has a great deal to say about moral and spiritual values, social issues such as prayer, fasting, pilgrimage and public affairs. These 'do's' and 'don'ts' are clearly stipulated.

A good Muslim must pray five times a day (before sunrise, at noon, in the afternoon, at sunset and at night).[15] He need not do so in a mosque if one is not available. Anywhere will do, so long as his heart and the ground chosen are clean. A Muslim lays a small carpet (*kilim* or *sajabada*) on the ground facing towards the East or, more accurately, the holy shrine (*ka'aba*) in Mecca. For God said, 'The whole earth has been purified for me for the worship of God. . . . Your Lord says "Pray unto me, I will answer your prayer"' (*The Forgiving One*, 40:61). When a person is travelling and is unable to pray, the noon and afternoon services can be combined. Similarly the sunset and the night prayers can be combined.

The Muslim year differs by ten days from the calendar year, hence the Muslim months do not always come at the same season. In the month of Ramadan the *Koran* prescribes fasting — 'Fasting is prescribed to you as it was prescribed for those before you, that you may attain to righteousness' (*The Cow*, 2:184). A good Muslim is required, throughout the month, to abstain from food, drink and sexual intercourse from dawn to sunset. The fast is obligatory upon every adult, with certain exceptions (those who are sick or are travelling, a woman with child or those who are old and find the severity of the fast too hard to bear).

The month of fasting being a lunar month, comes eleven days earlier every year thus rotating through the year so that in every part of the world it falls in all seasons of the year. This naturally entails great hardship to some Muslims — those who live in the tropics or in the Scandinavian lands, for instance. I have heard of Muslims working and living in Norway and Sweden who fly back to the Middle East for the month of Ramadan for they find it physically difficult to fast in northern climatic conditions. Fasting is a good psychological factor for it 'levels' all — rich and poor alike. The rich experience the pangs of hunger and thirst as much as the poor: 'Hunger and privation cease to be mere expressions and become an experience shared in common' (*Islam*).

Westerners who travel on business or holiday in Muslim lands find this abstention from food and drink from dawn to sunset during the month of Ramadan 'bizarre' and unbearable. My advice has always been to try and understand the moral and religious laws of their hosts and not to ostensibly appear to be breaking the people's sacred mode of living. Most, if not all, hotels and restaurants in the Meghrib will serve non-Muslims even though they refrain from drinking even a glass of water themselves.

There are those who 'forget' to fast. They justify this omission by quoting a saying of the Prophet, 'When one forgets and eats and drinks, he should complete his fast, for Allah made him eat and drink' (*A Manual of Hadith*).

The Koranic law is very specific about what a good Muslim should eat. The first condition is that it must be lawful (*halal*).[16] The second condition is that it should be good (*tayyib*), or fit for eating (not unclean or offensive to one's taste). One must be moderate in regards to quantity and quality: 'And eat and drink and be not immoderate, for He does not love the immoderate' (*The Heights*, 7:31).

God's name must be invoked before animals are slaughtered. And the Koran states to all Muslims:

---

15 This is called *Salat*.
16 Equivalent to Jewish *kashrut* — kosher. This carries the double significance of being earned lawfully as well as not being prohibited.

*'It is lawful for you to eat the flesh of all beasts other than that which hereby
is announced to you.
Game is forbidden while you are on a pilgrimage.
You are forbidden carrion, blood and the flesh of swine.
You are forbidden the flesh of slaughtered animals, and of those beaten
or gored to death . . .'*

The Table, 5:3–5:4

Fish is permitted, as are all vegetables, fruits and dairy food. A Muslim is meant to be tolerant towards non-Muslims. He is advised to eat with Jews and Christians. 'The game of the sea is that which has been hunted, and its food is that which is cast forth. And Ibn Abas said, Eat of the game of the sea whether it is [killed] by a Christian or a Jew or a Magician' (*A Manual of Hadith*).

All kinds of intoxicants are prohibited. This not only applies to drinks, but also to drugs.

During the last ten days of Ramadan some people stay in the mosque and devote themselves to Koranic studies and the remembrance of God. A good Muslim is also expected (if his means are sufficient) to go on a pilgrimage to Mecca once in his life. There, setting aside all earthly thoughts, he must devote himself to God.

*'Here am I. O Allah, here am I,
Here am I. There is no associate with thee;
All praise is thine and all Bounty;
There is no associate with thee.'*

Life has always been hard in desert and steppe lands. Nature often has been cruel to the Bedouin. Floods, famine and drought have created a sturdy, hard personality, but there were times when even the Bedouin and the Fellah found themselves in despair. Such a time was in the thirteenth century when the great historian Abd al-Latif al-Baghdadi visited Egypt and North Africa. Droughts and famine of unsurpassable scale ravaged the land and drove the people to inhuman extremes. I quote, not to sentimentalise, but to give an idea of the kinds of suffering that the North African people have undergone during their history, and also to illuminate the contract between man and God which runs in the very soul of a good Muslim.

*'They could no longer hold out any hope of the rise of the Nile, and in consequence,
already the price of commodities had risen. The provinces were made desolate by
drought; the inhabitants foresaw an inevitable scarcity, and the dread of the famine
excited tumultuous movements among them. The inhabitants of villages and of
country districts retired to the principal towns of the provinces, a large number
emigrated. . . . When the sun had entered the sign of the Ram, the air was corrupted,
the plague and contagion began to make itself felt, and the poor, pressed by the
famine which struck them always, ate carrion, corpses, dog and the excrement and
the filth of animals. This went on for a long time, until they began to eat little
children. It was not rare to surprise people with little children roasted or boiled . . . .'*

This gruesome tale, from *The Eastern Key*, continues with his description of parents eating their own children, whole villages making a business of killing and selling children, and how the government and God finally punished those 'animals'. It is accompanied by a succinct moral: 'This craze for eating one another became so common among the poor that the greater number of them perished in this way . . .' — a Satanic solution to the world's poverty problem?

With such glimpses of the past with its woe and suffering it is perhaps understandable why the Meghribi puts up with the deprivation and 'ill-faith' that is his lot. Indeed, he or she not only puts up with it, but accepts it as God's will, and is content. Back in the fourteenth century Ibn Khaldun wrote (in *The Mugaddimah*) about the tribe of Mudar, from the region of Hijaz: 'The Mudar inhabited a country without agriculture or animal produce. They were kept from the fertile plains, rich in grain . . . [but] they had no envy of the abundance of [those regions]. They often ate scorpions and beetles. They were proud to eat *ilhiz* — that is camel hair ground with stones, mixed with blood and then cooked.'

Even today a quick visit to the kasbahs and medinas of North Africa will reveal the all too obvious horrors of malnutrition. 'Most of them show the same symptoms. Malnutrition! The staple food was flour paste, or semolina with olive oil and red pepper sauce to flavour, and steamed vegetables. Meat was only eaten five or six times a year — the diet was monotonous and lacking in vitamins and protein' (*Tunisia*). Naturally the governments are working to solve such basic human problems, but unfortunately malnutrition is still prevalent though, 'thank God', on the decline.

When the North African countries gained their independence they lost expertise in all branches of industry and agriculture. The *colons* left in their millions taking their skills with them. Villages emptied of the young who either emigrated to Europe (France and Germany) or migrated to the cities. Agriculture, and especially viniculture, came to a dismal standstill, and many industrial projects were abandoned for good. But man is a productive animal. The new governments soon got the wheels of industry turning again, and with massive investments in industry, mining and co-operatives, the countryside that had stagnated under a cover of brown dust is gradually turning a bright green.

Life is changing fast and for the good in the Meghrib, and yet in some respects it has stood still since the days of the Almoravids and the Almohads. This is particularly so in Morocco, where there seems to be very little that is different between this following brief sketch of sixteenth-century Fez (from *Description de l' Afrique* by Leo Africanus), and the Fez of today. Africanus described Fez as a large city with 100 hostelries, with inns situated in the centre of the city in the neighbourhood of the Mosque of the Kairawannians. (Innkeepers formed an influential corporation. There was a system of 'self-service' in those inns, but one had to prepare one's own food!) The Fezians, Africanus continued, ate three times a day: after the dawn prayer (bread, fruit and a gruel); after the afternoon prayer (a light meal in winter and a substantial meal in summer); and between sunset and the night prayer. This last was the main meal of the day, comprising bread, couscous and semolina and also dairy produce. The bazaars of Fez were full of all the known vegetables of the day; particularly popular were (and still are) carrots, turnips and gourds. Meat was scarce: the poor were condemned to an unwilling diet of vegetarianism, while the middle classes — traders, landlords etc — had mutton, goat, beef, chicken, pigeon and plenty of fish (shad). The very rich naturally had plenty of everything!

Reading the work of Africanus (who incidentally was a Muslim slave converted to Christianity) one is permitted to wonder whether time has stood still in the medinas of Morocco or Algeria — but then momentary thoughts are shattered by the motor-car horns, the TV aerials that rival the minarets, and the wailing chants from the radios clashing with the thoughtless tom-toms of the West's primitive children. And the Meghribi smiles an enviable smile. He is content with his lot. He knows his place in this mysterious universe. Allah is merciful, is understanding, is kind and all remembering.

'I have never seen poorer people in my life, and I have never seen happier people.' So comments the young, eager American do-gooder (in *Tunisia*), not really understanding the soul of the Meghribians. Happiness is a state of mind. The Meghribi is happy for he is content with God, himself and his life.

Characteristics of the Cuisine

'Sri utaiyib la takul f sogalu ikun msiyib — Buy and cook, don't eat at the market even though it is given for nothing'

Moorish saying

There have been five major culinary influences on the Meghribi cuisine: the nomadic Berbers and Arabs; the food of the native people themselves; the Spanish-Moorish; French and Italian; and the Ottoman and Middle Eastern Arab.

The most influential was naturally the food of the native inhabitants — the Berbers. This is found in such dishes and cooking methods as couscous, tajine, the popular *harira* soups and the rich vegetable and fruit stews. The nomad's cuisine, on the other hand, was very poor. 'Many persons we used to know restricted themselves to goat's milk. They drank from the udder some time during the day or at breakfast. This was their only food for fifteen years' (*The Mugaddimah*). The Bedouin lived on grains, dates, milk, the meat of their animals (sheep and camels) and creatures that live in the desert and steppes such as locusts, goats, gazelles, scorpions etc. A very poor cuisine indeed.

When the Muslims entered mainland Spain they found themselves surrounded by lavish greenery and a much richer culture. They soon adapted themselves to this luxury and a new culinary culture was developed — that of Andalusia. This rich culture was perhaps the most influential of all for it virtually revolutionised the food of the Sultans and the rich, and in time it penetrated the homes of the ordinary citizens of Morocco and Tunisia — when the Moors were thrown out of Spain they migrated to the two aforementioned lands rather than to Algeria and Libya. The Andalusian style is best reflected in the stews and desserts, in the incorporation of fruits and nuts into dishes, the wider use of olives and olive oil, and the sophisticated additions of spices and herbs. Andalusians preferred olive oil while the nomads only had *smen* (clarified butter) or animal fats. This divergence of taste is best illustrated when comparing recipes from the Mediterranean coastline with those of the steppe lands. Indeed, the

Moroccan cuisine goes so far as to label dishes cooked with fat or butter *kdra*, and those with olive oil (or the local favourite — peanut oil) as *mqualli*. Indeed, in the late seventeenth century the Berber poet Mouh Ait Messaoud even coined a few lines in praise of butter rather than olive oil (he was no doubt of nomadic origin):

'Let us go and clear the forests,
And bring back great wealth.

Men of wisdom listen to me
Pay attention to what I say.

Nowadays poetry unfortunately for her
Is shared between Hand and Saddi.

Those who do not have oil at home
Ask for butter at other homes.'

Poèmes Kabyles Anciens

While the Andalusian, deprived of all the goodness of his land, wept for home:

'In Andalusia cloths are white
that folks in mourning wear,
The custom's right . . . I bear its truth
In every greying hair
that grieves for my lost youth.'

Arabic-Andalusian Casidas, Abu-l-Hasan al-Husri

The most important influence on the Algerian cuisine however was that of France. This is most obvious in the use of tomato purée, sweets and starters that have more than an accidental touch of metropolitan France. Algerians use little spice in their food. Their cooking techniques are simpler than those of Morocco where abundant use is made of saffron, coriander, caraway and marjoram. In short, Algerian dishes tend to be less 'exotic' than those of Central Morocco — from the region of Fez and Marrakech — where one can safely say the truest North African dishes originate.

The Tunisian cuisine has a strong Italian influence, as indeed has the Libyan. This is particularly obvious in the widespread use of pasta, tomato purée and rice as opposed to couscous grains. In Libya, in addition to the Italian influence, there is perhaps a much stronger one of Ottoman origin. This is the cooking of the Middle Eastern Arabs and the Turks of Anatolia. Dishes such as *doulmah* — vegetables stuffed with meat, rice and nuts — and Middle Eastern sweets like *sahleb*, *muhlahibah* and *bahlawah* are all of eastern Arab origin and not Meghribi.

The greatest anomaly that one sees today in the Meghrib is the deliberate down-grading by the North African of his original, native food against that of the French. Search as one may, one is hard-pressed to find reasonably priced restaurants serving good local food. The choice is either a cheap, filthy (by western standards) snackbar or a very expensive, pseudo eating house that offers music, cabaret and a few Meghribi dishes! There is no happy medium as yet because the middle-class North

African still lives in the shade of the all prevailing French culture.

This is a pity for the North African cuisine is undoubtedly one of the great and original cuisines of the world. Limited perhaps, due to geographical restrictions, but superb within those limits, reflecting the amount of time and wealth of imagination that man has devoted in order to create something worthy for himself and his Creator.

'All praise is due to Allah who has given us to eat and drink and has made us obedient to His will.'

chorbat
— soups —

Tradition has it that during Ramadan the gates of Heaven are opened, the gates of Hell closed and the Devils chained. It also expresses the belief that whosoever observes the Ramadan Fast will obtain forgiveness of all his sins. Fasting is one of the four 'Pillars of the Faith' and is regarded by all – including those who do not normally carry out their daily religious requirements – as a must. The end of each day's fast is announced by the firing of a cannon and the start of a long, leisurely meal. In North Africa, and particularly in Morocco, this fast is broken with a few spoonfuls of a classic soup called *harira*.

Harira is of Berber origin, hence pre-Islamic. It is a nourishing soup which has many variations, some with fresh and dried vegetables, or with rice or pastry dough, some with meat, chicken, liver or gizzard.

Some people eat *harira* in winter for breakfast – this is especially true of the peasants of Dar Makhzen, while the middle classes of Fez (Morocco) eat *harira* after their meals as a refreshment for it is claimed that *harira* acts as a relief from liver congestion, cleansing one's stomach after a rich and filling meal. The tastiest *hariras* are sold in the small café-restaurants of Fez and Marrakech in Morocco.

I have included several *harira* recipes below. During the thirty days of Ramadan it is traditionally eaten with dates or honey cakes such as *grioush* or *briouats*. I suggest you serve them with bread and dates.

harira

This first recipe is the traditional one of lentils and coriander and it has
a marvellous flavour and aroma. If fresh coriander is not available use fresh
parsley instead. The flavour is not as authentic, but still delicious.

stock
110g (4oz) lamb or mutton, diced
2 or 3 small meat bones if available
225g (8oz) small whole peeled onions or 1 medium onion, coarsely chopped
25g (1oz) butter
1 teaspoon salt
1/2 teaspoon black pepper
1/4 teaspoon powdered saffron
1.8 l (3 pints) water
110g (4oz) whole lentils, rinsed
Juice 1 lemon

tadouira
675g (1¹/₂lb) tomatoes, blanched, peeled and rubbed through a fine sieve
or 4 tablespoons tomato purée
1.2 l (2 pints) water
1 teaspoon salt
2 tablespoons flour mixed to a smooth paste with 300ml (1/2 pint) cold water
8 tablespoons finely chopped parsley
2–3 tablespoons finely chopped coriander or extra parsley

Place the meat, bones, onion, butter, salt, pepper, saffron and water in a large
saucepan and bring to the boil. Lower the heat, cover the pan and simmer for 30
minutes. Remove the lid, add the lentils and lemon juice and replace the lid. Continue
to simmer for a further 30–45 minutes or until lentils and meat are cooked.

Meanwhile prepare the *tadouira* by placing the sieved tomatoes or purée in a
saucepan and stirring in the water and salt. Bring to the boil and simmer for 10
minutes. Strain the stock from the large saucepan into the tomato liquid. Add the flour
mixture and stir well.

Place the parsley and coriander in a liquidiser with a little of the soup and blend
until smooth. Stir into the soup. Bring back to the boil, stirring constantly. Taste and
adjust the seasoning if necessary. **Serves 6**

harira min himass

harira with chickpeas

Chicken is often the meat base for this *harira* from the Kabyle mountain regions
of Algeria. The Kabyles are the most important of the Berber Confederations
in Algeria. They have preserved their language and customs and, to a great extent,
the purity of their Berber blood.

Serve with bread or, if you wish to be more authentic,
with fresh or dried dates and dried figs.

50g (2oz) butter
225g (1/2lb) raw chicken (e.g. 1 breast, boned), skinned and cut into small pieces
110g (4oz) chickpeas, soaked overnight in cold water
1 medium onion, coarsely chopped
8 tablespoons finely chopped parsley
1 teaspoon black pepper
1/4 teaspoon powdered saffron
2 teaspoons salt
1 teaspoon cinnamon
1.8 l (3 pints) water
110g (4oz) long-grain rice, rinsed thoroughly under cold running water
2 tablespoons flour mixed with 450ml (3/4 pint) water until smooth
2 eggs, lightly beaten

garnish
Juice 1 lemon

Melt the butter in a large saucepan. Add the chicken pieces, drained chickpeas, onion, parsley, pepper, saffron, salt and cinnamon and fry for 2–3 minutes, stirring frequently. Add the water and bring to the boil. Cover the pan, lower the heat and simmer for about 1 hour or until the chickpeas are tender.

Add the rice and simmer for a further 15–20 minutes. Stir in the flour mixture and bring to the boil, stirring constantly. If the mixture is too thick add a little more water. Remove the soup from the heat and stir in the beaten eggs. Serve in bowls with a little lemon juice squeezed over the top.

You can substitute kidney beans for the chickpeas and crushed vermicelli for the rice. **Serves 6-8**

harira bidaouiya

bedouin soup

This delicious soup is a Moroccan speciality which is popular with the nomads in the south of the country.

The eggs will separate when added to the soup – this is a characteristic of many *harira* soups and it gives them an interesting texture and appearance.

3 tablespoons oil
350g (12oz) leg or shoulder of lamb, trimmed of fat and cut
into strips 1/2cm (1/4in) thick and 2.5–3.5cm (1–11/2in) in length
1/2 teaspoon turmeric
1/2 teaspoon ginger
3 large tomatoes, blanched, peeled and passed through a fine sieve
1 small onion, finely chopped
4–5 inner sticks of celery, finely chopped
2 teaspoons salt
1 teaspoon black pepper
1/2 teaspoon cinnamon
1.8 l (3 pints) water
3 tablespoons crushed vermicelli or orzo pasta
2 eggs, lightly beaten

To serve
Juice 1 lemon

Heat the oil in a large saucepan, add the strips of meat and fry for a few minutes until browned and coated with oil. Add the turmeric, ginger, tomato pulp, onion, celery, salt, pepper, cinnamon and water. Stir well and bring to the boil. Cover the pan, lower the heat and simmer for about 45 minutes or until the meat is tender.

Add the vermicelli or orzo, stir well and simmer, uncovered, for 8–10 minutes or until tender. Turn off the heat and leave for 3–4 minutes, then gently stir in the beaten eggs. Pour the soup into individual bowls and sprinkle each with a little lemon juice.
Serves 6-8

harira kerouiya

caraway harira

Caraway (*carum carvi*) is extremely popular with North Africans for its many digestive qualities as well as its flavour. It relieves uterine cramps, promotes the secretion of milk and is particularly good for infants as a stomach settler. This simple soup is full of aroma as it also contains fresh mint and gum arabic (mastic) which can be bought at good Middle Eastern and Indian stores.

1.8 l (3 pints) water
2 tablespoons flour mixed to a smooth paste with 150ml (1/4 pint) water
4 sprigs fresh mint
1½ teaspoons salt
1½ tablespoons caraway seeds, pounded to a powder with a mortar and pestle
2 grains gum arabic, powdered
Juice 1 lemon

Place the water in a large saucepan and bring to the boil. Stir some of the hot water into the flour mixture and then pour it through a fine strainer back into the pan. Bring back to the boil, stirring constantly.

Pick the mint leaves from the stalks and place in a mortar with the salt. Pound vigorously and then stir into the soup. Stir in the powdered caraway seeds and gum arabic and bring back to the boil. Simmer for 15 minutes, taste and adjust seasoning if necessary. Stir in the lemon juice and serve.

A skin will form on this soup if allowed to cool, therefore serve immediately or remove the skin with a slotted spoon before reheating. **Serves 6**

harira mkhinza

This is a summertime soup that is usually prepared at the feast of Aid el Kebir. Here the caraway is replaced by '*peumus boldus*' – boldowood or *baldoh el faghiyah* – a plant that grows most generously in the gardens of North Africa.

Often 450g (1lb) lamb's liver is thinly sliced and added to the soup. The remaining ingredients are as in the soup above.

'My love was like a young gazelle,
Her eyes when she looked upon me
Made me to hide my own in the dark
For they were brighter than the sun shining in water,
My love had breasts
Rounder than the pomegranates
That made me desire to pluck them,

My love had lips
Redder than a flower
And her skin was whiter than milk,
My love had feet
Smaller than petals of the jasmine
And swifter than the feet of an antelope,
So that she fled away and escaped me;
But when her eyes were turned the other way from me
I was no longer dazzled but could see,
And my legs became longer than the legs of a camel . . .
My love is like a flower that I have gathered,
And she is mine.'
By Bus to the Sahara

harira marrakchia

kidney bean harira

This is a meatless soup from Morocco.

110g (4oz) dried, skinned kidney beans, rinsed
1.8 l (3 pints) water
1 tablespoon *khli* fat (see recipe in Glossary) or 1 tablespoon oil
or 15g (1/2oz) butter
2 tablespoons flour mixed to a smooth paste with 150ml (1/4 pint) cold water
1 teaspoon paprika
1/2 teaspoon chilli pepper
11/2 teaspoons salt
1/4 teaspoon cumin
75g (3oz) rice, vermicelli or orzo pasta
4 tablespoons finely chopped coriander

To serve
Juice 1 lemon

Place the beans in a saucepan, cover with cold water and bring to the boil. Simmer for 2 minutes, turn off the heat and set aside for 1 hour. Drain.

Place the beans in a large saucepan, add the water and fat and bring to the boil. Cover the pan, lower the heat and simmer until the beans are tender. Stir a little of the hot soup into the flour mixture and then pour back into the pan. Bring to the boil, stirring constantly.

Add all the remaining ingredients except the lemon juice and stir well. If adding rice simmer for 15–20 minutes or until tender. If adding pasta simmer for 8–10 minutes or until tender. Taste and adjust seasoning if necessary. Pour into bowls and sprinkle with lemon juice. **Serves 6-8**

A similar soup is called *Askif*, the name give to *harira* by the Tachelait tribes of central Morocco. It uses peeled and cubed turnip instead of kidney beans and barley or maize instead of rice. They also make a *harira* using 350g (12oz) thinly shredded cabbage and omitting the kidney beans and rice.

harira bil halib

harira with milk

'We gave him milk to drink, he became a partner in the cow' Moorish proverb

This soup is from the desert region of Algeria where the Sahara
has shaped a hardy yet simple nomadic folk whose praises Wilson MacArthur
sang in the following terms:

'Along them came swinging band after band of nomads, small, dark, stalwart people, with open smiling faces, the women unveiled and carrying themselves with a bold and fearless grace. They walked with long, easy, swinging strides, tirelessly eating up the miles while the camels, laden high with the impedimenta of a wandering people, plodded in solemn procession with their noses in the air. The impression was not easily forgotten – an impression of fierce pride, of enduring stamina and of unquenchable vitality, the vitality that has made these people survive, through twelve centuries, in perpetual hardship and penury. But how different for the nomads of the western world, the furtive, stealthy Romany who wanders over Europe defiant of control yet sneaking a livelihood from his unwilling hosts. These people have chosen to live out their lives in the wilderness, and the wilderness has stamped them with its own indelible brand.' Auto Nomad in Barbary

The nomads – mostly Berbers – have milk and semolina and with them they have evolved this simple soup. It is quite bland and not to everyone's taste.

1.8 l (3 pints) milk
15g (1/2oz) butter
1 teaspoon salt
1/4 teaspoon black pepper
3 tablespoons fine semolina mixed to a smooth paste with
150ml (1/4 pint) cold milk
1 egg yolk

garnish
2 tablespoons melted butter
A little chopped fresh mint or coriander (optional)

Bring the milk to the boil in a large saucepan. Add the butter, salt and pepper and simmer over a low heat for 5 minutes. Stir several tablespoons of the hot milk into the semolina mixture and then pour back into the pan, stirring constantly until the soup comes to the boil. Lower the heat and simmer for 10 minutes, stirring frequently.

Beat the egg yolk with a fork and stir into the soup. Remove the pan from the heat and serve immediately. If the soup is left to cool a skin will form – remove this with a slotted spoon before reheating. Pour the soup into individual bowls, spoon a little melted butter into the centre of each and sprinkle with the chopped mint or coriander if you wish. **Serves 6**

shahriyet el-hamrak

This simple Moroccan variation uses vermicelli or a fine spaghetti instead of the semolina.

1.2 l (2 pints) milk
600ml (1 pint) water
1 teaspoon salt
175g (6oz) vermicelli or fine spaghetti, crushed
25g (1oz) butter

garnish
3 teaspoons sugar
1¹/₂ teaspoons cinnamon

Bring the milk and water to the boil in a large saucepan. Add the salt, vermicelli or spaghetti and butter. Stir well and bring back to the boil. Lower the heat and simmer for about 8 minutes, stirring occasionally, or until the vermicelli is tender. To serve pour the soup immediately into bowls and sprinkle 1/2 teaspoon of sugar and 1/4 teaspoon of cinnamon into each bowl.

If this soup is left to stand for any length of time it will thicken considerably; therefore, when reheating, add more liquid. **Serves 6**

harira hara bi smid

spicy semolina soup

Semolina, with its various sizes of grain, is part of the staple diet of North Africans and it is not surprising therefore that it is used widely in soups. The recipe below comes from western Algeria and in particular from the mountain villages of Aurès. Delicious and filling.

4 tablespoons oil
2–3 cloves garlic, crushed

11/2 teaspoons salt
1 tablespoon paprika
1 teaspoon harissa (see Glossary)
450g (1lb) tomatoes, blanched, peeled and chopped
1.8 l (3 pints) water
2 medium potatoes, peeled and cut into 1cm (1/2in) cubes
110g (4oz) couscous (coarse semolina)

garnish
3 tablespoons finely chopped coriander

Heat the oil in a large saucepan, add the garlic, salt, paprika and harissa and fry gently for 2–3 minutes. Add the tomatoes and simmer for 5 minutes. Add the water and bring quickly to the boil. Simmer for 5 minutes. Add the potato cubes and cook for 5 minutes. Stir in the couscous and simmer for 15 minutes. Sprinkle the coriander into the soup and serve immediately. **Serves 4-6**

nafah

aniseed semolina soup

Aniseed (*pimpinella anisum*) has a fragrant odour and seeds with a sweet taste. It promotes digestion, improves appetite and promotes milk production in nursing mothers. This soup, and the variation given, is usually served to mothers before or immediately after giving birth. Needless to say it can be eaten at other times as well! Both recipes are from Morocco, but the soups are found throughout the Meghrib under different names.

1.8 l (3 pints) water
110g (4oz) couscous
1 teaspoon paprika
1/4 teaspoon powdered saffron
1 teaspoon salt
25g (1oz) butter
1/2 teaspoon black pepper
1 level tablespoon powdered aniseed diluted in 90ml (3fl oz) water

Bring the water to the boil in a large saucepan. Stir in all the remaining ingredients except the aniseed and bring back to the boil. Lower the heat and simmer for about 20 minutes or until the couscous grains are soft and swollen. Stir in the diluted aniseed and remove from the heat. Serve immediately.

Traditionally this soup is served with fresh dates although dried ones are equally good. **Serves 6**

tadeffi

This soup is made with flour or semolina, garlic, saffron, thyme and mint. To prepare bring 1.8 l (3 pints) water to the boil in a large pan. Mix 50g (2oz) flour or fine semolina to a smooth paste with a little water and stir into the water together with 1 teaspoon salt, 2 cloves garlic, 1/2 teaspoon black pepper, 1/3 teaspoon saffron, 1/2 teaspoon ground ginger and 3 tablespoons fresh thyme and 1 tablespoon fresh mint, both finely chopped. Stir constantly until the soup comes to the boil and thickens. Simmer for 10 minutes.

Just before serving remove the garlic cloves, crush them and return to the soup. Serve with a little oil sprinkled into each bowl. **Serves 6**

A particularly exhilarating but (dare I say) noisy characteristic of the people of the Meghrib is the incantation of '*You-You*'. '*You-You*' is the equivalent of 'Hip, Hip, Hooray' or 'Olé' yet it is much more than these exclamations of happiness or of triumph. '*You-You*' is a way of life, '*You-You*' is one's tongue shaking up and down in one's mouth – very fast!

'*You-You*' is the exhortation to the world that a child is born, or is circumcised, that a wedding is taking place or a pilgrim has just returned from Mecca. '*You-You*' was the telephone, the church bell, the Mullah's chant, the radio or television of yesteryear. It was the means with which people informed others of their happiness, good fortune and state of mind – and they still '*You-You*' whether it is in a Paris concert hall, at a gathering for a *kif* (party), outside the gates of Old Jerusalem, in a luxury Rabat or Algiers apartment or in the tents of the Saharan wilderness.

After a child's birth the mother is offered, as well as *tadeffi*, another soup called *marga*. This is a light hen chicken soup (if it's a boy) or cockerel soup (if it is a girl). On the seventh day after the birth all the relatives gather to 'name' the child. This naming ceremony takes place after breakfast which traditionally consists of several kinds of soup (*harira* or semolina), different kinds of *rghaifs* (see page 299), rice puddings, tea or coffee, cakes and *sellou* (see page 252). A lamb is then sacrificed in the child's honour. The oldest male in the group kills the animal, dedicating it to God for naming him/her so and so. A little salt and sugar is sprinkled over the sacrificial spot. The child's name is loudly announced and the '*You-You*' commences to the accompaniment of drums, tambours and other regional instruments. '*You-You-You*' – to us this day a child is born!

osbane es'smid

semolina balls in lamb soup

A delicious and filling soup from Algeria. The sauce of lamb, tomatoes, lentils and spices has tasty semolina balls in it.

4 tablespoons oil
1 onion, finely chopped
225g (8oz) lamb or mutton (or veal), cut into 1cm (1/2in) cubes
1 teaspoon salt
1 teaspoon paprika
1/4 teaspoon cinnamon
1/2 teaspoon harissa (see Glossary)
1 tablespoon finely chopped coriander (optional)
2 tablespoons finely chopped parsley
1 tablespoon finely chopped mint or 1/2 tablespoon dried mint
3 large tomatoes, blanched, peeled and chopped
1.8 l (3 pints) water
175g (6oz) whole lentils, ringed

Semolina Balls

375g (12oz) medium semolina
1/2 onion, very finely chopped
1 tablespoon finely chopped coriander (optional)
1 tablespoon finely chopped parsley
1 tablespoon finely chopped mint or 1/2 tablespoon dried mint
1 teaspoon salt
1/2 teaspoon black pepper
1 egg
90ml (3fl oz) oil
90ml (3fl oz) water

Heat the oil in a large saucepan, add the onion and fry until soft. Add the meat and fry, turning frequently, until evenly browned. Add the salt, paprika, cinnamon, harissa, coriander, parsley, mint and tomatoes and stir well. Cook over a low heat for 10 minutes, stirring frequently. Add the water and lentils and bring to the boil. Lower the heat and simmer for 20 minutes.

Meanwhile prepare the semolina balls by placing the semolina, onion, herbs, salt and pepper in a large bowl. Add the egg and oil and mix well. Now add enough of the water to make a malleable dough which holds together. Keeping your palms damp, roll the mixture into apricot-sized balls.

When the soup has been simmering for about 20 minutes add the semolina balls

and continue to cook for a further 30 minutes or until the meat and lentils are tender. Taste, adjust seasoning if necessary, and add a little more water if the soup is too thick for your taste. Place a few balls in each bowl and spoon the soup over them.
Serves 6-8

bazin

semolina dough

'Il bazin amoud el din – Bazin is the pillar of a person's life and religion' Libyan saying

In 1845 James Richardson was treated to a feast of *bazin* in the deserts of Libya. He recalled the incident in some detail in that marvellously chatty book *Travels in the Great Desert Of Sahara, 1845–1846*. *Bazin* (sometimes also called *aseeda*) is a true classic of the desert – the food of the nomad whether Berber, Arab, Tuareg or African.

Well, what is *bazin*? I would like Richardson to take over now and tell you what it is and how it was eaten in the town of Ghadames 150 years ago.

'This morning there was a grand gourmandizing of bazeen, in celebration of the nuptials of the two daughters of my taleb. The feast was given by the fathers of the young men. Nearly the whole of the male population of the Ben Wezeet, besides strangers and the Arab soldiers, went to dig, and dip, and dive into the huge bowl of bazeen, some three or four hundred adults, besides boys . . . after they had swallowed half a dozen mouthfuls, they immediately retired and left the coast clear for the rest, and thus the ceremony was soon got through. . . . My taleb, as a matter of course, called upon me to go to the festa. I found the festive hall to be a smallish oblong room, the walls of which were garnished with a number of little looking-glasses, polished brass basons, and various other small matters. . . . In the centre of the room was placed an enormous wooden dish, full of bazeen, or thick boiled pudding made of barley-meal, with olive oil, and sauce of pounded dates poured upon it. Every person ate with his hands, rolling the pudding into balls and dipping the balls into oil and date-sauce. A great piece of carpeting was laid round the bowl, to be used as a napkin to wipe the hands and mouth. The wooden dish or bowl might have been three feet in diameter, and was replenished as fast as emptied with masses of boiled dough, oil and date-sauce. There was suspended over it, two or three feet above, a wicker roof, to prevent the dirt from falling into it when the people stood up all around and wiped their hands. The visitors squatted down together, encircling the bowl, in numbers of about eight or ten.'

Here then is this classic of the desert. The first recipe is just for the dough which is often eaten, as described above, with melted butter, honey and lemon juice.

110g (4oz) fine semolina
4g (¹/₈oz) yeast
150ml (¹/4 pint) tepid water

To cook
150ml (¹/4 pint) water
30ml (1fl oz) oil

To serve
25g (1oz) butter, melted
60-90ml (2–3fl oz) honey
Juice 1 lemon

Place the semolina in a bowl. Mix the yeast with a little of the tepid water until smooth and add to the semolina. Gradually knead in the remaining water and beat with a wooden spoon for 2–3 minutes. The mixture should have a batter-like consistency. Cover with a cloth and set aside in a warm place for 30 minutes.

Bring the cooking water to the boil in a small pan. Lower the heat and slowly pour the batter into the pan stirring constantly and crushing the mixture against the side of the pan. Continue to cook for several minutes, stirring constantly, until the dough forms a soft ball. Remove from the heat.

When cool enough to handle add the oil and knead it in well. Shape the dough into a ball and place on a greased serving plate. Traditionally bazin is eaten with one's fingers with a little melted butter, honey and lemon juice poured over it.

This traditional recipe is the basis for several soups, two of which I give below.

bazin maraquat dadjaj

bazin with chicken soup

Bazin
See recipe above

Soup
1 chicken breast, skinned
1 onion, finely chopped
350g (³/4lb) carrots, peeled and diced
1.2 l (2 pints) water
1 teaspoon salt
¹/2 teaspoon black pepper

Place all the soup ingredients in a large saucepan and bring to the boil. Lower the heat, cover the pan and simmer for 30 minutes.

Meanwhile prepare the *bazin* as described in the recipe above and shape it into walnut-sized balls. Add these to the simmering soup and cook for a further 10–15 minutes. Remove the chicken breast, discard the bones and cut the flesh into small pieces. Stir back into the soup, heat through and serve. **Serves 6-8**

bazin min chorba bil hout

bazin with fish soup

This Algerian fish soup is from the south-eastern Sahara bordering onto the Fezzan region of Libya.

Bazin
See recipe above

Soup
450g (1lb) white fish (heads, tails etc or steaks)
5 tablespoons oil
2–3 cloves garlic
3 tomatoes, blanched, peeled and passed through a sieve
1 tablespoon tomato purée
2 bay leaves
1 sprig fresh thyme or 1 teaspoon dried thyme
3 tablespoons finely chopped parsley
1¹/₂ teaspoons salt
¹/₂ teaspoon black pepper
¹/₂ teaspoon harissa (see Glossary)
¹/₄ teaspoon saffron (optional)
1.8 l (3 pints) water

Rinse the fish and dry with kitchen paper. Place on the base of a large pan and pour in the oil. Fry gently for 15–20 minutes, turning occasionally. Remove from the heat, transfer the fish to a plate and set aside to cool. When cold discard the skin and bones and cut the flesh into bite-sized pieces.

Meanwhile prepare the *bazin* as described in its recipe and shape it into walnut-sized balls.

Place all the remaining soup ingredients in the pan and stir well. Bring to the boil, lower the heat and simmer for 30 minutes. Add the fish pieces and cook for a further 10 minutes. To serve either place some bazin balls in each soup bowl and pour the soup over them or drop them into the soup for the last 10 minutes of its cooking time.

Some people like to mince the fish flesh finely before adding it to the soup.

chorbat bouzellouf

lamb's head soup

This soup, which is highly popular throughout the Mediterranean lands, the Middle East and Asia proper, is rarely found in Britain and Europe. This is a shame as it is tasty. Order the head from your butcher in advance and ask him to skin and quarter it for you. In North Africa of course the cook can just nip down to the souk and choose his own!

1 lamb's head, quartered and thoroughly rinsed
75g (3oz) chickpeas, soaked overnight in cold water and drained
2 tablespoons oil
1 large onion, finely chopped
1 teaspoon salt
1/2 teaspoon black pepper
75g (3oz) vermicelli, crushed into 3.5–5cm (1¹/2–2in) lengths
1 egg yolk
Juice 1 lemon

Garnish
2 tablespoons finely chopped parsley

Three-quarters fill a large pan with lightly salted water, add the head and chickpeas and bring to the boil. Remove any scum. Lower the heat, cover the pan and simmer for 1 hour or until the chickpeas are tender. Remove the head and set aside until cool enough to handle. Measure the stock and make up to 1.8 l (3 pints) with water if necessary.

Heat the oil in a small pan, add the onion and fry gently until soft and golden. Add to the stock together with the salt and pepper and stir well.

Remove any meat on the head, including the tongue, cut into small pieces and add to the soup. Bring the soup back to the boil, add the vermicelli and simmer for about 7–8 minutes or until just tender. Taste the soup and adjust seasoning if necessary. Remove from the heat. Beat the egg yolk and lemon juice together in a small bowl, pour into the soup and stir well. Serve immediately, sprinkled with parsley. **Serves 6-8**

churbat dajaj bil hilba

chicken soup with hilba

A tasty chicken soup from Tripoli, Libya. It is a dark red colour. If you wish, you can increase the quantity of *hilba*. Sometimes rice or crushed vermicelli or orzo pasta is added to the soup.

2 tablespoons *smen* (see Glossary) or 25g (1oz) butter
1 onion, chopped
1.25–1.5kg (2^1/$_2$–3lb) chicken, cut into 6 pieces and skinned
3 ripe tomatoes, blanched, peeled and chopped
1 tablespoon tomato purée
1 teaspoon salt
^{1}/$_4$ teaspoon black pepper
^{1}/$_4$ teaspoon saffron
1.8 l (3 pints) water
1 tablespoon *hilba* (see Glossary)
3 tablespoons finely chopped parsley

Heat the *smen* or butter in a large pan, add the onion and fry until soft and golden. Add the chicken pieces and fry for a few minutes, turning frequently. Add the tomatoes, tomato purée, salt, pepper, saffron and water and stir well. Bring to the boil, lower the heat, cover the pan and simmer for about 45 minutes or until the chicken is tender.

Add the *hilba* and parsley, stir well and simmer for a further 20–30 minutes. Serve in individual bowls with one piece of chicken in each. **Serves 6**

djari byad

chicken soup constantine-style

Constantine (Algeria) was once known as Cirta which, when occupied by Rome, was re-named Constantina. During the Arab invasions it suffered grievously and, after a short period of independence, it fell to the Ottoman Turks and was subject to the Dey of Algiers. Today Constantine is the third largest city in Algeria, but still retains many characteristics of her ancient past.

'I wandered through the street markets. Many of the shops were still no more than walled boxes, even if they offered modern hardware or draperies. More intriguing were the peasants – some squatting by little heaps of vegetables, others offering a couple of live fowls – you could take them as they were, or the vendor would wring their necks. Other peasants were more unusual if less hygienic. Instead of selling

a sheep to a butcher, they had killed it in their village, cut it up and now offered sections of its body for sale. One man would hold a leg of mutton in his hand, the next a confused heap of liver and other offal. No one seemed to bother about smells or flies.' North African Journey

Make sure that your chicken is oven ready – there is a limit to being a stickler for authenticity! This is a thick and filling soup which is a meal on its own when served with bread.

50g (2oz) *smen* (see Glossary) or butter
1 onion, finely chopped
450g (1lb) chicken flesh (2 breasts)
Salt and black pepper
1.8 (3 pints) water
175g (6oz) minced meat
2 tablespoons finely chopped parsley
2 egg yolks
1 level tablespoon cornflour
75g (3oz) vermicelli or rinsed rice
Juice 1 lemon

Garnish
1 tablespoon finely chopped fresh parsley, mint or coriander

Melt the butter in a large pan, add three-quarters of the onion and fry until soft. Add the chicken and fry for a further 3–4 minutes, turning occasionally. Season with $1^1/2$ teaspoons salt and $1/2$ teaspoon black pepper, add the water and bring to the boil. Lower the heat, cover the pan and simmer for 30 minutes.

Meanwhile place the minced meat in a bowl, add the remaining onion, the parsley and a little salt and pepper. Add one of the egg yolks and knead the mixture thoroughly until well blended. Keeping your hands damp, form the mixture into marble-sized balls.

When the chicken flesh is cooked remove it to a plate. Strain the stock and return it to the pan making up to 1.8 l (3 pints) with water if necessary. Bring to the boil, add the meatballs and simmer for 15 minutes. In a small bowl mix the cornflour to a smooth paste with some of the hot stock, pour into the pan and stir constantly until the soup thickens slightly.

Remove and discard the chicken bones and cut the flesh into small pieces. Return to the pan together with the vermicelli or rice and simmer for 7–8 minutes to cook the vermicelli or for 15 minutes to cook the rice. Remove from the heat. Beat the remaining egg yolk with the lemon juice and stir into the soup. Serve immediately sprinkled with the garnish. **Serves 6**

chmeunka

tripe soup

There was a time, indeed not so long ago, when British High Streets boasted of their tripe shops. There was a chain of restaurants-cum-butchers-cum-grocers, UCP, where tripe was proudly displayed in shop windows. It is now quite difficult to find tripe, which is a pity. This recipe is from Tunisia and it is wonderful on a cold winter's day. Serve with bread.

900g (2lb) tripe, washed thoroughly
2.5 l (4 pints) water
2 teaspoons salt
150ml (1/4 pint) oil
4 large carrots, peeled and diced
4 turnips, peeled and diced
4 cloves garlic, crushed
1 teaspoon harissa (see Glossary)
1/2 teaspoon ground coriander
1 teaspoon paprika
3 bay leaves
1/2 teaspoon black pepper

Garnish
Juice 2 lemons
2 tablespoons finely chopped parsley

Cut the tripe into 5cm (2in) pieces and place in a large saucepan. Add the water, salt and oil and bring to the boil. Lower the heat, cover the pan and simmer for 1 hour. Occasionally lift the lid and remove any scum.

After 1 hour add the remaining ingredients, cover the pan and simmer for a further hour. Taste and adjust seasoning if necessary. Serve in individual bowls garnished generously with the lemon juice and parsley. **Serves 6-8**

chorbat el hout ramazan

festive fish soup

Traditionally served during the month of Ramadan, this is a delicious, spicy soup.

6 tablespoons oil
2 onions, finely chopped
1 clove garlic, crushed
1 teaspoon cayenne pepper
1 teaspoon salt
1/2 teaspoon cumin
2 tablespoons tomato purée
1.8 l (3 pints) water
675g (1¹/₂lb) mixed fish (monkfish, whiting etc), cleaned and washed
110g (4oz) pearl barley, rinsed thoroughly under cold water and drained
Juice 1 lemon

Garnish
2 tablespoons finely chopped parsley

Heat the oil in a large saucepan, and the onions add fry until soft and turning golden. Add the garlic, pepper, salt, cumin and tomato purée, stir well and fry for 2–3 minutes. Add the water and fish, stir well and bring to the boil. Lower the heat, cover the pan and simmer for 20 minutes or until the fish is tender. Remove fish with a slotted spoon and transfer to a large plate. When cool enough to handle remove and discard all bones, cut flesh into bite-sized pieces and return to the soup.

Add the pearl barley, return to the boil, lower the heat, cover the pan and simmer for a further 20–30 minutes or until barley is soft. Stir in lemon juice. Serve garnished with the parsley. **Serves 6**

chorbat el khodra meknesi

vegetable soup meknes-style

This is a rich and filling soup, with the meat and vegetables finely chopped. Popular throughout Morocco, but especially in the region of the ancient imperial town of Meknes which, during the reign of Sultan Moulay-Ismail (see Introduction), experienced a period of great prosperity. It is what survives from this period – the Place El-hadim, Bab-el-Mansour and Moulay-Ismail's tomb – that makes the town an important stopping place on a trip to Morocco.

25g (1oz) butter
175g (6oz) lamb or beef, cut into 1cm (¹/₂in) cubes
175g (6oz) carrots, peeled and diced
1 large turnip, peeled and diced
1 onion, finely chopped
1 leek, finely chopped
1 stick celery, finely chopped

2 small meat bones, optional
1¹/2 teaspoons salt
¹/2 teaspoon black pepper
¹/4 teaspoon ground saffron
1.8 l (3 pints) water
675g (1¹/2lb) tomatoes, blanched, seeded and chopped
175g (6oz) potatoes, peeled and diced
3 tablespoons finely chopped coriander or parsley

Melt the butter in a large pan, add the meat and fry for several minutes until evenly browned. Add the carrots, turnip, onion, leek and celery and fry for a few minutes, stirring frequently. Add the bones, salt, pepper, saffron and water, stir and bring to the boil. Lower the heat, cover the pan and simmer for 45 minutes.

Add the tomatoes, potatoes and coriander or parsley, stir, cover and simmer for a further 15–20 minutes or until the potatoes are cooked. Taste to check the seasoning and add a little more water if necessary. **Serves 6**

chorba khodra

vegetable soup

This simple soup from the Algerian side of the Atlas mountains makes a tasty, light start to a main meal.

2.5 l (4 pints) water
1¹/2 teaspoons salt
¹/4 teaspoon black pepper
4 carrots, peeled and diced
2 turnips, peeled and diced
1 leek, finely chopped
2 large potatoes, peeled and diced
1 stick celery, finely chopped
110g (4oz) chopped spinach
1 courgette, diced
1 large tomato, blanched, peeled and chopped
1 tablespoon oil
¹/2 teaspoon paprika
2 teaspoons salt
¹/2 teaspoon harissa (see Glossary)
¹/2 teaspoon cinnamon

Place the water, salt and pepper in a large saucepan and bring to the boil. Rinse the vegetables and add to the pan together with the remaining ingredients. Stir and bring back to the boil. Lower the heat, cover the pan and simmer for 30 minutes.

At this point you can serve the soup as it is. However, it is often puréed first. If you do purée the soup then you may like to add a little more water to get the thickness you prefer. In which case adjust the seasoning accordingly. Bring back to the boil and serve. **Serves 6-8**

chak-choukat el khobz

bread soup

'The thinnest bread finds itself married to bread' Algerian saying

Here is an old recipe from the mountains – and, no doubt, the plains. Bread when stale is not wasted, but made into a fine, warming soup much appreciated on wintery nights up there on the slopes of the mighty Atlas mountain range – the geological backbone of the lands of the Meghrib. It extends for more than 2000 kilometres (1200 miles) from Agadir in the south to Tunis in the north east.

Soup made from bread is not indigenous to North Africa, it appears in most 'peasant' cuisines of the world. Harissa gives this recipe its North African touch.

15g (1/2oz) butter
4 tablespoons oil
1 onion, finely chopped
2 large tomatoes, blanched, peeled and chopped
1 tablespoon tomato purée
1/2 teaspoon harissa (see Glossary)
11/2 teaspoons salt
1/2 teaspoon black pepper
2 potatoes, peeled and cut into 1cm (1/2in) cubes
1.8 l (3 pints) water
375g (12oz) stale bread cut into 2.5cm (1 in) cubes

Heat the butter and oil in a large saucepan, add the onion and fry until soft and golden. Add the tomatoes, tomato purée, harissa, salt and pepper, stir well and fry for several minutes. Add the potatoes and water and bring to the boil. Lower the heat, cover the pan and simmer for 30 minutes.

Add the bread cubes, toss in the sauce, cover the pan and simmer for a further 10 minutes. The bread cubes will soften and swell. Serve this delicious and filling soup piping hot. **Serves 6**

kemia
— hors d'oeuvres and salads —

One of the great Middle Eastern traditions is the laying of a large and sumptuous *mezzeh* table, where scores of small dishes are served, all filled with raw or cooked vegetables, olives, pickles, small grilled meatballs and salads, etc. No other cuisine in the world can compete with a Lebanese *mezzeh* spread, but the North Africans do have a good go! *Aadou* in Tunisia and *Kemia* in Algeria are the equivalent of the Middle Eastern *mezzeh* and the Russian *zakouski*. At their simplest they include plates of almonds, walnuts, pistachios, salted pumpkin or melon seeds as well as grilled and salted cashew nuts. There will always be a few plates of olives (violet, green or black, see Glossary), some white cheese (*zib zeena*), all kinds of pickled vegetables as well as various cooked or grilled vegetables – some of which are given below.

A *kemia* may also include several types of *breiks*, fish dishes, tajines etc and, of course, a large number of freshly prepared salads.

I start with a few Tunisian inspired *ajlouke* dishes which are usually served on a *kemia* table, but – as with most Middle Eastern and North African food – can be eaten as accompaniments to main dishes.

ajlouke el-badendjel

aubergine hors d'oeuvre

The aubergine or eggplant entered North Africa with the Arabs via Iran from its homeland in India. Subsequently it spread, with the Moors, via Spain to the rest of Europe and the New World. All the same, there are not many exciting aubergine dishes in the region – certainly nothing that matches those in the Turkish-Armenian cuisine.

Ajlouke el-Badendjel is a simple salad which is easy to prepare and makes a fine appetiser.

2 large aubergines, peeled and quartered
2 medium red peppers, halved
2 cloves garlic, crushed
1 teaspoon harissa (see Glossary)
1 level teaspoon powdered caraway
Juice 1 lemon
1¹/₂ teaspoons salt
3 tablespoons oil

Half fill a large saucepan with water and bring to the boil. Add the aubergines and red peppers and simmer for 30 minutes or until soft. Strain through a colander. When cool enough to handle squeeze the aubergine flesh between your hands to extract as much liquid as possible. Transfer the flesh to a bowl.

Chop the red peppers finely and add to the bowl together with all the remaining ingredients. Mash thoroughly with a fork. To serve spread the salad over a shallow plate and eat with bread. **Serves 6-8**

ajlouke-el-qar'a

courgette hors d'oeuvre

All *ajlouke* dishes are similar. In this recipe courgettes are boiled and then mashed with herbs and spices. Makes an excellent starter on a kemia table.

4 medium courgettes, topped, tailed, scraped and cut into slices
1 teaspoon harissa (see Glossary)
2 cloves garlic, crushed
Juice 1 lemon
1 level teaspoon ground caraway

1 level teaspoon coriander
1 teaspoon salt
3 tablespoons oil

Garnish
Black olives

Half fill a large saucepan with water and bring to the boil. Add the courgette slices and simmer for 20–30 minutes or until tender. Strain into a colander. When cool enough to handle squeeze the slices between your hands to extract as much water as possible. Transfer to a bowl and mash until smooth.

Add the remaining ingredients and mix well. Spread the salad out on a shallow dish and garnish with the olives. Eat with bread. **Serves 6**

qar'a magli

fried courgettes

An ever popular way of preparing courgettes and aubergines is to fry them in olive oil or to dip them in batter and then fry them.

frying in oil
2 large aubergines or 4 courgettes, cut into 1cm (¹/2in) rounds
Oil

Heat some oil in a pan until hot. Add a few of the aubergine slices and fry until golden brown on both sides, turning occasionally. Remove with a fork and drain on kitchen paper. Cook the remaining slices in the same way. Serve cold. Makes an excellent starter with a glass of whatever aperitif one likes, but best perhaps with a glass of *arak*, *boukha* (fig juice), anisette or pastis etc.

fried in batter
3 courgettes or 2 medium aubergines, cut into 1cm (¹/2in) rounds

batter
2 eggs
2 teaspoons oregano
1 teaspoon cumin
¹/2 teaspoon paprika
¹/2 teaspoon harissa (see Glossary)
¹/2 teaspoon salt
Oil for frying

In a small bowl mix together the eggs, oregano, cumin, paprika, harissa and salt.

Heat some oil in a pan. Dip a few of the vegetable slices into the batter and drop into the hot oil. Fry gently until golden on both sides, turning once. Remove with a slotted spoon and drain on kitchen paper. Cook the remaining vegetable slices in the same way. Serve hot or cold.

ajlouke el qar maghrabi

pumpkin hors d'oeuvre

'The pumpkin gives birth and the fence has the trouble'
– said when a woman has married a man with children from a previous marriage
and who make her angry. Moroccan saying

675g (1¹/₂lb) pumpkin, peeled and cut into 5cm (2in) pieces
2 cloves garlic, crushed
Juice 1 lemon
1 level teaspoon ground caraway
1 level teaspoon coriander
1¹/₂ teaspoons salt
3 tablespoons olive oil

Garnish
1 tablespoon finely chopped fresh mint or 1 teaspoon dried mint

Half fill a large saucepan with water and bring to the boil. Add the pumpkin pieces and simmer for 15 minutes or until soft. Strain into a colander. When cool enough to handle squeeze the flesh between your hands to extract as much water as possible. Transfer to a bowl and mash with a fork.

Add all the remaining ingredients and mix thoroughly. Spread on a shallow serving dish and garnish with the mint. Serve cold. **Serves 6**

mzoura

carrots in hot sauce

From Tunisia this delicious spicy dish makes an excellent starter or a fine accompaniment to grilled fish.

675g (1¹/₂lb) carrots, peeled and cut into thin rounds
4–5 tablespoons oil

2 cloves garlic, crushed
1 teaspoon harissa mixed with 5 tablespoons water (see Glossary)
1 teaspoon powdered caraway
4 tablespoons vinegar
1 teaspoon salt
1/2 teaspoon cumin
3 tablespoons finely chopped parsley

Half fill a saucepan with water and bring to the boil. Add the carrot slices and simmer for about 15 minutes or until just tender. Strain into a colander.

Heat the oil in a pan, add the garlic, harissa mixture, caraway, vinegar, salt and cumin and stir well. Mix in the carrots, cover the pan and cook for a further 10 minutes or until the liquid is greatly reduced. Remove from the heat, stir in the parsley and transfer to a serving dish. Serve hot or cold. **Serves 4-6**

batata-be-kamoun

potato with cumin

'How I shall water you oh cumin plant' – meaning that the debtor will pay
him his due when the cumin is watered, is never, because cumin is never watered.
Moroccan proverb

A delicious way of serving potatoes which is good as an appetiser, but also makes
an ideal accompaniment to grilled meats.

675g (1¹/₂lb) potatoes
1 teaspoon harissa mixed with 4 tablespoons water (see Glossary)
2 teaspoons cumin
1¹/₂ teaspoons salt
Juice 1 large lemon
4 tablespoons oil

Garnish
1 tablespoon finely chopped parsley

Rinse the potatoes, drop into a pan of boiling water and cook until just tender. Strain into a colander. Meanwhile put the harissa mixture, cumin, salt, lemon juice and oil into a large bowl and mix well.

When the potatoes are cool enough to handle peel and cut into 2.5cm (1in) cubes. Add to the bowl and toss well in the dressing. Pile into a serving dish, garnish with the parsley and serve cold. **Serves 4-6**

salatit batata

– potato with caraway –

A tasty Algerian salad which replaces the cumin with caraway.

Prepare the potatoes as described above. Heat 6 tablespoons oil in a pan, add juice 1 lemon, 1 teaspoon harissa mixed with 4 tablespoons water, 1 teaspoon powdered caraway and 1¹/2 teaspoons salt. Simmer until most of the liquid has evaporated. Add potato cubes and toss until well coated with the mixture. Transfer to a serving dish and leave until cold. **Serves 4-6**

salatit mischwia

grilled tomato and pepper salad

A classic Tunisian dish which is served as a starter and also as an accompaniment to meat and fish dishes. It is tasty, and simple to prepare.

6 large, firm, ripe tomatoes
3 large peppers
Juice 1 lemon
1 teaspoon salt
1/4 teaspoon black pepper
1 small onion, finely chopped
2 tablespoons finely chopped parsley
3 tablespoons oil

Garnish
Black olives

Arrange the tomatoes and peppers on a large baking tray and either roast in a hot oven (200C, 400F, Gas Mark 6) or cook under a hot grill for 15–20 minutes, turning occasionally until skins are wrinkled and burnt. Drop the vegetables into cold water immediately. Peel off the skins and chop the vegetables finely. Place them in a bowl and add the remaining ingredients and mix thoroughly. Transfer to a serving dish and garnish with the olives. **Serves 4-6**

salatit meuklia bi filfil

– fried tomato and pepper salad –

150ml (1/4 pint) oil
2 onions, thinly sliced
4 green peppers, seeded and cut into thin strips

4 large tomatoes, blanched and peeled
2 cloves garlic, crushed
1 teaspoon chilli pepper
1/2 teaspoon cumin
1 teaspoon salt

Heat oil in large frying pan, add onions and fry until soft. Remove with a slotted spoon and reserve. Add the sliced peppers to the pan and fry until soft. Chop the tomatoes and add to the pan together with the onions and remaining ingredients. Stir well and simmer until all the vegetables are cooked and most of the liquid has evaporated. Transfer to a serving dish. Excellent hot or cold. **Serves 4-6**

brouklou min anshouwa

cauliflower with anchovies

Anchovies are found in abundance on the Mediterranean coastline of the Meghrib. There are many similar dishes making use of small fish and vegetables – aubergines with sardines, courgettes with anchovies etc. Excellent as a starter, you can serve this dish hot or cold with pickles, bread or rice.

1 cauliflower, broken into florets
2 large potatoes, quartered
3 tablespoons oil
2 cloves garlic, crushed
1 teaspoon harissa (see Glossary) mixed with 5–6 tablespoons water
Juice 1 lemon
1 teaspoon powdered caraway
1 teaspoon salt
1 tin anchovies

Half fill a large saucepan with lightly salted water and bring to the boil. Add cauliflower and potatoes, lower heat and simmer for 8–10 minutes or until just tender. Strain into colander.

Heat oil in a large frying pan, add garlic, harissa mixture, lemon juice, caraway and salt and mix well. Remove anchovies from the tin and reserve six. Cut the remaining ones into small pieces and add to the frying pan. Cook over a low heat for about 5 minutes, stirring frequently.

Cut the potatoes into 2.5cm (1in) cubes and add them and the cauliflower florets to the pan. Stir gently to baste the vegetables with the pan juices. Cook gently for 4–5 minutes. Transfer to a serving dish and garnish with the reserved anchovies. **Serves 4-6**

— fresh salads —

The concept of salad (from the Latin *sal* – salt – presumably derived from the early Roman custom of dipping lettuce, cucumber or endive into salt before eating), as understood in Europe, did not exist until a few generations ago in the Meghrib. Vegetables were eaten raw with just a little lemon juice sprinkled over them. Even today a modest household table will have a plate of sliced tomatoes garnished with olives, or a plate of onions thinly sliced with radishes, cucumbers, olives and a few hard-boiled eggs all sprinkled with salt, olive oil and lemon juice or vinegar.

A typical hotel menu will offer a salad – Salad Marocaine – which is a large plate of grilled and chopped green peppers, tomatoes mixed in olive oil and garnished with black and violet olives. Another ever popular hotel salad is one called Bigarree – a mixed salad of asparagus, sliced beetroot, cubed potatoes, shredded cabbage, sliced cucumber, egg topped with mayonnaise, all garnished with lemon juice and olive oil. And in the last few decades, certain authentic North African 'salads' have been developed – most making use of the fruits and vegetables of the region such as oranges, olives, limes etc.

chalda karnoune

raw artichoke salad

2 lemons
4 medium artichokes
1 teaspoon salt
1/4 teaspoon black pepper
1/4 teaspoon paprika

Garnish
Slices of cucumber, spring onions and olives

Three-quarters fill a large bowl with cold water and stir in the juice of one of the lemons. Halve the other lemon.

Take one artichoke and cut off as much of the stem as possible. Pull off and discard any tough or bruised outer leaves. Lay on its side and slice off and discard the top third of the artichoke. Rub all the cut edges and the base with one of the lemon halves. Holding the artichoke in one hand place the thumb of that hand firmly on the lower part of each leaf and with the other hand snap back and pull off the leaf. The thumb will hold the meaty part of the leaf intact. Keep rubbing cut edges with the lemon. Spread out the top leaves and pull out the prickly, purple leaves surrounding the hairy choke. Use a teaspoon to scrape out and discard the choke. Squeeze lemon juice into the centre. Cut the artichoke in half and drop into the acidulated water. Repeat with remaining artichokes.

After 15 minutes remove the artichokes and drain. Slice thinly and transfer to a bowl. Squeeze the remaining lemon halves and pour the juice over the artichokes. Add the salt, pepper and paprika and toss the salad lightly. Arrange on a serving plate and garnish. **Serves 4-6**

chalda brouklou

raw cauliflower salad

This very simple, crisp Moroccan salad is easy to prepare.

1 small cauliflower
1 tablespoon finely chopped onion
3 tablespoons oil
Juice 1 large lemon
1 teaspoon salt
1/2 teaspoon black pepper
1/2 teaspoon paprika
1 tablespoon finely chopped parsley

Break the cauliflower into small florets, rinse and drain. Place the remaining ingredients in a salad bowl and mix well. Add the cauliflower and toss well. Chill for at least an hour before serving. **Serves 6-8**

Using the same ingredients as above fry the cauliflower florets in the oil until lightly browned and then proceed as above.

chalda brouklou sfaxinya

cauliflower salad à la sfax

This Tunisian favourite uses potatoes with the cauliflower. Sfax (Safagis) is the second largest city in Tunisia and faces the Mediterranean and the Kerkenna Islands. Since ancient times Sfax has been the centre of a rich land, as skilful irrigation and the moist air that comes from the nearby forests have created a fertile soil, rich and productive, where most of the country's olive trees are found. Those olives have survived from ancient times. They even endured the onslaught of the infamous nomadic Banu Hilal and Banu Sulaim tribes.

1 small cauliflower, broken into florets
2 large potatoes, peeled and quartered
1 teaspoon harissa mixed with 2 tablespoons water (see Glossary)
1 teaspoon powdered caraway
1/2 teaspoon coriander
1 teaspoon salt
3 tablespoons oil
Juice 1 large lemon

Half fill a large saucepan with lightly salted water and bring to the boil. Add the cauliflower and potatoes and simmer for 10 minutes or until just tender. Do not overcook. Strain into a colander.

Mix all the remaining ingredients together in a salad bowl. Add the vegetables and toss gently until well coated in the dressing. Refrigerate until ready to serve.
Serves 6-8

meslalla

olive salad

Beloved by all, this salad of olives (violet, black or green – see Glossary for preparation methods) appears almost everywhere, all the time. The olive and its oil were, and still are, venerated by the people of North Africa.

110g (4oz) washed and stoned olives (use mixed for attractive colouring)
Juice 2 large lemons
1 teaspoon paprika
1/2 teaspoon chilli pepper
1/2 teaspoon cumin
1 clove garlic, crushed
1 teaspoon salt
2 tablespoons oil
2 tablespoons finely chopped parsley

Mix all the ingredients together in a salad bowl and refrigerate before serving.
Serves 4-6

'The Marabout seeing my little stock of oil, burst forth with a violent panegyric on olive oil as he dipped his fingers into it and licked them, not much to my satisfaction – "Oil is my life! Without oil I droop, and am out of life; with oil I raise my head and am a man, and my family [wife] feels I am a man. Oil is my rum – oil is better than meat." So continued Mohammed, tossing up his head and smacking his lips.

'I have no doubt there is great strength in olive oil. An Arab will live three months on barley-meal paste dipped in olive oil. Arabs will drink oil as we drink wine.' Travels in the Great Desert of Sahara

— orange salads —

'A beautiful orange
Peeled off her rays
Inundated her colours
Into the horizons of the universe,
Suckling the still bright day
Which undressed inside out.'

Jardins de Marrakech

Olives, dates, oranges and lemons are the pride of the Meghrib. These subtropical fruits abound throughout the countryside. Olive groves spread for miles and miles, palm-trees forest the oases and people's back gardens are strewn with orange and lemon trees. Indeed, the wide modern boulevards of such towns as Fez, Oran, Tunis and Marrakech are decorated with orange trees and date palms. With the former (when in season) one simply has to stretch one's arm to reach the fruit, with the latter one has to climb (forbidden), or throw stones at the heavily laden bunches of fruit – an occupation universally loved by children!

It is not surprising that oranges appear extensively in North African cuisine. The surprise is that they do not play a still larger part, as for example citrus fruits do in modern Israeli and Californian cuisines; but then the North Africans are traditionalists at heart, not daringly experimental like the Americans.

However, as the recipes below show, there are some fine such recipes.

chalda bartogal wa zaitun

orange and olive salad

This first one incorporates both the olive and the orange. It is from Morocco and is simple, refreshing and excellent as a starter or an accompaniment to meat and poultry grills.

4 large oranges, peeled, white membrane removed
20–30 black olives, washed and stoned
Juice 1 small lemon
1 teaspoon salt

³/4 teaspoon cumin
¹/2 teaspoon chilli pepper or harissa (see Glossary)

Divide the oranges into segments and cut each of them into 3 pieces. Place in a salad bowl with the remaining ingredients and toss thoroughly. Refrigerate before serving. **Serves 6**

chalda bartogal wa jazar

orange and carrot salad

From Morocco, a plateful of golden taste and appearance which is ideal with all kinds of meat and poultry dishes.

450g (1lb) carrots, peeled and grated
2 large oranges, peeled and white membrane removed, then cut into thin rounds
¹/2 teaspoon salt
2 teaspoons orange blossom water
1 tablespoon caster sugar
Juice 1 large lemon

Place all the ingredients in a salad bowl and toss thoroughly. Refrigerate before serving. **Serves 4-6**

chalda bartogal wa fijil

orange and radish salad

'The radish is a good
And doubtless wholesome food,
But proves, to vex the eater,
A powerful repeater.
This only fault I find;
What should be left behind
Comes issuing instead
Right from the eater's head.'
Ibn Quzman, Anthology of Moorish Poetry

Here is a colourful and tasty salad excellent with grills and kebabs. The radishes used are the long variety, but round ones will do.

6 long radishes or about 12 round, fat radishes
2 large oranges, peeled, white pith removed, thinly sliced crossways
Juice 1 lemon
1 tablespoon orange blossom water
2 teaspoons caster sugar
1/2 teaspoon salt
1/2 teaspoon cinnamon

Rinse the radishes thoroughly under cold running water. Place in a bowl of cold water and leave to soak for 30 minutes, changing the water at least twice. Drain them and coarsely grate. Place in a salad bowl with the orange slices.

Mix the remaining ingredients in a small bowl and pour over the salad. Toss and refrigerate for 30 minutes before serving. **Serves 4-6**

salatit limoun

lemon salad

From Fez, this biting yet piquant salad is certainly different and is surprisingly delicious. Try with hot or cold meats and with bread and cheese.

2 ripe lemons, peeled
1 small onion, thinly sliced
3 tablespoons finely chopped parsley
1 teaspoon paprika
1/4 teaspoon chilli pepper
1/2 teaspoon cumin
8 violet olives, stoned
8 black or green olives, stoned
1 teaspoon salt
4 tablespoons oil

Place the lemons in a bowl of lightly salted cold water for 30 minutes. Remove and halve. Squeeze out and reserve the juice. Cut the lemon flesh into small pieces and place in a salad bowl. Add the remaining ingredients and half the reserved lemon juice and mix well. Serve. **Serves 4-6**

chalda loubia khadra

green beans with almonds

This is an unusual salad of green beans with mayonnaise and almonds.

I have no idea who first conceived the idea, but it was served to me at the home of an Algerian couple in good old Salford a few rainy months ago. So here it is, with a homely Moroccan proviso: 'Eat, don't ask.'

675g (1¹/₂lb) French beans, topped and tailed
3 tablespoons finely chopped parsley
150ml (¹/₄ pint) mayonnaise
1 teaspoon cumin
4 hard-boiled eggs, thinly sliced
50g (2oz) slivered almonds, toasted until golden
Black olives

Cook the beans in lightly salted boiling water for 8–10 minutes or until just tender. Strain into a colander and leave to cool.

Place the parsley, mayonnaise and cumin in a bowl and mix well. Add the beans and toss gently. Taste and adjust seasoning if necessary. Pile the mixture into the centre of a shallow dish. Arrange the sliced eggs around the edge and scatter the almonds and olives over the salad. Serve immediately. **Serves 6**

salatit feggous

cucumber salad

In this recipe the Meghribi will use the 'snake' or 'curving cucumber' – a type which is not readily available in Britain although I have managed to find a few in Indian grocery stores. *Feggous* is a long, thin vegetable which tends to be much drier than the ordinary cucumber. If *feggous* is not available I suggest that you use as an alternative the much smaller, 15cm (6in) long cucumbers which can also often be found in Indian and Middle Eastern stores – at least these have more flavour than the long, thick 'sticks' we are often obliged to eat. However, if the worst comes to the worst (and it often does) use ordinary cucumbers.

450g (1lb) feggous, washed and grated
¹/₂ teaspoon salt
1 teaspoon dried thyme, crushed
Juice ¹/₂ lemon
1 tablespoon sugar

If using ordinary cucumber drain in a fine sieve for 15 minutes before mixing. Place all the ingredients in a salad bowl and mix well. **Serves 4-6**

chalda khiar

– cucumber salad –

This is a Tunisian cucumber salad mixed with cream.

450g (1lb) cucumber, thinly sliced
2 tablespoons finely chopped fresh mint or 1 tablespoon dried mint
1/2 teaspoon salt
1/4 teaspoon black pepper
150ml (1/4 pint) single cream

Put the cucumber slices in a bowl of lightly salted water and leave for 10 minutes. Drain thoroughly. Place in a salad bowl with the remaining ingredients, toss and serve.
Serves 4-6

bekoula

mallow salad

Bekoula is the name given in the Berber dialect to the common mallow (*malva sylvestris*) – an annual or perennial plant found in waste land, rubbish dumps, fields and roadsides. It is also cultivated for medical purposes – it makes a good tea for treating coughs, bronchitis, lung catarrh etc. The plant has large green leaves rather like spinach. When not in season use either fresh spinach or flat-leafed parsley – this can be bought from most Indian and Cypriot shops – ask for Greek or Arab parsley.

110g (4oz) mallow or flat-leafed parsley or spinach, chopped
50g (2oz) parsley, finely chopped
25g (1oz) fresh coriander or tarragon, finely chopped
2 sticks celery including leaves, finely chopped
3 cloves garlic
Zest of 1/2 pickled lemon (see page 250, optional)
2 teaspoons paprika
1/2 teaspoon chilli pepper
1 1/2 teaspoons salt
4 tablespoons oil
10–12 black olives, stoned
Juice 1 large lemon

Place the chopped herbs and vegetables in a colander and rinse thoroughly under cold water. Shake off excess moisture and place in a large saucepan with the whole cloves of garlic. Cook over a medium heat for about 10 minutes, stirring frequently. Do not add any water as that retained by the vegetables will be sufficient. Remove garlic cloves, peel, crush and return to the pan. Add lemon zest, paprika, chilli powder, salt and oil, lower the heat and simmer until all the water has evaporated. Stir occasionally. Add the lemon juice and olives and cook for a further 2 minutes.

Transfer to a salad bowl and leave to cool. Taste, adjust seasoning if necessary and serve. **Serves 4-6**

salatit el bayd tarablousia

egg salad tripoli-style

Tripoli (not to be confused with her name-sake in Lebanon) is the capital of the people's Joumhouriet of Libya – an ancient land always sparsely populated. Herodotus wrote in The Histories: *'One thing I can add about this country, so far as one knows, it is inhabited by four races – of which two are indigenous and two not. The indigenous peoples are the Libyans and Ethiopians, the former occupying the northerly, the latter the move southerly parts. The immigrants are the Phoenicians and Greeks. I do not think the country can be compared for the fertility of its soil with either Asia or Europe, with the single exception of the region called Cinyps – this region however is quite different from the rest of Libya, and is as good for cereal crops as any land in the world.'*

Almost 2500 years later Libya is still a sparsely populated land with little agriculture, and is still populated by four races – Berbers and African blacks (the indigenous people), Arabs and Europeans – Greeks, Italians etc (the immigrants). Nothing much appears, on the surface, to have changed in all that time, but this is not so. Libya is one of the most socially dynamic lands in the world and most certainly, with Algeria, the most progressive and ambitious country in Africa – often to the great consternation of certain western countries. What Libya is doing today, Africa will do tomorrow.

Now for our salad. It is simple, cheap and wholesome. The eggs go very well with the lettuce, the olives give it colour and flavour and as for the mayonnaise – well, that is the imperialist influence for you! But it does taste nice.

2 Cos or 1 iceberg lettuce, washed and drained
2 tablespoons finely chopped parsley
50g (2oz) raisins
1 teaspoon paprika
4 tomatoes, thinly sliced
6 hard-boiled eggs, quartered lengthways
1/2 teaspoon cumin
5–6 tablespoons mayonnaise

Black olives

Shred the lettuce and place in a large salad bowl with the parsley, raisins and paprika. Mix well. Arrange the tomato slices and egg quarters over the lettuce. Sprinkle with the cumin. Dribble the mayonnaise attractively over the salad and decorate with the olives. **Serves 6**

salatit fassouliya

fresh kidney bean salad

This method of cooking vegetables is typically North African. The beans are cooked with herbs, spices and oil and then served cold. You can use this method to cook peas, broad beans, French beans etc.

900g (2lb) fresh, small kidney beans, topped and tailed
1 teaspoon paprika
1 clove garlic, crushed
4 tablespoons oil
2 teaspoons salt
3 tablespoons finely chopped coriander or parsley
Juice 1 lemon
Peel of 1/2 pickled lemon (see page 250), thinly sliced, or
thinly sliced peel 1/2 lemon plus
1 tablespoon vinegar
Handful olives, stoned

Garnish
2 hard-boiled eggs, quartered
1 large tomato, thinly sliced

Cut the beans into 5cm (2in) pieces and place in a saucepan with the paprika, garlic, oil and salt. Add just enough water to cover the beans by 1cm (1/2in). Bring to the boil, lower the heat and simmer for 8–10 minutes or until the beans are just tender.

Stir in the coriander or parsley, lemon juice, lemon peel and olives and continue to cook, stirring occasionally until all the water has evaporated. Transfer to a salad bowl and leave to cool, then decorate with the eggs and tomato slices. **Serves 6**

chalda roz gsentina

rice salad constantine-style

A speciality of the Algerian city of Constantine. It is similar to several French and Italian rice salads although rice, in fact, is very little used in North African cooking. If you wish, after preparing the salad you can press it into a decorative mould and then turn out and garnish.

110g (4oz) long-grain rice, rinsed thoroughly, cooked until tender and drained
2 tomatoes, finely chopped
50g (2oz) green beans, cooked
50g (2oz) peas, cooked
2 tablespoons finely chopped spring onions
2 tablespoons finely chopped parsley
75g (3oz) flaked tuna fish or chopped prawns
1 teaspoon cumin
Juice 2 lemons
6 tablespoons oil
1 teaspoon salt
1/2 teaspoon black pepper

Garnish
Handful of mixed green and black olives, stoned
2 hard-boiled eggs, sliced

Place the rice, tomatoes, beans, peas, onions, parsley, fish or prawns and the cumin in a large salad bowl and mix well.

Mix the lemon juice, oil, salt and pepper together and pour this dressing over the salad. Toss thoroughly, taste, then adjust seasoning if necessary. Either decorate the salad in the bowl with the garnishes and serve or press the salad into a mould, turn out, decorate and serve. **Serves 6-8**

— entrées —

The North African cuisine, much like its Middle Eastern relations, does not traditionally have an entrée course – all the food is laid on the table at the same time.
Entrées as such are of recent vintage, a European influence that first affected the
hotels and restaurants and latterly the homes of middle-class Meghribians. In this
chapter therefore I have included all dishes that are now usually served between the
soup and the main course.

bastela

I open this chapter with one of the great dishes of the world – *bastela*.
A masterpiece of flavour, colour, texture and imagination, it is reputed to be of
Syrian origin. I think not. It is undoubtedly a product of the Spanish-Moorish
culture that flourished from the ninth to the sixteenth centuries in Andalusia and
Valencia. Indeed the Valencian *pastel di carne* and Andalusian *pastel di pollo*
(*pastel* is a round cake or pie in Spanish) are nothing but the primitive origins of
this most exquisite Moroccan dish, the pride and glory of Fez.

There are two kinds of people in this world; those who have eaten *bastela* and
those unfortunates who have not! I am one of the fortunate ones, as are my wife
and my son Raffi (I was instructed to mention his name somewhere in this book).
We ate *bastela* in Morocco – not in Tangier, Rabat or Marrakech, but in Fez –
and it was magnificent. The original inhabitants of Fez were, of course, Andalusian
Moslems. They were not necessarily of Berber or Arab origin, and a fair number
were Spanish Christian converts. They brought to Fez their food, culture, poetry
and music when they were finally thrown out of Spain. They brought *bastela* which,
in time, changed from being a simple meat or chicken pie to a dish 'worthy
of kings'. It now consists of a filling of pigeons/doves with eggs and spices topped
with a layer of almonds, sugar and cinnamon and all wrapped in layers of thin
crispy pastry.

There are two slight drawbacks about *bastela*. Firstly, it is a little time-consuming to
make, therefore it is worth waiting for some festive occasion to make the effort.
The second drawback might be the pigeons! Although these can be obtained from
a few specialist shops, I suggest that you substitute poussins.

As for the pastry I suggest you use baklava filo which you can buy from many
Middle Eastern and continental shops. However, if you wish to be really
authentic use the *bastela* pastry – *malsougua* or *ouarka*, the recipe for which
I have included in the Glossary.

To prepare this dish you need a circular tin about 3.5cm (1¹/₂in) deep and 30–35cm
(12–14in) in diameter.

450g (1lb) filo pastry (15 sheets) or about 30 sheets *ouarka*

filling, fez style

110g (4oz) butter
450g (1lb) onions, very finely chopped
6 x 450g (1lb) poussins, halved
2 teaspoons salt
1 teaspoon black pepper

1/2 teaspoon saffron diluted in 1 tablespoon water
11/2 teaspoons cinnamon
3 tablespoons finely chopped parsley
6 tablespoons oil
175g (6oz) blanched almonds
50g (2oz) sugar
6 eggs, beaten
1 egg yolk

garnish
2 tablespoons icing sugar
1 tablespoon cinnamon

To make the filling, melt the butter in a very large saucepan. Add the onion, halved poussins, salt, black pepper, saffron, cinnamon and parsley. Cover the pan and cook over a low heat for 20 minutes, stirring frequently. If necessary add about 150ml (1/4 pint) water, but you may find that the poussins have produced enough liquid in which to cook. Cover the pan and continue to cook over a low heat until the meat is tender. Remove the poussins and, when cool enough to handle, remove and coarsely shred the flesh.

Meanwhile heat the oil in a small saucepan, add the almonds and fry, stirring constantly, until golden. Remove with a slotted spoon, drain on kitchen paper and then grind in a mortar. Place in a bowl and mix in the sugar and 2 tablespoons of the oil. Reserve remaining oil.

Return the saucepan in which the poussins were cooked to the heat, and continue to simmer until all the liquid has evaporated. Add the beaten eggs and cook over a low heat, stirring constantly until the eggs have set.

To assemble the bastela, first oil the large round tin, then cover it with 5 sheets of filo overlapping them so that at least 10cm (4in) of each sheet hangs over the edge of the tin. Place 2 more sheets over the base trimming off any corners which are too large to fit into the tin. Sprinkle the egg mixture evenly over the base and cover with 2 more sheets of filo, again trimming away any excess pastry. Spread the pieces of poussin over the pastry. Cover with another 2 sheets of pastry and then sprinkle the ground almond mixture evenly over the top. Fold the overhanging pastry in over the filling, brushing the edges to hold them down. Place the remaining 4 sheets of pastry over the top so that at least 10cm (4in) of each sheet overhangs the edge of the tin. Tuck these ends in under the bastela as though making a bed. The pie should be no more than 3.5cm (11/2in) thick.

Brush the surface with some of the reserved oil and then with the egg yolk. Place in an oven preheated to 350F, 180C, Gas Mark 4 and cook for 20 minutes. Remove from the oven, turn onto a large tray and then slide back upside down into the tin. Return to the oven and cook for a further 20 minutes. To serve, turn out onto a large serving dish, almond layer uppermost, and decorate with the icing sugar and cinnamon. Serve immediately, and eat with your hands please. No knives and forks.
Serves 8-10

filling, marrakech style

25g (1oz) butter
450g (1lb) onions, grated
6 x 450g (1lb) poussins, halved
2 tablespoons finely chopped parsley
1¹/2 teaspoons black pepper
1/2 teaspoon ginger
1/4 teaspoon nutmeg
1 tablespoon cinnamon
1/2 teaspoon saffron diluted in 2 tablespoons water
2 teaspoons salt

egg layer

600ml (1 pint) chicken stock
1 large onion, grated
6 tablespoons chopped parsley
12 hard-boiled eggs, chopped
2 tablespoons cinnamon
Juice 1 large lemon

Place ingredients, from butter to salt, in a large pan, cover and cook over a low heat for 20 minutes, stirring frequently. Add a little water if necessary, recover and simmer until the poussins are tender. Remove from the pan and, when cool enough to handle, remove and coarsely shred the flesh.

Meanwhile, to make the egg layer, simmer the chicken stock with grated onion and chopped parsley until the onion is tender and the mixture is virtually a dry paste. Place in a bowl and add to it the chopped hard-boiled eggs, cinnamon and lemon juice. Knead this mixture well.

Prepare the *bastela* as above but incorporating only two layers of filling – shredded poussin and egg. Cook as preceding recipe, decorate with icing sugar and cinnamon and 15–20 toasted whole almonds.

trid

layered pancakes with pigeon

'Don't marry an old woman, even though you will eat young pigeons and lamb's meat with her' i.e. the most delicious food Moroccan saying

'If the rich eat bastela, what of the poor?' 'They have trid.'

Trid – the poor man's *bastela* – is another speciality of Fez. The pancakes, made with *rghaif* batter (see Glossary) are layered with pigeon, chicken or lamb. These pancakes are not cooked in a frying pan, but in a round earthenware pot called *qdra dial trid*. The pot has a big opening at each end. The embers are placed inside the pot which is then laid on supporting stones. I suggest you use a large saucepan or tin with a smooth base placed upside down over a simmering pan of water.

Poussins are a very satisfactory substitute for pigeons, but you can also use either a 1.5–1.75kg (3–4lb) chicken or 675g (1¹/2lb) lamb cut into 1cm (¹/2in) pieces.

Rghaif dough (but omit the yeast, see Glossary)

filling
1.75kg (4lb) poussins (pigeons) or chicken or meat (see above)
3 large onions, finely chopped
1 teaspoon pepper
¹/4 teaspoon saffron
50g (2oz) *smen* or butter (see Glossary)
5cm (2in) stick cinnamon

garnish
2 tablespoons cinnamon
2–3 tablespoons icing sugar

First prepare the filling by halving the poussins or pigeons (or chicken pieces or chopped meat) and placing them in a large saucepan. Add the remaining filling ingredients, cover the pan and place over a low to medium heat. Cook for 15 minutes, stirring frequently. If you think the mixture needs a little water add 5–6 tablespoons, but you will probably find that the meat and onions give off enough liquid. Continue to simmer, covered, for a further 30–45 minutes or until the flesh is tender. Remove the halved poussins or chicken pieces etc and set aside until cool enough to handle. Meanwhile continue to simmer the onion sauce until the liquid has evaporated. Bone and chop the meat coarsely, return to the pan, stir well and set aside. Reheat when it is time to layer the pancakes.

Prepare the dough as described on page 299, and divide into 24 balls. Turn a large saucepan or baking sheet, which is at least 30cm (12in) wide and has a smooth bottom, upside down over a pan of simmering water. Lightly oil your hands and a working top, take a ball of dough and gently stretch it in all directions until it forms a paper-thin sheet. Do not use a rolling pin. Do not worry too much if there are one or two holes! Now pick it up and place on the upturned pan. It is much easier to do this if you have someone to help lift the other end. Cook for about 30 seconds and then turn over and cook the other side for the same length of time. Remove and place in the bottom of a large, suitably sized ovenproof casserole. Prepare and cook 2 more pancakes in the same way and layer in the casserole. Now sprinkle the top pancake with one-quarter of the cinnamon and icing sugar. Prepare and cook 3 more pancakes and layer in the casserole. Spread half the filling evenly over the pancakes. Prepare and cook 3 more pancakes and layer over the filling. Sprinkle with another quarter of the cinnamon and icing sugar. Prepare and cook 3 more pancakes and layer in the pan. Spread with the remaining filling. Prepare, cook and layer the remaining pancakes, sprinkling a further quarter of the cinnamon and icing sugar halfway through. Top the last pancake with all the remaining cinnamon and icing sugar.

Cover the casserole and place in an oven preheated to 400F, 200C, Gas Mark 6. Bake for 15–20 minutes, remove and serve immediately. Cut into wedges and accompany with lemon wedges and salad. **Serves 6**

rhhaif-el-farrani

agrisse-filled pancakes

Now, if you cannot even afford *trid*, your only other choice is *rghaif-el-farrani*! A marvellous choice in my opinion. Made with *rghaif* dough these pastries are filled with onion, parsley, pepper, cumin and *agrisse* – the leftovers of *khli* (see Glossary). I have substituted minced meat for the *agrisse*. This recipe will make about 20 pancakes and so I suggest you halve the propo rtions if they are to be eaten as a starter. In Morocco these pancakes are eaten as savouries or as a light lunch with a glass of mint tea. I would add to that a bowl of salad of your choice.

Rghaif dough (see Glossary)

filling
225g (8oz) agrisse or minced meat
225g (8oz) onion, finely chopped
4 tablespoons finely chopped walnuts or almonds
2 tablespoons finely chopped parsley
1/2 teaspoon salt
2 teaspoons paprika
1 teaspoon chilli pepper
1 teaspoon cumin

First prepare the filling. If using minced meat place it in a small pan with the onion and fry for 15–20 minutes, stirring frequently until the meat is cooked. Stir in the remaining ingredients and set aside to cool. If using agrisse simply mix all the ingredients together well in a bowl.

Prepare the *rghaif* dough as described in the Glossary and divide it into 40 walnut-sized balls and place on a lightly oiled surface. Now lightly oil your hands and a working top, take one ball, flatten it and gently pull and stretch it in all directions to make a paper-thin sheet. Do not use a rolling pin. Place a soupspoonful of the filling in the centre and fold the edges over to form a square. Now stretch out another ball of dough in the same way. Place the filled pancake in the centre of this sheet with its smooth side uppermost. Fold the edges over in the same way. Place this square, stuffed pancake on a lightly oiled tray. Continue to prepare and stuff the pancakes until you have used up all the ingredients. Place each stuffed pancake on the baking sheet leaving a little space between each. Flatten them slightly with your fingers. Bake in an oven preheated to 375F, 190C, Gas Mark 5 for about 30 minutes or until golden. Serve immediately. **Makes 20**

m'hadjeb

pancakes filled with onion and tomato

An Algerian speciality which is similar to the previous recipe. The pancakes should be made with very fine semolina and not sifted flour as with rghaif, but the latter is equally good. This is a much lighter dish and makes a fine starter, savoury or a light lunch if served with a bowl of salad.

Rghaif dough (see Glossary), but made with fine semolina

filling
3 large onions, chopped
2 tablespoons *smen* or 25g (1oz) butter (see Glossary)
3 ripe tomatoes, blanched, peeled and coarsely chopped
1 teaspoon harissa
1 teaspoon salt
1/2 teaspoon cumin

Prepare the filling by frying the onions in the butter until soft and transparent. Add the remaining ingredients and cook for a further 5–10 minutes, stirring frequently. Set aside to cool. Prepare and cook the pancakes as described above.

Traditionally these pastries are cooked in a tajine dish and sprinkled with oil while cooking to keep them soft and tender, but the method above will do just as well. **Makes 20**

breiks
— stuffed pastries —

What *bastela* is to Morocco, *breiks* are to Tunisia (also known as bourek in Algeria and *briouat* in Morocco). They are paper-thin pastries filled with vegetables, meat, chicken, rice, eggs etc. They are very like the Ottoman-Turkish boregs from whence the name.

The pastry dough for *breik* is unique. I am not sure whether it is Tunisian or Moroccan, but both claim it as theirs. There is a slight difference: malsougua, the Tunisian, is made with semolina, and *ouarka*, the Moroccan, is made with sifted flour. For preparation of this latter dough see the Glossary.

You can substitute the *breik* dough with commercial filo pastry, packets of which are sold in Middle Eastern and Indian shops. This pastry unfortunately lacks the thinness and transparent quality of *ouarka* pastry, but it is still a satisfactory substitute.

These pastries are usually folded in one of three ways – in squares, triangles or cylinders.

squares

Cut the pastry sheets into strips about 12.5 x 30cm (5 x 12in).
Cut and fill one sheet at a time and cover the rest with a tea towel to prevent them drying out. When you have used up all the filling wrap any remaining sheets up and store in fridge or freezer for future use. Place 1 heaped teaspoon of the filling about 2.5cm (1in) in from the short edge nearest you and flatten it slightly.
Fold as illustrated below.

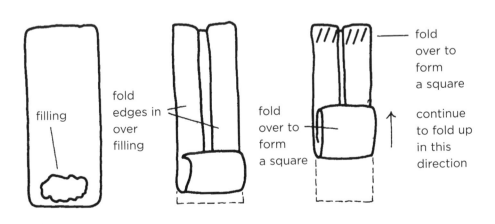

filling

fold edges in over filling

fold over to form a square

fold over to form a square

continue to fold up in this direction

fold over to form a square

triangles

Cut pastry as described in Squares above. Place a heaped teaspoon about 2.5cm (1in) in from the short edge nearest you and fold as illustrated below.

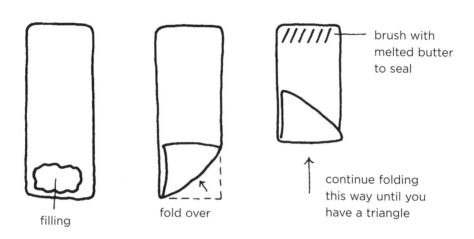

filling

fold over

brush with melted butter to seal

continue folding this way until you have a triangle

cylinders

Cut the pastry as described in Squares above. Place 1 heaped teaspoon of the filling about 2.5cm (1in) in from the edge nearest you and spread it into a ridge. Roll up as illustrated below.

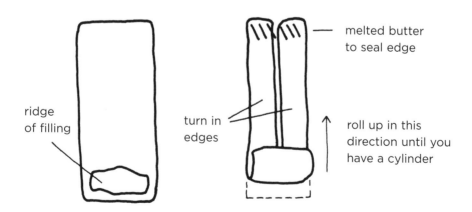

ridge of filling

turn in edges

melted butter to seal edge

roll up in this direction until you have a cylinder

bourek felfel

pepper breik

From Algeria, this *breik* is nearer to the Middle Eastern *borek* than most Tunisian *breiks*. The dough is similar to that used in the famed *cerkez pufboregi*, Circassian meat boreks. You can fry these *breiks* or bake them in the oven.

Sometimes the pepper *chakchouka* filling is replaced by a slice of cheese – Cheddar, feta or haloumi.

meat filling
275g (10oz) minced meat
1 small onion, grated
1 tablespoon finely chopped parsley
1 tablespoon *smen* or 15g (1/2oz) butter (see Glossary)
1 teaspoon salt
1/2 teaspoon black pepper

pepper *chakchouka*
4 green peppers
1 green chilli pepper, finely chopped, or 1 teaspoon harissa
2 tomatoes, blanched, peeled and finely chopped
2 cloves garlic, crushed
2 tablespoons oil

dough
450g (1lb) plain flour
1 teaspoon salt
2 eggs
4 tablespoons oil
150ml (1/4 pint) mixed milk and water
75g (3oz) *smen*, or butter, melted

First prepare the meat filling by mixing all the ingredients together in a saucepan and frying over a medium heat, stirring regularly, for about 20 minutes or until cooked. Set aside to cool.

Meanwhile to prepare the *chakchouka* place the whole green peppers under a hot grill or in a hot oven and cook, turning regularly until the skins are dark brown and wrinkled. Remove and, when cool enough to handle, peel off the skin, discard the seeds and chop the flesh. Place in a frying pan with the remaining ingredients and fry for 12–15 minutes, stirring frequently. Set aside to cool.

To prepare the dough sift the flour and salt into a large bowl and make a well in the centre. Add the eggs and oil and mix with a wooden spoon. Knead for about 10 minutes gradually adding enough of the milk and water mixture to make a soft, smooth dough. Shape the dough into a large ball and dust with flour. Divide into 18 lumps and roll into small balls. Sprinkle a working top with flour and roll out one of the balls as thinly as possible into a circle about 17.5–20cm (7–8in) in diameter. Set aside on a floured top and brush its upper surface with a little of the melted butter. Roll another ball out as thinly as possible, place it on top of the first one and then brush its upper surface with melted butter. Continue rolling out the balls, brushing the upper surface of each circle with butter and then stacking them on top of each other. Sprinkle a large part of the work top generously with flour and place the stack of circles in the centre. Flour the rolling pin and roll out the pile of circles until you have one very large, very thin sheet of dough.

Cut the pastry into 10cm (4in) squares or circles. Place 1 teaspoon of the meat filling and 1 teaspoon of the pepper mixture in the middle of each, dampen edges with cold water and fold in half to form a triangle (if pastry is cut into squares) or a semi-circle (if cut into circles). Seal the edges with the prongs of a fork. Continue until you have used up all the dough and filling.

If deep-frying, heat sufficient oil in a large pan to fry the *breiks*, a few at a time, until golden. Remove with a slotted spoon and drain on kitchen paper. If baking, place on lightly greased baking trays, brush with a little beaten egg and bake in an oven preheated to 400F, 200C, Gas Mark 6 for 15–20 minutes or until risen and golden. Serve hot. **Makes 24–26**

breik bil batata

potato breik

This tasty *breik* recipe is from Tunisia, as are many of the recipes I have given in this section.

12 sheets *ouarka* (see Glossary) or about 18–20 strips filo cut as in
Squares on page 69
Oil for frying

filling
350g (12oz) potatoes, peeled and cubed
2 eggs
1 onion, finely chopped
2–3 cloves garlic, chopped
1 teaspoon salt
1/2 teaspoon black pepper
4 tablespoons finely chopped parsley

For the filling, place the potatoes in a saucepan with one of the eggs (to hard-boil it) and cover with water. Bring to the boil and simmer until the potatoes are tender. Drain, remove egg and mash potatoes. Meanwhile heat 2 tablespoons oil in a frying pan, add the onion, garlic, salt and pepper and fry for about 5 minutes or until the onion is soft. Stir in the parsley. Add the mashed potatoes and the raw egg and mix thoroughly. Chop the hard-boiled egg finely.

Either place 1 tablespoon of the filling on one-half of a sheet of *ouarka* and fold over to form a semi-circle, or fill the strips of filo as described above. As you finish them cover with a tea towel to prevent them drying. When they are all prepared add enough oil to cover the base of a large frying pan by about 5cm (2in) and heat. Add a few *breiks* at a time and fry until golden on both sides, turning once. Remove with a slotted spoon and drain on kitchen paper. Serve immediately. **Serves 6**

briouat bil kafta

minced meat *breiks*

A Moroccan speciality, *briouats* are *breiks* that are usually filled with minced meat – as in this recipe – or with Mergues sausages (see Glossary). Roll the sausages in *ouarka* sheets about 15 x 20cm (6 x 8in) to make cylindrical *breiks* the size of the sausages and then fry.

Brains are also often used as a filling, but by far the most popular *briouats* are those filled with minced meat or rice. This is a standard recipe for kafta *briouat*.

12 sheets *ouarka* (see Glossary) or about 18–20 strips filo cut as in Squares on page 69

filling
2 tablespoons oil
250g (9oz) minced meat
1 teaspoon cumin
1 teaspoon paprika
1/2 teaspoon chilli pepper
3 tablespoons finely chopped parsley
1 tablespoon finely chopped fresh coriander
1 small onion, finely chopped
1 teaspoon salt
3 eggs, beaten
1 teaspoon cinnamon

garnish
Cinnamon
Icing sugar

Heat the oil in a saucepan, add the meat, cumin, paprika, chilli pepper, parsley, coriander, onion and salt and cook over a moderate heat, stirring frequently for about 20 minutes or until the meat is cooked. Pour the eggs over the meat, sprinkle with the cinnamon and cook for a further 3–4 minutes, stirring constantly. Remove from the heat and leave to cool.

Now prepare and cook the *breiks* as described in *Breik* Bil Batata (page 72). Sprinkle with cinnamon and icing sugar and serve hot. **Serves 6**

breik bil djaj

breik with chicken filling

12 sheets *ouarka* (see Glossary) or about 18–20 strips filo cut as in Squares, page 69

filling
350g (12oz) chicken breast
1 onion, peeled and quartered
1 large potato, peeled and quartered
1 teaspoon salt
4 tablespoons finely chopped parsley
1 large egg
1/4 teaspoon black pepper
1/2 teaspoon paprika

To prepare the filling place the chicken and onion in a saucepan, add about 900ml (1½ pints) of water and bring to the boil. Lower the heat and simmer for 20 minutes. Add the potatoes and salt and simmer for a further 20 minutes or until potatoes are cooked. Drain into a colander.

When cool enough to handle remove skin and bones from the chicken and discard. Chop the chicken flesh, onion and potatoes and place in a bowl with the remaining ingredients. Mix well and, when cold, prepare *breiks* as described in *Breik Bil Batata* (page 72). **Serves 6**

briouat bil-roz

rice-filled *breiks*

These make excellent starters, savouries or entrées when served with salads.

12 sheets *ouarka* (see Glossary) or about 18–20 strips filo cut as in Squares, page 69

240ml (8fl oz) milk

150ml (5fl oz) water

75g (3oz) long-grain rice, rinsed thoroughly under cold running water

25g (1oz) butter

1/2 teaspoon salt

1 teaspoon caster sugar

1 tablespoon orange blossom water

2 tablespoons oil

50g (2oz) blanched almonds

garnish

Icing sugar

Cinnamon

Place the milk and water in a saucepan and bring to the boil. Add the rice, butter and salt, lower the heat and cook for 15 minutes, stirring frequently. Stir in the sugar and orange blossom water and cook for a further 8–10 minutes, still stirring frequently. Remove the pan from the heat and leave to cool, but stir from time to time. Meanwhile heat the oil in a small pan, add the blanched almonds and fry until golden. Remove with a slotted spoon and pulverise either in a mortar or in a blender. Add the powdered almonds to the rice mixture and stir well.

When the mixture is cold prepare and cook the *breiks* as described in *Breik Bil Batata* (page 72). Sprinkle with a little icing sugar and cinnamon and serve hot.

Serves 6

bourek hout

fish-filled *breiks*

A delicious *breik* which makes an excellent starter or entrée.

12 sheets *ouarka* (see Glossary) or about 18–20 strips filo cut as in Squares, page 69

filling

350g (12oz) white fish steaks, grilled, fried or poached

1 clove garlic, crushed

4–5 tablespoons chopped parsley

1 teaspoon salt

1/2 teaspoon black pepper

Juice 1/2 lemon

50g (2oz) stale bread, soaked in water

2 hard-boiled eggs, finely chopped

Remove and discard any fish bones and skin, then flake the flesh and place in a bowl. Add the garlic, parsley, salt, pepper and lemon juice. Thoroughly squeeze as much moisture as possible from the bread and add to the bowl. Mash the ingredients well with a fork. Stir in the chopped hard-boiled eggs.

When the mixture is cold prepare and cook the *breiks* as described in *Breik Bil Batata* (page 72). Serve hot. **Serves 6**

Below are several variations of *breiks* which have, as their filling, whole raw eggs which cook as the *breiks* are fried. In the first recipe the filling is simply a seasoned egg while in the others the eggs are accompanied by a variety of mixtures – onion, fish, meat etc.

They make excellent savouries, appetisers or a light lunch when served with salads. The pastry for these *breiks* is either *ouarka* (see Glossary) or sheets of filo.

to fill the pastry

ouarka:

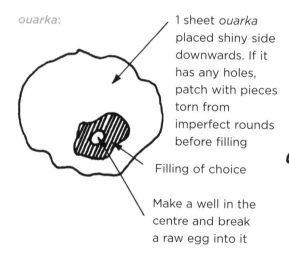

1 sheet *ouarka* placed shiny side downwards. If it has any holes, patch with pieces torn from imperfect rounds before filling

Filling of choice

Make a well in the centre and break a raw egg into it

Fold *ouarka* sheet in half. The upper side is sticky and should seal, but do not worry if the edges do not seal completely

filo:

Spread out 1 sheet filo and brush with melted butter. Fold into quarters. Brush with butter. If not a square, fold over edges to make about 15 x 15cm (6 x 6in)

Filling of choice

Make a well in the centre and break a raw egg into it

Brush edges with beaten egg, fold over and press edges to seal

breik bil bayd

breik with egg

'Better an egg today than a hen tomorrow' Libyan proverb

These simple, tasty and cheap egg *breiks* are the pride of the Tunisian housewife.

12 sheets *ouarka* (see Glossary) or 12 sheets filo pastry
110g (4oz) butter, melted } if using filo
1 egg, beaten
Oil for frying

filling
12 eggs
Salt
Pepper

Prepare the *breiks* using either *ouarka* or filo as described on page 76. Season each egg with a little salt and pepper before you enclose it. Do not worry if a little of the egg white escapes. Place the *breiks* under a tea towel as you prepare them to prevent them drying out before frying.

To fry add enough oil to a large frying pan to cover the base by about 1cm (1/2in) and heat. Carefully slide 1 or 2 *breiks* into the oil. Fry for about 30 seconds and then prick the pastry with a fork. Turn the *breiks* over and fry for 2–3 minutes or until nicely browned on both sides. The length of time you leave the *breiks* to cook will depend a little on how well done you like your eggs! Remove the *breiks* with a slotted spoon and keep hot while you fry those remaining in the same way. Serve hot with lemon wedges.
Serves 6

breik bil bayd we bsal

breik with egg and a parsley and onion stuffing

This is a very tasty *breik*.

12 sheets *ouarka* (see Glossary) or 12 sheets filo pastry
110g (4oz) butter, melted } if using filo
1 egg, beaten
12 eggs
Oil for frying

6 tablespoons water
4 tablespoons finely chopped parsley
2 onions, finely chopped
2 cloves garlic, finely chopped
1 teaspoon salt
1/2 teaspoon black pepper

To prepare the filling, place all the ingredients in a saucepan and cook over a moderate heat until the onions are soft and the liquid has evaporated. Remove and cool.

Now make the *breiks* as described in the diagrams on page 76 and fry following instructions for *Breik bil Bayd* (page 77). **Serves 6**

breik bil toune

breik with egg and tuna fish

You can use salmon instead of tuna if you wish, and if you can't get fresh fish, the tinned variety is very successful.

12 sheets *ouarka* (see Glossary) or 12 sheets filo pastry
110g (4oz) butter, melted ⎫
1 egg, beaten ⎭ if using filo
12 eggs
Oil for frying

filling
275g (10oz) tuna (if fresh, cook it first)
3 tablespoons finely chopped parsley
Juice 1/2 lemon
1/2 teaspoon salt
1/4 teaspoon black pepper

First prepare the filling by removing any skin and bones from the fish and flaking the flesh into a bowl. Add the remaining ingredients and mix well.

Now prepare the *breiks* as described in the diagrams on page 76. Do not worry if a little of the egg white escapes. Place the *breiks* under a tea towel as you make them to prevent them from drying out. To fry follow instructions for *Breik bil Bayd* (page 77). Serve hot with lemon wedges. **Serves 6**

breik lham

breik with meat and egg filling

Delicious and filling pastries.

12 sheets *ouarka* (see Glossary) or 12 sheets filo pastry
110g (4oz) butter, melted
1 egg, beaten
} if using filo
12 eggs
Oil for frying

filling
225g (8oz) lean meat cut into 1cm (1/2in) pieces or 225g (8oz) minced meat
2 tablespoons oil
5–6 tablespoons water
1 onion, finely chopped
1 large potato, peeled and cut into 1cm (1/2in) pieces
2 cloves garlic, crushed
4 tablespoons finely chopped parsley
1 teaspoon salt
1/4 teaspoon black pepper
1/2 teaspoon paprika
1 egg

Place all the filling ingredients except the egg in a saucepan and cook, covered, over a low heat until the meat and potatoes are cooked and the liquid has evaporated. Remove from the heat. If you have cooked pieces of meat then pass the mixture through a mincer. If you have used minced meat then mash the mixture with a fork until the potato pieces are broken up and well blended. Set aside to cool, then add the egg, and mix well to bind the ingredients.

Prepare the *breiks* as described in the diagrams on page 76 and fry according to instructions for *Breik bil Bayd* (page 77). **Serves 6**

bourek annabi

annaba-style *breiks*

A speciality from Annaba (Bône), the fourth largest city in Algeria.
It is a considerable seaport for the phosphates, iron ore, timber, livestock, wine and cereals of eastern Algeria.

This *breik*, also popular in Tunisia, makes a rich and filling meal.

Serve it with lemon wedges.

12 sheets *ouarka* (see Glossary) – in Algeria better known as dioul
– or 12 sheets filo pastry
110g (4oz) butter, melted
1 egg, beaten } if using filo

filling
2 tablespoons *smen* or 25g (1oz) butter
2 spring onions, chopped
2 cloves garlic, chopped
225g (8oz) minced meat
3 tablespoons parsley
110g (4oz) grated cheese (Cheddar, haloumi etc)
1 teaspoon salt
1/2 teaspoon black pepper
2 large potatoes, boiled and mashed

To prepare the filling melt the butter in a pan and fry the spring onions and garlic for 2–3 minutes, stirring frequently. Add the meat and fry for 15–20 minutes, stirring occasionally, until cooked. Remove from the heat and stir in the parsley, cheese, salt and pepper.

To make the *breiks* lay out sheets of pastry (folded according to diagrams if using filo) and spread a thin layer of mashed potato over one half. Add a little of the meat filling and make a light well in the centre. Carefully break an egg into it – do not worry if a little of the white escapes. Fold the *breik* as described in diagrams on page 76. Continue to make them until you have used up all the ingredients and place them under a tea towel until you are ready to fry them. Fry as described in instructions for *Breik bil Bayd* (page 77). **Serves 6**

Annaba, or Bône, was the ancient city of Hippone – the scene of many of the labours of the African-born St Augustine (of Hippo) who 'devoted his life and his not inconsiderable talents to bolstering up the tottering Roman Empire by combating the many heresies that weakened the spiritual power upon which, since it military might had declined, it was forced to rely' (*Auto Nomad in Barbary*). St Augustine died in Hippone while the Vandal hordes were battering the city gates. All was destroyed save the Basilica and its splendid library. The saint's body was removed and transported first to Cagliari (Sardinia) and then to Pavia. But the poor saint was not left to rest in peace. In 1842 his tomb was opened and his right arm was detached and borne off to be deposited (with all due pomp and circumstance) in his native cathedral of Bône.

bayd
— egg dishes —

'The first day a guest is fed on chicken, the second day egg and the third day ful (beans).'

Eggs are widely used in the North African cuisines, much more so than in Europe and the rest of the Middle East. This is due mainly to the fact that they are often substituted for meat. The latter is scarce, expensive, and there is often little choice.

'On first starting, some of the more respectable had a few hard-boiled eggs, with which the Jews most frequently travel; and the others had a little pickled fish' (*Travels in the Great Desert of Sahara*).

In Djema El Fna – 'Meeting-Place of the Dead' or more aptly 'Sinner's Rendezvous' where once the bodies of executed criminals were exposed to view, but which now is a vast open space, a cross between a bazaar, a circus and a huge amphitheatre filled with people from all over the world – Berber dancers, Saharan snake-charmers and European tourists all rub shoulders in what is perhaps one of the most exciting places to be, at any time of the day and any day of the year. In Djema El Fna they sell hard-boiled eggs and jacket potatoes stuffed with hard-boiled eggs for a few pence each and there is nothing more appetising than to wolf down a stuffed jacket potato in the middle of Marrakech with half a dozen children apeing every twitch of nose and eye. Naturally you have obliged them first by treating them to a filling snack!

In the 2-metre-square restaurants of any Meghribi kasbah one is offered a hard-boiled egg sprinkled with a little salt, black pepper and cumin which one is expected to eat as one would an apple.

Of the numerous egg dishes, I have selected a few starting with a simple omelette and finishing with a relatively rich festive dish called *minina*.

maguda bil bsal

onion omelette

There is a Moroccan saying that goes something like this – 'The Rifian kills his brother for the sake of an onion.' The story is that a Rifian – from the Rif mountain ranges of north-east Morocco, populated mainly by Berbers – once saw a person carrying a bag full of what he assumed were gold coins. He sneaked up on this person and knifed him to death. Much to his dismay, and Allah's, the bag contained onions. He of course was ignorant of that equally astute Moroccan expression 'Between the onion and its skin one gets nothing but a stink' – and he did! All this to introduce a recipe for an onion omelette, and one, moreover, from Algeria!

A simple dish which is delicious with bread and a salad.

2 tablespoons oil
75g (3oz) *smen*, **ghee or butter, melted**
3 onions, cut crossways into thin rounds
12 eggs
1¹/₂ teaspoons salt
¹/₂ teaspoon black pepper

Heat the oil and half the butter in a large frying pan, add the onions and fry gently for 20–30 minutes or until soft.

Meanwhile break the eggs into a bowl, and add the salt, pepper and remaining butter. Whisk well and pour evenly over the onions. Cook over a low heat until just set. Lift the edge of the omelette from time to time to check when the base is golden. Remove from the heat, transfer to a large serving plate and serve. **Serves 4–6**

maguda bil djaj

chicken omelette

Magudas are not omelettes as we understand them in Britain. They are hardly ever soft, creamy or light. *Magudas* (in Berber) or *ooja* or *ajja* (from the Arabic *eggah*) are firm, thick – usually 2.5cm (1in), but sometimes more – and always filled with vegetables, meat, chicken, brains etc.

Magudas are eaten hot or cold, cut into segments and served as appetisers or on a buffet table. They also make an ideal lunch or supper dish.

This is a Tunisian recipe.

450g (1lb) chicken breast
12 eggs
50g (2oz) stale bread, soaked in water
1¹/₂ teaspoons salt
¹/₂ teaspoon black pepper
2 tablespoons oil

to serve
Lemon wedges

Place the chicken breast and 2 of the whole eggs in a saucepan, cover with water and bring to the boil. Lower the heat and simmer for about 20 minutes or until the chicken is cooked. Remove from the heat and transfer chicken to a large plate. Reserve the cooking liquid. When cool enough to handle bone the chicken and cut the flesh into small pieces. Place in a large bowl. Squeeze as much liquid as possible from the bread and add to the bowl together with the salt and pepper. Shell the hard-boiled eggs, chop coarsely and add to the bowl. Break remaining eggs into the bowl and beat lightly with a fork.

Heat oil in a large frying pan and pour in chicken mixture. Lower heat, cover the pan and cook for about 10–15 minutes, shaking the pan occasionally to prevent it sticking. When the top of the omelette is just set place a plate over it and turn the pan upside down. Slide the omelette back into the pan and cook for a further 5 minutes. Remove pan from the heat, pour 90ml (3fl oz) of reserved cooking liquid over omelette and leave to stand for 4–5 minutes. Transfer to a large serving plate, cut into wedges and serve with the lemon wedges. **Serves 6**

maguda bil lham

meat omelette

Similar to *Maguda bil Djaj* this recipe makes a rich, thick and filling omelette. Serve hot or cold.

175g (6oz) lean meat, cut into 1cm (1/2in) pieces
12 eggs
1 small onion, chopped
4 tablespoons finely chopped parsley
3 cloves garlic, peeled
11/2 teaspoons salt
1/2 teaspoon black pepper
1/2 teaspoon paprika
150ml (1/4 pint) water
4 tablespoons oil
50g (2oz) stale bread, soaked in water

to serve
Lemon wedges

Place the meat, 2 of the whole eggs, onion, parsley, garlic, salt, black pepper, paprika, water and 2 tablespoons of the oil in a large saucepan. Bring to the boil, lower heat, cover pan and simmer for about 20 minutes or until meat is tender. Stir occasionally. Remove eggs and continue to simmer the mixture, without the lid, until the liquid has evaporated. Transfer mixture to a large bowl and leave to cool. Shell the hard-boiled eggs, chop coarsely and add to the bowl. Squeeze as much liquid out of the bread as possible and add to the bowl. Break the remaining raw eggs into the bowl and mix with a fork.

Heat the remaining oil in a large frying pan and pour in the egg mixture. Lower heat, cover the pan and cook for 10–15 minutes, shaking pan occasionally to prevent sticking. When the top of the omelette is just set place a plate over it and turn pan upside down. Slide the omelette back into the pan and cook for a further 5 minutes. Remove pan from the heat and slide omelette onto a large serving plate. Cut into wedges and serve with the lemon wedges. **Serves 6**

maguda bil hout

fish omelette

Any kind of fish will do for this omelette. A *maguda* of fish roe, particularly of herring, is very much appreciated in Tunisia.

12 eggs
350g (12oz) fish, boned and cut into 2.5cm (1in) pieces
4 tablespoons finely chopped parsley
2 cloves garlic, crushed
Juice 1 lemon
1¹/₂ teaspoons salt
¹/₂ teaspoon black pepper
50g (2oz) stale bread, soaked in water
2 tablespoons oil

to serve
Lemon wedges

Place 2 of the whole eggs in a small saucepan, cover with water and boil for 10 minutes. Place the fish pieces, parsley, garlic, lemon juice, salt and pepper in a large bowl. Squeeze as much liquid from the bread as possible and add to the bowl. Shell the hard-boiled eggs, chop coarsely and add to the bowl. Break the remaining eggs into the bowl and mix with a fork.

Heat oil in a large frying pan and pour in the fish mixture. Lower the heat, cover the pan and cook for 10–15 minutes, shaking the pan occasionally to prevent the omelette sticking. When the top of the omelette is just set place a plate over it and turn pan upside down. Slide the omelette back into the pan and cook for a further 5 minutes. Remove pan from the heat and slide the omelette onto a large serving plate. Cut into wedges and serve with the lemon wedges.

A traditional Moroccan wedding song sung by *neggafates* (bridal assistants), from *Traditions et Coûtumes des Communautés Musulmanes et Juives*.
  'See how she is the most beautiful,
  She is tender as a young pigeon,

She is lithe as a sugar cane.
She has the delicacy of honey on the tip of a needle,
She has the softness and transparency of dates
She has the flesh of a fish
She is the saltless beauty.
Here she is. Look, admire,
The lord and his prophet Sidna Mohammad
Have graced her and their blessing is upon her.'

maguda bil badendjel

aubergine omelette

You can prepare courgettes, carrots, potatoes and other vegetables
in the same way. A simple, but effective and filling dish, serve it with a fresh salad,
some home-made pickles and bread.

2 large aubergines
4 cloves garlic, crushed
2 tablespoons finely chopped parsley
1 teaspoon powdered caraway
1/2 teaspoon coriander
11/2 teaspoons salt
1/2 teaspoon black pepper
1/4 teaspoon chilli pepper
1/2 teaspoon paprika
10 eggs
3 tablespoons oil

to serve
Lemon wedges

Place the aubergines in a hot oven or under the grill and cook until the skins are black and the flesh soft when poked with a finger. Remove and leave until cool enough to handle. Peel off the skin, scraping off and reserving any flesh that comes away with it. Place the flesh in a bowl and mash with a fork. (If using other vegetables cook and purée in the normal way.) Add the garlic, parsley, caraway, coriander, salt, black and chilli peppers and paprika. Mix well. Break the eggs into the bowl and mix thoroughly.

Heat the oil in a large frying pan and pour in the egg mixture. Lower the heat, cover the pan and cook for 10 minutes, shaking the pan occasionally to prevent sticking. When just set place a plate over the omelette, turn the pan upside down and then slide the omelette back into the pan. Cover and cook for a further 5 minutes. Transfer to a serving plate, cut into wedges and serve with the lemons. **Serves 6**

ooja bil mergues

spicy sausage omelette

Spicy Tunisian sausages with green peppers and tomatoes make
a fine lunch when served with a fresh salad and bread. You can substitute the
Mergues (see Glossary) with thin Italian, Polish or Spanish chorizo sausages.

You can also incorporate potatoes, sautéed lightly in oil.

4–5 tablespoons oil
675g (1¹/₂lb) spicy Mergues sausages, cut into 2.5cm (1in) rounds
2 cloves garlic, crushed
¹/₂ teaspoon harissa diluted in 3 tablespoons water (see Glossary)
1 teaspoon powdered caraway
2 teaspoons paprika
4 large tomatoes, blanched, peeled and quartered
1¹/₂ teaspoons salt
6 tablespoons water
5 medium green peppers, seeded and cut lengthways into 1cm (¹/₂in) strips
9 eggs

garnish
Salt and pepper
1 tablespoon finely chopped parsley or tarragon

Heat oil in a large frying pan, add sausage rounds and fry, turning frequently until evenly browned. Stir in the garlic, diluted harissa, caraway, paprika, tomatoes, salt and water. Stir well, cover the pan and simmer over a low heat for about 30 minutes or until the mixture is thick. Stir occasionally to prevent sticking. Add the peppers, cover and cook for a further 10 minutes.

Beat the eggs in a bowl and pour evenly over the sausage mixture. Cook over a low heat, stirring constantly. Do not overcook. The eggs should retain a creamy consistency. Season with a little salt and pepper and garnish with the parsley or tarragon. Serve immediately. **Serves 6**

In Morocco *khli* (see Glossary) is cooked with its fat and with eggs to make a tasty omelette.

bayd bi zaitun

olive omelette

Most 'standard' omelettes – tomato, cheese etc – are prepared, but as well as these there are several that are typically Moroccan or, more accurately, North African. One such dish is this simple one of eggs and olives. The olive and its tree hold a prominent place in the mythology of the Meghribians. The olive tree is held to be sacred because the name of God (Allah) is supposed to be written on its leaves. Another superstition assures that olive oil helps the memory, but the eating of olives causes oblivion – which brings us nicely to a story about an olive lover.

Once, at a wedding feast, a guest was busy eating up all the olives. A fellow guest was rather annoyed and, desirous of teaching him a lesson, said, 'Do you know that eating too many olives will make you lose your memory?'

The first man, a few black olives in his mouth, half a dozen in the palm of his hand and his eyes feasting on a full plate of violet and green olives, muttered, 'Yes, what you say is so, indeed. For each time I take an olive I have already forgotten the one I ate before.'

225g (8oz) black olives, stoned
9 eggs
3 tablespoons finely chopped parsley
1/2 teaspoon powdered caraway
1/2 teaspoon cumin
1 teaspoon salt
1/2 teaspoon black pepper
25g (1oz) butter

garnish
1 teaspoon paprika
1 tablespoon finely chopped parsley or tarragon

Cut the olives into small pieces. Break the eggs into a bowl, add the chopped olives, parsley, caraway, cumin, salt and pepper and beat thoroughly.

Heat the butter in a large frying pan, pour in the egg mixture and cook over a low heat until only just set. If possible the top should be slightly runny. Remove from the heat, fold the omelette over and slide onto a serving plate. Sprinkle with the paprika and parsley or tarragon. **Serves 6**

ooja bi selg

spinach omelette

Spinach, leek, parsley, onion, tomato and many other vegetables are used in *ooja* omelettes, but spinach is undoubtedly the most popular. In Britain in recent times spinach has reappeared in our kitchens. It was, after all, very popular until about the turn of the previous century when it disappeared.

In the Mediterranean lands spinach has always been popular. Not only has it many 'good' qualities – its leaves contain a high level of iron and potassium – but it has a great affinity with eggs, garlic, onion and yogurt.

This simple omelette from Libya is strictly a love affair between spinach and eggs.

675g (1^1/$_2$lb) fresh spinach or 350g (^{3}/$_4$lb) frozen leaf spinach
8 eggs
1 teaspoon *hilba* (see Glossary)
^{1}/$_2$ teaspoon black pepper
2 teaspoons salt
2 tablespoons *smen* or 25g (1oz) butter

If using fresh spinach first rinse it very thoroughly under cold running water, then place in a large saucepan and cook in its own juices until tender, stirring frequently. Drain and when cool enough to handle squeeze out any excess water and chop. If using frozen spinach first thaw it thoroughly then place in a saucepan and cook in its own juices until tender. Drain and when cool enough to handle squeeze out excess moisture and then chop.

Break the eggs into a bowl, add the *hilba*, pepper and salt and beat with a fork. Stir in the chopped spinach. Melt the *smen* or butter in a large frying pan and pour in the egg-spinach mixture. Cook over a low heat for 10-15 minutes or until set. Either turn the omelette over and cook for a few more minutes or brown the top under a hot grill. Transfer to a large plate, cut into wedges or lozenges and serve with a fresh salad.
Serves 4-6

bayd magli bi dersa

scrambled eggs in a piquant sauce

Everyday fare for the average Tunisian. A delicious, simple egg dish flavoured with garlic and harissa. You can increase their quantities if you are a sucker for punishment – most Tunisians are!

3 tablespoons oil
4 cloves garlic, finely chopped
1 tablespoon tomato purée diluted in 120ml (4fl oz) water
1 teaspoon harissa or more (see Glossary)
1¹/2 teaspoons powdered caraway
1 teaspoon coriander
1/2 teaspoon paprika
1¹/2 teaspoons salt
9 eggs

garnish
Some black olives
1 tablespoon finely chopped parsley or tarragon

Heat oil in a large frying pan, add garlic and fry for 1 minute, stirring frequently. Add diluted tomato purée, harissa, caraway, coriander, paprika and salt, mix well and simmer for 5 minutes.

Break the eggs into a bowl and beat with a fork; Pour into the frying pan and stir thoroughly. Cook over a low heat for 5-7 minutes or until just set. Transfer to a large serving plate, garnish and serve hot. **Serves 4-6**

bayd magli bil qar'a

scrambled eggs with courgettes

900g (2lb) small courgettes, washed, topped and tailed
2 teaspoons salt
1 teaspoon black pepper
3 tablespoons oil
2 cloves garlic, finely chopped
6 eggs
2 tablespoons milk
2 tablespoons finely chopped tarragon or mint or
1 tablespoon dried tarragon or mint
1 tablespoon *smen* or 15g (¹/2oz) butter

garnish
1/2 teaspoon cumin

Cut the courgettes into ¹/2cm (¹/4in) rounds, sprinkle with half the salt and pepper and set aside for 30 minutes. Heat the oil in a large frying pan, add the garlic and fry for 30 seconds. Add the courgette slices and fry for 5-7 minutes, turning several times until nicely browned. Meanwhile break the eggs into a bowl, add the milk, remaining salt and pepper and tarragon or mint and mix well.

Add the *smen* or butter to the frying pan and turn the courgettes in it as it melts. Pour the egg mixture evenly over the courgettes and stir gently. Cook over a low heat for 5-7 minutes. The eggs should retain a creamy consistency so do not overcook. Transfer to 1 large plate, sprinkle with the cumin and serve immediately. **Serves 6**

— chakchouka —

The *Larousse Gastronomique* has this to say about one of the most striking dishes of the Meghrib: 'A dish made of sweet or strong peppers, tomatoes, little marrows (zucchinis) or aubergines (eggplants), cut in pieces and fried in olive oil with garlic and onion, the whole either mixed with beaten eggs or not as the case may be, and cooked for a few minutes on a slow fire.' So far so good, but it fails to inform that *chakchouka* is one of the most popular and beloved dishes of the Meghrib as well as the most versatile.

There are so many *chakchouka*-labelled recipes that it has been very difficult to choose or arrange them, for they can be soups, salads, stews and even tajines. There will be several *chakchouka* dishes appearing throughout this book, but in this chapter are included those that can be regarded as entrées, that have an 'eggy' connection.

chakchouka-el-yahoud

jewish-style chakchouka

'Sleep in the beds of Christians, don't eat their food; eat the food of Jews, but don't sleep in their beds.'

This recipe, which was given to me while on a visit to Jerusalem, is a Jewish-style *chakchouka*. A great number of Israelis are, of course, of North African origin and they took with them to their new land much of their Meghribian culture.

Served throughout the length and breadth of Israel in all cafés, restaurants, hotels and bars.

3-4 tablespoons oil
2 medium onions, coarsely chopped
2 cloves garlic, chopped (optional)
5 large tomatoes, finely chopped
1 large red pepper, seeded and thinly sliced
6 eggs
1 teaspoon salt
1/2 teaspoon black pepper

Heat the oil in a large frying pan, add onions and garlic and fry, stirring frequently, until golden. Add chopped tomatoes and pepper slices, lower the heat, cover the pan and cook gently for 20 minutes.

Remove cover and break eggs over the surface. Stir gently to break the yolks. Replace the cover and cook for a further 3-4 minutes or until the eggs are set. Remove from the heat, sprinkle with the salt and pepper and serve immediately. **Serves 4-6**

chakchouka-bil-badendjel

aubergine chakchouka

A standard recipe from Algeria.

5-6 tablespoons oil
2 large green or red peppers, seeded and thinly sliced
3 large tomatoes, coarsely chopped
3 medium aubergines, peeled, quartered and cut into 2.5cm (1in) slices
2 cloves garlic, chopped
2 tablespoons finely chopped parsley
6 eggs
11/2 teaspoons salt
1/2 teaspoon black pepper

Heat oil in a large frying pan and add peppers, tomatoes, aubergine slices, garlic and parsley. Mix thoroughly, lower the heat, cover the pan and simmer for 15-20 minutes, stirring occasionally. Add a little more oil if necessary as aubergines have an unquenchable thirst for oil.

Remove lid and break the eggs over the mixture stirring gently with a fork to break the yolks. Cover the pan again and cook for a further 3-4 minutes or until the eggs are set. Remove from the heat, sprinkle with the salt and pepper and serve immediately. **Serves 6**

chakchouka-bil-brouklou

cauliflower chakchouka

This is a Tunisian recipe which is similar to the one above. It makes a delicious and filling meal with or without the hot, spicy Mergues sausages.

4-5 tablespoons oil
1 onion, chopped
3 carrots, scraped and cut into thin rounds
2 cloves garlic, crushed
1 tablespoon tomato purée
2 teaspoons salt
1/2 teaspoon powdered caraway
1/2 teaspoon black pepper
2 potatoes, peeled and cut into 2cm (3/4in) cubes
1/2 cauliflower, broken into florets
225g (8oz) fresh broad beans, shelled and with skins removed
225g (8oz) Mergues sausages, cut into 2.5cm (1in) pieces (see Glossary)
600ml (1 pint) water
6 eggs

Heat oil in a large frying pan, add the onion, carrots and garlic and fry for several minutes, stirring frequently, until the onion is soft. Add all the remaining ingredients except the eggs, mix well and bring to the boil. Lower the heat, cover the pan and simmer for about 30 minutes or until the vegetables are tender. Remove the lid and continue to simmer until the liquid has evaporated.

Break the eggs over the mixture stirring gently with a fork to break the yolks. Cover the pan and cook for 3-4 minutes or until the eggs are set. Remove from the heat and serve immediately. **Serves 6**

chakchouka-bil-khodra

This Algerian recipe makes use of courgettes. Follow the recipe above, but replace the cauliflower with 350g (12oz) courgettes cut into 2cm (3/4in) rounds.

Another popular dish, *Chakchouka-bil-Karnoun*, uses the same ingredients as the cauliflower *chakchouka* but replaces the cauliflower with 4 artichokes.

This great love of the Meghribians for eggs – raw, boiled, scrambled, poached etc – has become a legend. Wilson MacArthur in *Auto Nomad in Barbary* tells of an amusing incident when he met an egg seller in the middle of the Sahara.

'We paused for a drink. Within five minutes of our stopping a figure rose, as it seemed, out of the ground near the road and came striding over. His face was intent, he was in haste to reach us before we drove away, and as he approached the window he looked at us with an anxious grin. From the folds of his burnous he produced a handful of eggs and thrust them towards us.

'The troops used to say that no matter where you stopped in the middle of the desert an Arab would bob up and offer eggs. This sudden apparition made us too light-headed for serious conversation, but, having no more francs – the last had been spent on petrol – I offered cigarettes. The dweller in the wilderness was not impressed. English cigarettes were good, he knew; but cigarettes, to him, had only the commercial value of the cheapest Tunisian brand. And eggs were eight francs each.

'By what magic of bush telegraph he acquired this knowledge we could not guess. Are the latest market prices broadcast through the deserts of North Africa by some means unknown to the European mind, restricted as it is by its materialism? We could only speculate; the vendor in the wilderness knew the correct value of the wares he offered.

'I tried to strike a bargain; my supply of cigarettes from Gibraltar was running sadly low and I was loath to see it shrink still farther; yet food was more essential. I prepared to make a sacrifice. But a chance discovery in the course of pantomime saved my cigarettes. The eggs were hard-boiled. Hard-boiled eggs we neither of us liked and would not have. Disconsolate, the desert tradesman saluted and withdrew, his simple faith in the immutability of life shattered.

'Had not the British always demanded hard-boiled eggs, since they had no means of cooking eggs while they raced after Rommel? And we rejected hard-boiled eggs! In any case must not all eggs be hard-boiled almost as soon as they are laid, so that they can be preserved a little while? Truly the world is hard and the way of the foreigner incomprehensible.'

minina

brain and chicken omelette

This is a Tunisian dish of brains, eggs and chicken, a thick omelette which is served cold. It is always prepared in large quantities (as with the recipe below) for special occasions and feast days. *Minina* is served at a *La Nzaha* – a picnic in the countryside where town-dwelling Meghribians go whenever they get the chance. They sing, dance, pick flowers and are often accompanied by professional singers and musicians. Carpets are laid, whole lambs – *mechoui* – are cooked under a hurriedly arranged wood pit. Couscous is served and sherbet-type drinks, as well as bottles of the famed *Sidi Harazem* mineral waters, are toasted to life, happiness and '*baraka*' – luck.

Minina will make an excellent accompaniment on a buffet table. However, you can easily halve or quarter the quantities if you wish.

1 calf brain or 2 lamb brains
1 tablespoon vinegar
1.5kg (3lb) chicken, cut into pieces
30 eggs
1 tablespoon salt
1 teaspoon black pepper

Place the brains in a bowl, add sufficient cold water to cover, and add the vinegar. Leave to soak for 30 minutes. Meanwhile place the chicken pieces and 6 of the whole eggs in a large saucepan, cover with water and bring to the boil. Lower the heat and simmer for about 30 minutes or until the chicken is tender. Remove the chicken and eggs from the pan to cool and reserve the stock

Grease well an ovenproof dish about 30cm (12in) in diameter or 25cm (10in) square and at least 7.5-10cm (3-4in) deep. Now find a baking tin large enough to hold the greased dish and add water to the depth of 2.5cm (1in). Place the tin with the water in an oven heated to 400F, 200C, Gas Mark 6.

Rinse the brains under cold running water and remove arteries and outer membranes. There should be no traces of blood. Cut the brains into small pieces and place in a large bowl. Bone the chicken pieces and either pass the flesh through a mincer or chop finely. Add to the large bowl.

Shell the hard-boiled eggs and carefully remove the whites leaving the yolks intact. Cut the whites into thin slices and add to the bowl. Break the remaining eggs into the bowl, season with the salt and pepper and mix all the ingredients together until well blended. Pour into the greased dish and smooth over with the back of a spoon. Arrange the hard-boiled egg yolks decoratively on the surface without touching each other. Cover with an oiled sheet of foil and stand the dish in the baking tin with the water. After 3 minutes reduce the heat to 350F, 180C, Gas Mark 4 and cook for 45 minutes or until cooked. Remove the foil and cook for a further 5 minutes to brown.

Reheat the chicken stock, turn off the oven and pour 150ml (1/4 pint) of the stock evenly over the omelette. Leave for 10 minutes and remove from the oven. Leave to cool and then unmould and serve cold. Cut into wedges and serve with lemon.
Serves about 15

djeghlellou be za'tar

snails with thyme

'He remained fasting for a year and breakfasted on snails' Moroccan proverb

These snails – also called *boubbouche* – are much smaller than the Burgundy variety and are white with black circles. They are served in their stock which is made with herbs, spices and orange peel. This stock is claimed by many to cleanse the blood, to induce energy and to be beneficial for all kinds of stomach troubles.

The recipe below is from Algeria, but this dish is equally popular in Morocco, particularly in Fez where they grow in abundance in the fields. Liquorice root, green tea and gum arabic (or mastic) can all be bought in health-food shops.

About 900g (2lb) snails
1½ teaspoons caraway seeds
1½ tablespoons thyme
½ teaspoon paprika
1 small onion, finely chopped
1 tablespoon tomato purée
¼ teaspoon green (or ordinary) tea
2 tablespoons finely chopped fresh mint
1 small piece liquorice root (ark sous)
Skin of ½ bitter (Seville) orange
Skin of ½ small orange
1 whole green chilli pepper
½ teaspoon powdered gum arabic (mastic)
1 teaspoon salt

Scrape away the chalky substance sealing the shells. Rinse for several minutes under cold running water. Place in a bowl, cover with salted cold water and add 1 tablespoon of vinegar. Leave to soak for 2 hours. Then rinse once more. Half fill a large saucepan with water and bring to the boil. Add the snails and blanch for 5-7 minutes. Drain into a colander and cool under running water.

Meanwhile bring 1.2 l (2 pints) water to the boil in a large saucepan and add all the remaining ingredients. Simmer for 2-3 minutes and then tip in the snails. Cover the pan, lower the heat and simmer for 1½-2 hours. When the snails come away from their shells easily and are no longer rubbery they are cooked. Taste and adjust seasoning if necessary. Allow the snails to cool in their stock. Just before serving reheat, pour the contents of the pan into a large bowl and serve. **Serves 6**

edjeidjette es serdine

fried sardine rissoles

Use fresh sardines if available, but this Algerian recipe also works well with other small fish like sprats. Serve with a fresh salad.

About 900g (2lb) sardines
2 eggs
1 onion, finely chopped
2 tablespoons finely chopped parsley
1 teaspoon salt
1/4 teaspoon black pepper
1/2 teaspoon cumin
Flour
Oil for frying

to serve
Lemon wedges

Scale, cut off the heads and bone the fish. Rinse for several minutes under cold running water and then drain. Transfer the fish to a large bowl and mash firmly with a fork. Add the eggs, onion, parsley, salt, pepper, cumin and 1 tablespoon of flour, and mix thoroughly. Put 50g (2oz) flour on a plate for the coating. Take a tablespoon of the mixture, shape it into a ball and press gently between your palms to flatten slightly. Coat generously with flour and set aside. Prepare the remainder of the mixture in the same way.

Heat some oil in a deep pan and gently fry the rissoles, a few at a time, until cooked through and golden on both sides. Remove with a slotted spoon and serve warm with lemon wedges. **Serves 6**

mokh megli

fried brains

Once considered one of the choicest morsels of all by Greeks, Romans, Carthaginians and, no doubt, Uncle Tom Cobley and all. In Britain today brains, and sweetbreads as well, have virtually disappeared from our tables, which is a shame. Brains were once (in Greece of the fifth century BC) 'a compulsory eat, for it was like eating the heads of one's parents!' – a real delicacy.

450g (1lb) lamb or calf brains
1 tablespoon vinegar
1 teaspoon salt
1/2 teaspoon black pepper
2 cloves garlic, finely chopped
15g (1/2oz) butter
1 tablespoon oil

garnish
1 tablespoon finely chopped parsley
Lemon wedges

Place the brains in a bowl, add the vinegar and cover with cold water. Set aside for 30 minutes then rinse under cold running water and drain. With a pointed knife remove and discard arteries, outer membranes and any traces of blood. Cut brains into 2.5cm (1in) pieces. Place salt, pepper and garlic in a bowl, add the pieces of brain, toss well and leave for 15 minutes.

Heat butter and oil in a frying pan, add brain mixture and fry for 10-15 minutes, stirring occasionally. Transfer to a serving dish, garnish with the parsley and lemon and serve hot with bread. **Serves 4**

A deep-fried version uses the same quantity of brains as above. Parboil brains in water with 2 tablespoons lemon juice for 10 minutes. Drain. Plunge immediately into cold water and then cut into pieces. Mix 2 tablespoons lemon juice and 2 tablespoons oil in a bowl, add pieces of brain and marinade for 30 minutes. Drain and dry on kitchen paper. Roll in seasoned flour, dip in beaten egg and deep fry. Sprinkle with 1/2 teaspoon each chilli pepper and cinnamon and serve with lemon wedges.

And may Allah be merciful to your brains.

khodrat
— vegetables —

'Vegetables are the pride of the dining table.'

Thus goes an Arab saying, but it is a Middle Eastern expression and not one that will easily apply to the Meghrib. An urban North African is not much enamoured of vegetables on their own. His palate has been spoilt by the delectable taste and flavours of tajines which, though they do use fruits and vegetables, are essentially meat-based dishes. The urban Meghribi loves meat because there is little of it around and meat is a good sign of prosperity – and the urban Meghribi loves to appear sophisticated, urbane and prosperous.

It is in the *bled* – the countryside – that most of the tasty vegetable dishes are found. There the peasants make clever use of their aubergines, asparagus, thistles, gourds, all kinds of beans, mallow etc. And it is to the vast hinterland we go for our first recipe – a simple one of lentils in a spicy sauce called *dersa*. This sauce, an Algerian favourite, is made with garlic, cumin and cinnamon and pops up in many meat and vegetable dishes in this chapter and in Everyday Dishes. I have included a standard dersa recipe in the chapter on Sauces and Pickles, but since there are several variations a few will appear with the individual recipes chosen.

ades bil dersa

lentils in spicy dersa sauce

Eaten on its own or as an accompaniment to all kinds of meat. Also particularly good with 'watery' tajine dishes.

375g (12oz) whole lentils, cleaned, rinsed and soaked in cold water for 2 hours
1 tablespoon *smen*, ghee or butter
1 onion, finely chopped
2 bay leaves

dersa sauce
2 cloves garlic, crushed
1 whole chilli pepper, finely chopped or 1 teaspoon chilli powder
1 teaspoon salt
1/4 teaspoon cinnamon
1 teaspoon cumin
1/4 teaspoon black pepper
750ml (1 1/2 pints) water

Half fill a large saucepan with lightly salted water and bring to the boil. Drain the lentils and add to the pan. Simmer for 5-7 minutes, drain and reserve. In a small bowl mix together all the sauce ingredients and reserve.

Melt the *smen*, ghee or butter in a saucepan, add the onion and fry until soft and turning golden. Add the sauce and the bay leaves and bring to the boil. Stir in the lentils, boil for 1 minute, cover the pan, lower the heat and simmer for about 20 minutes or until the lentils are tender and the liquid is reduced. Serve immediately. **Serves 6-8**

I have often wondered what we in Europe – particularly those of us who live in Britain, the Emerald Isle and the hinterland of Central Europe – would be eating today if the potato had not been introduced. Potatoes are an integral part of our European diet. In Africa they are of lesser importance but this, I hasten to add, does not mean that the North Africans have ignored this 'newcomer' to their ancient cuisine. On the contrary they (as befits their character) have adapted it to their social tastes and needs. It is therefore for both culinary and curiosity interests that I have included these recipes. See what can be done with a little imagination!

batata bil zait

potatoes in olive oil sauce

A tasty potato dish which can be eaten hot or cold.

1.5kg (3lb) potatoes, peeled
150ml (1/4 pint) olive oil
4 cloves garlic, thinly sliced
1 tablespoon tomato purée
1 teaspoon harissa (see Glossary)
1 teaspoon cumin
1/2 teaspoon salt
3 tablespoons finely chopped parsley

Cut the peeled potatoes into 2cm (3/4in) thick round slices. Heat the oil in a large saucepan, add the garlic, tomato purée, harissa, cumin and salt and stir well. Add 900ml (11/2 pints) water and the potato slices and mix well. Bring to the boil. Lower the heat and simmer for 15 minutes.

Add the chopped parsley and stir in carefully. Simmer for a further 5-10 minutes or until the potatoes are tender. Serve hot or cold. **Serves 6**

batata fliyon

In this recipe from the region of Oran in northern Algeria the chopped parsley is replaced by wild mint – *Mentha sylvestris* – which grows nearby in abundance. Use 2-3 tablespoons whole or coarsely chopped fresh mint leaves, which give a refreshing taste to the potatoes. The remaining ingredients are as above.

batata bil selg

potato with spinach

Selg is a kind of spinach that grows in the wild. Since it is not available in Britain I have throughout this book replaced it with spinach.

1 clove garlic, chopped
1 whole chilli pepper, coarsely chopped or 1 teaspoon chilli powder
1 teaspoon salt
90ml (3fl oz) water
5 tablespoons oil
1 teaspoon paprika

1/4 teaspoon black pepper
225g (1/2lb) fresh spinach, thick stems and coarse and discoloured leaves discarded
1.25kg (about 2¹/2lb) potatoes
4 eggs, beaten

Place the garlic, chilli pepper and salt in a mortar and crush to a paste. Place in a small bowl and mix in the water. Heat the oil in a large saucepan, stir in the chilli mixture, paprika, black pepper and 600ml (1 pint) water. Bring to the boil, lower the heat and simmer for 5-10 minutes. Meanwhile wash the spinach very thoroughly under cold running water. Set aside to drain. Peel the potatoes, rinse well and cut them into 1cm (1/2in) thick rounds. Add the spinach and potatoes to the saucepan, stir and simmer for about 30 minutes or until the potatoes are tender. Pour the eggs evenly over the vegetables and cook for a further 3-4 minutes. Serve hot or warm. **Serves 6**

batata maglia bil dersa

spicy fried potatoes

Fried potatoes North African-style with a hot sauce. They are an excellent accompaniment to grilled meats and Mergues sausages (see Glossary).

1.5 kg (about 3lb) potatoes, peeled and washed
Oil for frying
1 clove garlic, finely chopped
1 teaspoon harissa (see Glossary)
2 teaspoons salt
1 teaspoon ground caraway

to serve
2 tablespoons vinegar
1/2 teaspoon black pepper

Cut the potatoes into 1/2-1cm (1/4-1/2in) thick rounds and then into 1/2-1cm (1/4-1/2in) sticks. Soak in cold water for 20 minutes and then pat dry.
　　Meanwhile add sufficient oil to cover the base of a large saucepan by 1cm (1/2in) and heat. When hot add some of the potato sticks and fry until cooked and golden. Remove with a slotted spoon and drain on kitchen paper. Cook the remaining potato sticks in the same way. (You can deep fry them in a chip pan if you wish.)
　　When all the potatoes are cooked pour off most of the oil leaving only about 3-4 tablespoons in the pan. Add the garlic, harissa, salt and caraway and fry for 1 minute. Stir in 60ml (2fl oz) water and bring to the boil. Simmer for 3-4 minutes. Add the fried potatoes and stir well to coat with the sauce. Simmer for a few minutes to evaporate excess liquid. Pile the potatoes into a dish, sprinkle with the vinegar and black pepper and serve. **Serves 6**

badendjel bil bsal

aubergine with onions

900g (2lb) aubergines
1¹/₂ teaspoons salt
6 tablespoons oil
2 cloves garlic, crushed
3 onions, chopped
5 ripe tomatoes, blanched, peeled and coarsely chopped
¹/₂ teaspoon harissa (see Glossary)
¹/₄ teaspoon black pepper
3 tablespoons finely chopped parsley

Cut the aubergines crossways into 1cm (¹/₂in) thick slices, place in a colander, sprinkle with 1 teaspoon of salt and set aside for 30 minutes. This will remove any bitterness. Rinse thoroughly under cold water and pat dry. Heat the oil in a large saucepan, add a few of the aubergine slices and fry until golden on both sides. Remove and drain on kitchen paper. Fry the remaining slices in the same way adding more oil if necessary. Keep them warm.

If necessary add a little more oil to the pan, add the garlic and onions and fry until soft and turning golden. Return the aubergine slices to the pan and add the tomatoes, harissa, remaining salt and pepper and stir gently. Cover the pan and simmer gently for about 30 minutes, stirring occasionally. Spoon into a serving dish, sprinkle with the parsley and serve immediately with a rice pilav or on a bed of couscous. **Serves 6**

bissara

hillsmen's bean purée

One day a town dweller met a peasant hillsman and asked, 'What would you do, my good man, if you were to become a Sultan?'
The jbli (hillsman) replied, 'If I were a Sultan I would eat every day bissara.'

This dish, like most other vegetable dishes, is eaten by the hillsmen of Morocco and Algeria because meat is scarce. *Bissara* is also served at weddings. The guests, upon arrival, take a few spoonfuls of this purée and then sit in their allotted places. And of course there will be the cries of 'You-You'. It makes a fine appetiser.

450g (1lb) shelled broad beans with grey skins removed
2 fresh chilli peppers, thinly sliced and with seeds discarded

1 teaspoon cumin
1 teaspoon paprika
3 cloves garlic, crushed
1/2 teaspoon salt
2 tablespoons olive oil

to serve
Juice 1 lemon

Half fill a large saucepan with water and bring to the boil. Add the beans and simmer for about 30 minutes or until very tender. Drain and place in a bowl. Crush the beans with a wooden spoon to reduce to a purée. Add all the remaining ingredients and mix well until smooth and blended. Spread the mixture over a shallow serving dish, sprinkle with the lemon juice and serve with bread. **Serves 4**

kahrmus riffi

aubergine purée, rif-style

The Rif chain of mountains in northern Morocco have been inhabited for centuries by Berber tribes who have managed to retain much of their ethnic and cultural purity. The Riffian is a hardy, carefree, freedom-loving person who has finally accepted 'the will of Allah' (i.e. his lot) in this vainglorious world. He lives simply, eats simply and according to Moroccan folklore, is simple. Richard Hughes' wonderful stories in *In the Lap of Atlas* attest to that. Ish-Ha the fool (a cross between the legendary Antar of Arabic folklore and Nasreddin Hoça of Anatolia with a touch of carefree Meghribian thrown in) 'was the greatest Fool there has ever been in the world. He was so great a Fool that when he was a boy and his mother told him to watch the door while she went into the market to buy food he lifted
the door off its hinges and carried it with him down the street to where he could play with the other boys without ceasing to watch it . . .'

The Riffian is no fool by any means. He is the descendant of proud folk who have seen empires and nations crumble and disappear. Yet he is still here, on the mountains, like an eagle waiting.

2 large aubergines, hulls removed
4 teaspoons salt
75ml (2¹/₂fl oz) oil
2 cloves garlic, finely crushed
1/2 teaspoon black pepper
1 teaspoon paprika

1/2 teaspoon marjoram
garnish
1 tablespoon olive oil
1 teaspoon cumin
Black olives

Half fill a large saucepan with water and bring to the boil. Add the aubergines and 3 teaspoons of the salt, and simmer until soft. Drain and set aside until cool enough to handle. Then peel off the skins scraping off and retaining any flesh that comes away with them. Chop the flesh coarsely.

Heat the oil in a large frying pan, and the remaining salt, the garlic, black pepper, paprika, marjoram and aubergine flesh. Stir well and cook over a medium heat, mashing frequently with a wooden spoon until the mixture becomes a purée. Transfer to a shallow serving dish, spread smoothly over the surface and garnish with the oil, cumin and olives. Serve with bread. **Serves 4**

chakchouka qsentiniya

constantine-style ratatouille

The 'classic' ratatouille should include aubergines, courgettes, onion, tomatoes and peppers. This Algerian version is loosely labelled ratatouille. It is in fact a *chakchouka* (see page 90), but undoubtedly sometime in the past both these dishes had one original source.

6 tablespoons, oil
4 cloves garlic, finely chopped
900g (2lb) onions, cut into thin rounds
150ml (1/4 pint) water
900g (2lb) tomatoes, blanched, peeled and chopped
1 dried chilli pepper, soaked in cold water for 1 hour
2 teaspoons salt
4 eggs
2 tablespoons finely chopped parsley

Heat the oil in a large frying pan, add the garlic and sliced onions and fry until soft. Add the water, bring to the boil, lower the heat and simmer for about 10 minutes. Add the chopped tomatoes and the chilli pepper – either whole or thinly sliced – and simmer for a further 10 minutes. Stir in the salt.

Break the eggs over the vegetables and tilt the pan from side to side to spread evenly. Sprinkle the parsley over the top and cook for 3-5 minutes or until the eggs are just cooked and then remove from the heat and serve immediately. **Serves 6**

lubia marrakechiya

white beans marrakech-style

From Marrakech, one of the most exciting cities in Africa – about which more later.
This dish of white beans with eggs and saffron is typical of Moroccan cooking.
Serve with bread or rice.

350g (3/4lb) white beans, soaked overnight in cold water or
675g (1¹/2lb) tinned beans, drained
1 large onion, finely chopped
2–3 cloves garlic, finely chopped
900ml (1¹/2 pints) water
150ml (1/4 pint) oil
3 tablespoons finely chopped parsley
2 teaspoons salt
1/4 teaspoon saffron diluted in 3 tablespoons water
1/2 teaspoon black pepper
4 eggs, beaten

garnish
2 tablespoons finely chopped tarragon, mint or parsley

Drain the soaked beans and place in a large saucepan with the onion, garlic and water
and bring to the boil. Lower the heat and simmer for about 1 hour or until the beans
are tender. Add a little more water if necessary. (If using tinned beans simmer them in
about half the water for 20 minutes.)

Meanwhile in a small pan heat the oil, add the parsley, salt, pepper and diluted
saffron and simmer for 3-4 minutes. Pour this mixture into the bean pan, stir well and
simmer for a further 12-15 minutes or until most of the water has evaporated. Pour the
beaten eggs over the mixture, stir gently and cook for 1-2 minutes. Remove from the
heat and serve immediately sprinkled with the garnish of your choice. **Serves 6**

'In the furrows of history,
She has ploughed a glory
of prestigious epic
in an epoch of mystery.
Marrakech the beautiful
She reflects in her waters,
Stretches out into her past
Fierce and rebellious.

Her branches up to the sun
In languorous winter
She walks upon awakening
With a loving look.
At night gentle and melancholy
Strolling the wings of
Your nostalgic past . . .'

Abdelmajid Ramadan, Chants du Moghreb

hmissa bil dersa

chickpeas with a spicy sauce

Chickpeas (*Cicer arietinum*) grow profusely, or should I say willingly, in arid and semi-arid regions. A highly nutritious legume – still under-used in Europe and the USA but not, I hasten to add, in Mexico or South America.

Chickpeas are at their best in Indian, Middle Eastern and North African cuisines. There are three varieties – black, red and white – but the latter is by far the most commonly used. They have an earthy, nutty flavour. The most famed chickpea-based dish is perhaps the Syrian classic *hummus-bi-tahina*, a purée of chickpeas with a sesame cream called tahina which has been popularised in recent years by Cypriot and Middle Eastern restaurants.

The dish below is very simple and filling with a standard Algerian dersa-based sauce. Serve it with bread or all types of grilled or roast meats.

150ml (¼ pint) oil
2 cloves garlic, finely chopped
1 teaspoon chilli pepper
1 teaspoon paprika
¼ teaspoon black pepper
1 teaspoon cumin
2 tablespoons tomato purée
1.25 l (2 pints) water
450g (1lb) chickpeas, soaked overnight in cold water
1½ teaspoons salt

Heat the oil in a large saucepan, add the garlic, chilli pepper, paprika, black pepper and cumin and fry for 30 seconds. Stir in the tomato purée and water and bring to the boil. Drain the chickpeas and add to the pan. Lower the heat and simmer for 45-60 minutes or until the chickpeas are tender. Add a little more water if necessary. Season the mixture with the salt and simmer until most of the liquid has evaporated. Serve immediately. **Serves 6**

All kinds of dried beans and peas can be prepared in this way. Add herbs and spices if you wish – thyme, basil, coriander, caraway, cinnamon etc.

brouklou bil dersa

cauliflower in dersa sauce

A typical Algerian dish which is simple, tasty and filling.

1 large cauliflower, trimmed and broken into florets
4 tablespoons oil
2 cloves garlic, chopped
2 ripe tomatoes, blanched, peeled and chopped
1 teaspoon salt
1/2 teaspoon black pepper
1 teaspoon paprika
1 teaspoon harissa (see Glossary)
4 tablespoons long-grain rice, washed thoroughly under cold running water
2 teaspoons coriander

Half fill a large saucepan with lightly salted water and bring to the boil. Add the pieces of cauliflower and simmer for 5 minutes. Drain into a colander.

In a large saucepan heat the oil, add the garlic, tomatoes, salt, pepper, paprika and harissa and fry for 1-2 minutes, stirring constantly. Add 300ml (1/2 pint) water, bring to the boil and simmer for 10 minutes. Add the rice, coriander and cauliflower, stir gently and simmer until the rice is cooked and the sauce reduced, stirring gently occasionally, Serve immediately. **Serves 6**

masloug

gourd tlemcen-style

A fascinating dish, which is primitive and classic at the same time, from the Tlemcen region of north-west Algeria bordering Morocco.

Clever use is made of jujube (*Ziziphus jujuba/Ziziphus sativa*), better known in English as Indian jujube. It is a fruit of Indian origin which grows in warm climates. The actual fruit is olive-sized and covered with a smooth, leathery red skin. Dried jujubes are used to sweeten medicines and as throat pastilles, as they are soothing to both the throat and chest.

The Tlemcen people use gourd, by which I mean any member of the *Cucurbitaceae* family – which includes, amongst others, pumpkin, marrow, summer squash etc. Most of these can be bought at some time during the year from Indian grocers and some good greengrocer shops. I suggest you use pumpkin or marrow.

450ml (3/4 pint) water
1 tablespoon *smen*, ghee or butter
1/4 teaspoon black pepper
1/4 teaspoon ginger
1/2 teaspoon cinnamon
1 onion, finely chopped
1/2 teaspoon salt
1/4 teaspoon saffron diluted in 2-3 tablespoons water
225g (1/2lb) dried jujubes
1.5kg (3lb) pumpkin, marrow etc, peeled and cut into 5cm (2in) cubes
1 tablespoon icing sugar
3 tablespoons orange blossom water

Place the water in a large saucepan and bring to the boil. Add the butter, black pepper, ginger, cinnamon, onion, salt, diluted saffron and jujubes, lower the heat and simmer for 15 minutes. Add the pumpkin or marrow cubes and cook for a further 10-12 minutes, stirring occasionally.

Gently stir in the icing sugar and orange blossom water and simmer for a further 3-5 minutes. By this time the vegetables should be tender and the sauce well reduced. Arrange the pumpkin cubes on a plate and pour the sauce and jujubes over the top. Serve hot. **Serves 6**

Below is a very sophisticated dish from the 'Kairwan of Algeria' for Tlemcen was not only the capital of a kingdom, but also a holy city with an incredibly chequered history. Tlemcen was so near Morocco that it attracted the attention, and whetted the appetites, of her greedy Sultans who constantly laid siege to her triple walls. Once a siege lasted for eight years, and the hapless inhabitants of Tlemcen were reduced to eating rats and even human bodies. Then a wise man (probably a distant relation of Ish-Ha the Fool) proposed a stratagem – the last two sheep of the town were fattened on the last sack of grain and allowed to escape the fortified walls. The Moroccan forces were dismayed, despairing of reducing a town so well provisioned. They hastily abandoned their siege and returned home licking their wounds, instead of honey. For a Berber adage propounds 'lick honey with your little finger' (i.e. don't be too greedy)!

And this brings us to the next recipe which is one of onions and honey. It is a fascinating purée of onions flavoured with ras-el-hanout and honey. It is simple but well worth trying, for, in the words of another Arab saying, 'An onion with a friend is a roast lamb.' How true, but wouldn't it be even nicer to have both roast lamb and onion together!

mzgaldi

onion and honey purée

Onion cooked with brown sugar or honey is also a traditional English remedy
for colds and bad chests. Serve with any roast or grilled meat. I probably shouldn't
mention it, but I like it with pork chops!

3 tablespoons oil
450g (1lb) onions, finely chopped
1¹/2 tablespoons ras-el-hanout (see Glossary)
1 teaspoon salt
3-4 tablespoons pure honey

Heat the oil in a saucepan, add the onions and fry for 5-10 minutes, stirring frequently,
until soft. Add the ras-el-hanout and salt and continue to cook, still stirring frequently,
until the onions have turned into a purée. Stir in the honey and simmer for a further 3-
4 minutes. Serve hot. **Serves 4-6**

foul gnaoua

negro musician's beans

This very simple dish is a particular favourite of the Negro *Gnaouiya* sect –
an unorthodox branch of Islam conjoined with earthy African myths. Most, if not all,
Gnaouans are musicians and the name has come to denote a simple, repetitive and
pulsating kind of music – a cross between Arab and African rhythms, with simple
yet haunting melodies. These musicians are found everywhere in Morocco
and across in Algeria. They are poor by religious choice, but undoubtedly rich
spiritually. It is said that there are many saints amongst their number.
I have included quite a few *Gnaouiya* recipes in this book.

150ml (¹/4 pint) oil
450g (1lb) white kidney, cannellini or pea beans, soaked overnight in cold water
2 cloves garlic, crushed
1 onion, finely chopped
2 teaspoons paprika
¹/2 teaspoon black pepper

1.2 l (2 pints) water
1 teaspoon salt
Juice 1 lemon
garnish
2 tablespoons finely chopped tarragon or parsley

Heat the oil in a large saucepan and add the drained beans, garlic, onion, paprika and black pepper. Fry gently for 10-15 minutes, stirring frequently. Add the water and bring to the boil. Lower the heat and simmer for about 1-1½ hours or until the beans are tender and the water has virtually evaporated. Stir in the salt and lemon juice and remove from the heat. Transfer to a serving dish, garnish and serve hot or cold.
Serves 6

sansafil maghli

fried salsify

Salsify (*tragopogon orientalis*), also known as the oyster plant, from the family *Compositae*, is still (nearly 300 years after its introduction to Britain) relatively unknown. This is a pity for it is a very interesting vegetable – rather like a long, thin, brown parsnip – which is highly prized in southern Europe and North Africa. You may be able to find it in Indian grocery stores and I have, just recently, seen it in the greengrocery department of one of the large supermarkets.

As well as being excellent with meat and fish dishes this recipe, from Tripoli in Libya, makes a fine hors d'oeuvre.

675g (1½lb) salsify, topped and tailed
Oil for frying

batter
110g (4oz) plain flour, sifted
1 teaspoon baking powder
1 egg
1 tablespoon olive oil
150ml (¼ pint) water
¼ teaspoon harissa (see Glossary)
½ teaspoon cumin
¼ teaspoon dried thyme
1 teaspoon salt

Lemon wedges

Wash the salsify under cold running water using a scrubbing brush if necessary to remove all the sand. Cut each root in half. Half fill a large pan with lightly salted water and bring to the boil. Add the salsify and simmer for 30 minutes. Strain into a colander and rinse under cold running water. When cool enough to handle peel the skin off the salsify and cut the roots into 7.5cm (3in) pieces.

To prepare the batter mix all the ingredients together in a shallow bowl. Heat sufficient oil to cover the base of a large frying pan by 5cm (2in). Dip several pieces of salsify in the batter and fry in the fat until crisp and golden. Remove with a slotted spoon and keep warm while you cook the remaining salsify in the same way. Serve hot with the lemon wedges. **Serves 6**

tbikha selg bi roz

spinach with rice and almonds

Rice is not widely used in North Africa – the exceptions being Libya and Egypt where the Arab grain, rice, predominates over couscous. This simple and filling dish from Algeria can be eaten on its own or as an accompaniment to meat or fish-based dishes.

900g (2lb) fresh spinach
1 clove garlic
1 dried chilli pepper, soaked in 5 tablespoons cold water
1 teaspoon salt
150ml (1/4 pint) oil
1 teaspoon paprika
1/2 teaspoon black pepper
4 tablespoons long-grain rice, rinsed thoroughly under cold water
300ml (1/2 pint) water
2 tablespoons blanched almonds, toasted until golden under a hot grill

Discard thick stems and discoloured leaves of spinach and rinse remainder thoroughly under cold running water. Drain and chop coarsely. Bring a large saucepan half filled with lightly salted water to the boil. Add the spinach and cook for 5 minutes. Drain into a colander.

Meanwhile in a mortar or blender crush the garlic, chilli pepper with its water, and the salt. Transfer this mixture to a large saucepan, add the oil, paprika and black pepper and fry gently for 5 minutes, stirring frequently.

When cool enough to handle squeeze as much water as possible from the spinach and add to the pan. Stir in the rice and water and simmer for about 20 minutes, stirring occasionally, until the rice is tender and the water absorbed. Transfer the spinach mixture to a large serving dish and sprinkle with the toasted almonds. **Serves 6**

tbikha foul wa karnoune

artichoke and bean stew

A rich, filling fresh vegetable stew from Algeria.

1.5kg (about 3lb) artichokes
675g (1¹/₂lb) French beans, stringed, topped and tailed,
and cut into 5cm (2in) pieces
350g (³/₄lb) peas
150ml (¹/₄ pint) oil
2 cloves garlic, finely chopped
2 tablespoons finely chopped fresh coriander, parsley or thyme
1 tablespoon tomato purée diluted in 4 tablespoons water
2 teaspoons salt
¹/₂ teaspoon harissa (see Glossary)
1 teaspoon black pepper

garnish
2 tablespoons finely chopped fresh mint or 1 tablespoon dried mint

Prepare the artichokes as described in the recipe given for Chalda Karoune (page 51).
Place the beans and peas in a large saucepan and add all the remaining ingredients except the artichokes. Cook over a low heat for about 30 minutes or until the vegetables are tender, stirring frequently, Add the artichokes, cover the pan and simmer for a further 30 minutes, stirring occasionally. When the artichokes are cooked spoon the mixture into a serving dish and sprinkle with the mint. **Serves 6**

mechoui
— grilled meats —

'Now how many Christian cooks, I wonder, could roast a sheep (or even a chicken) so tenderly that you could pinch off a mouthful without difficulty between finger and thumb? Yet that is what the Moroccan chefs do – in the houses of natives I found it as tender as butter – cooked, too, with stuffing, with gravies tasting of spices and olives and cumin seeds that no "Cordon bleu" would be ashamed of.' In the Lap of Atlas.

Mechoui (in classical Arabic, to grill or barbecue) has in the Meghrib come to mean the grilling of a whole lamb or sheep over charcoal. Along with the goat, the sheep is at once North Africa's curse and blessing. In the rainless months, hills, fields and entire pastures are dry and brown, yet these creatures (suppliers of vital necessities such as milk, meat and wool) go on relentlessly munching. For the North African (much more so than for the Middle Easterner) the lamb is a symbol of prosperity; and a *mechoui* of lamb roasting whole in a mud oven or over wood is a special treat, one which is reserved for feast days, marriages and saints' days. In Morocco the sheep is also sacrificed for the feast of Aid-el-Kebir which not only marks the end of the Ramadan pilgrimage to Mecca, but also commemorates Abraham's sacrifice of a ram in place of his son Isaac.

Choose a young lamb, tie up its legs,
'Bismillah!' – in the name of God!

A sharp knife is plunged into the animal's carotid artery to kill it, and blood spurts out profusely. The cut (near the throat) is then washed seven times. Then, above the joint of one of its legs – between flesh and skin – a cut is made with the knife and a long piece of wood is pushed through. To remove the hide, someone begins to blow through this opening until the animal blows up and its front legs stiffen. The lamb is now inflated. As someone tightly closes the opening with his hands another cuts the hide between the thighs. The lamb is flayed like a rabbit. The head, legs and horns (if any) must not be touched. The carcass is very gently suspended with the help of two wood or metal poles so all the blood is drained out. The peritoneum (membrane lining the cavity of the abdomen) is reserved, as are the liver, heart and intestines. The kidneys are also kept as they make an excellent kebab. The head and feet are singed and then the lamb is ready to be grilled.

There are several methods of doing this – on a spit, under the ground and in specially prepared mud ovens. The first method – by far the most popular – is known throughout the world. It comprises a bed of glowing wood or hot coals about 120 x 180cm (4 x 6ft) and 45cm (18in) deep. The lamb is spitted on a long timber or metal rod, one end resting on a pile of stones or brick or a Y-shaped metal rod, while at the other end a man sits constantly turning the spit. The lamb is regularly basted with a mixture of *smen* or butter, salt and cumin. For an average 13.5kg (30lb) lamb use 900g (2lb) melted *smen* or butter mixed with 110g (4oz) salt and 50g (2oz) cumin. It takes 3-4 hours to cook a lamb in this way. The skin should be tight, crisp and golden, but not burnt. The lamb is then transferred to a large dish and served whole. The meat is succulent and tender, literally falling off its bones. Huge platefuls of rice and couscous are served as accompaniments in a joyous festive atmosphere.

Method two involves the digging of a shallow pit approximately 120 x 180cm (4 x 6ft) and 60cm (2 ft) deep. A bed of wood or charcoal is laid and lit. When the flames have died away and the embers are glowing the carcass of the lamb is laid on them and the whole is covered with earth. The baking process takes about 5-6 hours. When it is ready the lamb is removed and all the clinging earth and stones are brushed off. The lamb is then placed on a large tray which is shaken until the meat drops from the bones. The meat is transferred to another serving dish and sprinkled with salt, black pepper, thyme and other herbs and spices.

In the Middle Atlas ranges of Morocco and Algeria a remarkable oven is constructed in which the lamb is cooked suspended upside down. This oven is very similar to the Caucasian *tonir* or *tander* clay oven, but much larger. Although the latter are for permanent usage since most village cooking is done there – e.g. bread, stews, kebabs etc – the basic principle is the same. The Indian *tandoor* of course is the same, and is a speciality of mountain people. A typical North African oven is constructed with wet mud or broken bricks, stones etc. The oven has a conical base of 120cm (4ft) rising to a height of 150cm (5ft) and with a 50cm (20in) opening at the top and a small doorway at the front through which wood or charcoal is constantly fed. The fire is encouraged to roar until the inner walls are glowing with heat. After a time what is left of the glowing charcoal or wood is removed and only the embers are left. The carcass is suspended from the roof opening and held in place by a stout piece of wood or metal and both openings are closed – the top with a sheet of metal 'glued' to the walls with a little wood and the bottom bricked up and coated with wet mud. Several hours later – depending on the size and age of the lamb – the *mechoui* is ready.

mechoui marinade

Before grilling the lamb is usually coated inside and out with a marinade.
This one is typically Moroccan.

225g (1/2lb) *smen* or butter, softened
2 tablespoons coriander
5 cloves garlic, crushed
2 teaspoons cumin
2 teaspoons paprika
2 tablespoons salt
1 tablespoon black pepper

Place all these ingredients in a bowl and beat to a smooth paste. Spread it over the inside and outside of the lamb. Other herbs and spices that are often used include saffron, thyme, sage, savory, mint, marjoram, sweet basil, parsley etc.

fakhad kharouf mechoui

grilled leg of lamb

A more practical and modest grill is a leg of lamb (ask your butcher to remove the bone and leave the pocket). You can grill this over charcoal, under a grill or in an open pan in the oven. The marinade is typical of the High Atlas region of Algeria.

1.5-1.75kg (3-4lb) leg of lamb
2 tablespoons oil
2 teaspoons salt
1 teaspoon black pepper
1/2 teaspoon thyme
1/2 teaspoon rosemary
2 tablespoons chopped fresh mint or 2 teaspoons dried mint
1 tablespoon coriander
1 teaspoon chilli pepper
2 bay leaves
Oil for basting

Place the oil, salt and pepper in a small bowl and mix together. Brush the inside and outside of the meat with this mixture. In another bowl mix together the thyme, rosemary, mint, coriander and chilli pepper and rub this mixture over the inside and outside of the meat. Place the bay leaves in the pocket of the meat and sew up the end.

Pierce the leg of lamb with a long skewer and cook over glowing charcoal (or under the grill or in the oven) turning regularly and basting with a little oil occasionally for 2-3 hours or until cooked through. **Serves 6**

— kababs —

'And now hunger draws our thoughts to food. We can hunt the regulation meal at the cafés in the main street, or go further afield to one of the hotels or restaurants. Or we can lunch as we stand at a native kabob bar, and so save the time we should otherwise spend on elaborate eating. Now a kabob bar is the snack luncheon counter of the Arab; you will find one in every street in all the old cities of Morocco. Inside his small cavernous shop the cook stands behind his counter, on which rests a hollow stone boat filled with glowing charcoal. Beside the cook is a heap of spiced mincemeat, another of liver and fat cut into pieces the size of a farthing, and a pile of skewers. On one skewer he threads alternate pieces of liver and fat; round another he moulds with his hand a roll of mince. He dips them in pepper, lays them across the boat and turns them over the red charcoal till they are cooked crisp and brown. Then he takes a small flat cake of bread, slits it at the side, drops in the hot grill, and hands it to you for fifty centimes, or three-farthings.

'They are good, these kabobs.' By Bus to the Sahara

They certainly are!

Kababs (from the Persian *kabob* – to burn) are popular throughout the Meghrib, although both in variety and choices of marinades they fall well behind those of the Middle East. However, the repertoire is still substantial and rich for, apart from lamb and goat (either whole or cut into smaller pieces), kababs are made of turkey, chicken, pigeon and other small birds, rabbit, gazelle, jackal, hedgehog and locust – yes, locust! – and very tasty they are too. They are highly prized by the Tuaregs in the Saharan vastness. Indeed, locusts were recognised as an article of diet in the Mosaic law, some species being regarded as clean, others unclean. 'These of them ye may eat; the locust after his kind, and the bald locust after his kind, and the beetle after his kind, and the grasshopper after his kind' (*Leviticus*, 11-22). Probably the most famous locust eater was John the Baptist whose meat was 'locusts and wild honey' (*St Matthew*, 3-4).

But first, kababs made of lamb. These are usually either of chunks of meat or of minced meat. I have included one well-known recipe, *Quotban*, and several marinades, for a marinade makes a kabab.

quotban

moroccan lamb kabab

1.5kg (3lb) leg of lamb
Juice 2 lemons
150ml ($^1/_4$ pint) oil
1 teaspoon cinnamon
4 cloves garlic, crushed
5cm (2in) fresh root ginger, peeled and chopped
$^1/_2$ teaspoon chilli pepper
$1^1/_2$ teaspoons salt
$^1/_2$ teaspoon black pepper
675g ($1^1/_2$lb) beef suet, cut into 2.5cm (1in) cubes

Bone the lamb, trim off excess fat and cut the meat into 2.5cm (1in) cubes. Mix all the remaining ingredients except the suet in a large bowl, add the cubes of meat, turn to coat thoroughly and set aside for 4-6 hours. Turn occasionally.

Thread the meat cubes onto skewers alternating them with the suet cubes. Grill over charcoal for 10-15 minutes, turning frequently and basting with the remaining marinade, until the lamb cubes are tender and the suet is crisp. Serve immediately with rice, salad, home-made pickles, bread etc. **Serves 6**

marinades

The following marinades are all suitable for a 1.5kg (3lb) leg of lamb cut into cubes.

lemon marinade

A standard marinade used throughout the Meghrib, particularly by snack-bar cooks.

Juice 1 large lemon
$^1/_2$ teaspoon paprika
1 teaspoon salt
2-3 tablespoons olive oil

harissa marinade - from tunisia

Juice 1 lemon
1 tablespoon harissa mixed with 150ml (1/4 pint) water (see Glossary)
1 teaspoon powdered caraway
1/2 teaspoon coriander
1 teaspoon salt
3 tablespoons salt
3 tablespoons olive oil

onion marinade - from libya

Juice 1 lemon
1 large onion, cut into rings
1 teaspoon cumin
1 teaspoon salt
1/2 teaspoon black pepper
4 tablespoons olive oil

mint marinade - from fez

Juice 1 large lemon
Juice 1 orange
1 teaspoon salt
150ml (1/4 pint) water
12 mint leaves, finely chopped
2 tablespoons oil

kabab riffi

rif-style kabab

In Meghribi cooking it is rare that chunks of lamb are kababed on their own. They are almost always accompanied by other cuts of meat such as suet, liver, kidney, heart and of course, in Tunisia, Mergues sausages. A Tunisian kabab will often include most of the above meats at the same time.

1.5kg (3lb) leg of lamb, boned and trimmed
2 lamb's livers
2 kidneys in their fat
4-5 tablespoons finely chopped parsley
1 onion, finely chopped
2 tablespoons salt

Cut the lamb and livers into 2.5cm (1in) cubes, and mix the parsley, onion and salt together in a bowl. Remove the skin from the kidneys and then thread onto skewers and grill for 3-4 minutes, turning once, over charcoal. Slide off the skewers onto the parsley-onion mixture and mix well.

Thread the remaining meat onto skewers distributing the kidneys with their fat evenly between the cubes of lamb. Grill over charcoal for 10-15 minutes, turning regularly. Serve immediately with the parsley mixture and with olives and lemon wedges. **Serves 6**

kafta kababs

minced meat kababs

Kafta (from old Aramaic) is the general name given to all kinds of minced meat kababs – lamb, beef or a mixture of the two. These kababs are by far the most popular since, understandably, the meat used is cheaper. All kinds of herbs and spices are incorporated into the meat which gives the kabab extra flavour and aroma. A particularly good kabab from Morocco makes use of very hot ground pepper called *felfel sudani*. As this is not readily available here I suggest you mix 1/2 teaspoon chilli pepper with 1/2 teaspoon black pepper.

900g (2lb) lamb, minced once
110g (4oz) mutton or beef fat, minced once
2 teaspoons cumin
4 teaspoons paprika

1 teaspoon very hot ground pepper (*felfel sudani*, or see above)
3 tablespoons finely chopped parsley
3 tablespoons finely chopped fresh coriander or fresh mint
1 large onion, coarsely chopped
2 teaspoons salt
1 teaspoon cinnamon

Place all the ingredients in a bowl and mix well. Pass this mixture through the mincer and transfer to a large bowl. Keeping your hands damp knead the mixture for 3-4 minutes until very smooth then cover the bowl and set aside for 30 minutes.

Take a lump of meat about the size of an egg, pass a skewer through it and then, with a damp hand, gently squeeze the meat out until the kabab is thin and sausage-shaped. See that the ends are firmly stuck to the skewer to prevent the meat slipping round during cooking. Continue until you have used up all the meat.

Cook on a well-oiled grid for about 10 minutes, turning frequently. Serve with bread, rice or potatoes and with a bowl of fresh salad. **Serves 6**

kafta sahraouiya

saharan-style kabab

A very basic kabab from the Saharan vastness where bread and peanuts are added to the meat to compensate for the lack of herbs and spices.

Serve with a bowl of salad.

1.5kg (3lb) shoulder of lamb, boned and minced once
50g (2oz) fresh breadcrumbs
50g (2oz) chopped peanuts
1 onion, coarsely chopped
1 teaspoon salt
1 teaspoon dried mint

Mix all the ingredients together in a large bowl and then pass through a mincer. Continue as with *Kafta Kabab* (above). **Serves 6**

kouah

spicy liver kabab

This is a very popular dish that appears throughout North Africa. This recipe is from western Algeria, hence the use of harissa. In Morocco the hot spice, *felfel sudani*, usually replaces the harissa and of course that much loved Moroccan ingredient – suet – is also included. In Libya the livers are rolled in crushed cumin seeds.

Serve on a fried salad of chopped onion, parsley and coriander seasoned with harissa.

900g (2lb) lamb's liver, cut into 5cm (2in) cubes
Juice 1 small lemon
1¹/2 teaspoons salt
¹/2 teaspoon black pepper
2 teaspoons paprika
1 teaspoon cumin
60ml (2fl oz) oil

fried salad
2 large onions, thinly sliced
1 tablespoon harissa (see Glossary)
4 tablespoons finely chopped parsley
4 tablespoons finely chopped coriander (or mint or tarragon)

Place the liver cubes in a shallow dish, sprinkle with the lemon juice and set aside for 10 minutes. Meanwhile mix the salt, black pepper, paprika and cumin together in a bowl.

After 10 minutes pat the liver cubes dry, drop into the spices and rub them thoroughly into the meat. Thread the liver onto skewers and brush with a little of the oil – this helps the cooking as liver contains little fat and dries out easily. Grill over charcoal for about 10 minutes, turning occasionally, until the meat is tender and just cooked through – the inside should be slightly pink.

Meanwhile prepare the salad by heating the remaining oil in a frying pan. Add the onions and fry until soft and golden. Stir in the harissa and remaining herbs and fry for 2-3 minutes, stirring constantly. Remove from the heat and spread over a serving plate. Arrange the kabobs over the top and serve with lemon wedges, olives and salad.
Serves 6

boulfah

rif-style liver kabab

A liver kabab from the Rif region of Morocco. The liver is wrapped in caul and then grilled over charcoal. It is a most unusual dish and the nearest to it that I have encountered is the classic Cypriot *sheftalia* – barbecued sausages of minced lamb. However, the Cypriot *panna* (caul fat from the pig) will not do here because of religious requirements. Therefore ask your butcher to get you some sheep's caul. This should look like long strips of fat which, when opened, take on the appearance of lacy threads of fine tissue.

Once the liver is cooked there will be little trace of the caul except for a delicious flavour.

900g (2lb) lamb or calf liver, cut into thick slices
1 sheep's caul
2 teaspoons cumin
4 teaspoons paprika
1/2 teaspoon chilli pepper
1 teaspoon salt

to serve
Lemon wedges

Grill the liver slices for 1 minute on each side. Remove from the grill, cut the slices into 2.5cm (1in) cubes and place in a bowl. Mix all the spices together in a small bowl and add half of this mixture to the liver. Mix well so that all the cubes are evenly coated.

Meanwhile wash the caul, drain and spread it out flat. Sprinkle the remaining spice mixture evenly over it. Cut the caul into rectangles approximately 7.5 x 10cm (3 x 4 in). Carefully wrap each cube of liver in a piece of caul and then thread onto skewers. Grill over charcoal for 8-10 minutes, turning frequently. Serve immediately with the lemon wedges and a fresh salad. **Serves 6**

kabab-el-alb

heart kabab

These are delicious kababs. Serve them with olives, lemons, pickles, salads and bread. I have included two versions. The first is from Morocco, the second from Libya and both are very tasty.

You may find it necessary to order a calf heart in advance from your butcher. You can also – and here I speak from experience – try your local Indian or Pakistani butcher. They always seem to have unusual cuts like hearts, heads, feet, offal etc in store.

About 900g (2lb) hearts, washed, cleaned, fat and tubes removed
1 tablespoon paprika
1 teaspoon cumin
1/2 teaspoon chilli pepper
11/2 teaspoons salt

Cut the hearts into 2.5cm (1in) cubes, place in a colander and rinse under cold running water. Drain and pat dry with kitchen paper. Mix the spices together in a bowl, add the pieces of heart and mix thoroughly.

Thread onto skewers and grill over charcoal for about 10 minutes, turning frequently. Serve with lemon wedges, pickles and a salad of your choice. **Serves 6**

libyan kabab

About 900g (2lb) calf or ox heart, washed, cleaned, fat and tubes removed
1 teaspoon chilli pepper
11/2 teaspoons salt
2 cloves garlic, crushed
3 spring onions, very thinly sliced
1/2 teaspoon black pepper
150ml (1/4 pint) oil
2 bay leaves

to serve
Fresh vegetables (radishes, quartered onions, sliced cucumbers, olives etc)
Lemon wedges

Cut the meat into 2.5cm (1in) cubes, and rinse in cold water. Drain and dry. Mix the remaining ingredients together in a bowl, add the cubed meat and mix thoroughly. Cover and marinate overnight.

Thread the meat onto skewers and grill over charcoal for about 10 minutes, turning frequently, or until cooked. Serve immediately with chosen garnishes. **Serves 6**

djej kababet

chicken kabab

In Europe chicken is undoubtedly the most popular bird for grilling, not only because of its availability and reasonable price, but also because the texture of the flesh is very suitable for any form of roasting.

In North Africa one can still purchase chicken, and indeed most fowl, *au naturel*. Oven-ready and pre-cooked chicken have as yet not arrived. Although one can buy the slaughtered and dressed birds from a few butchers who cater mostly for the middle classes, the usual thing is to go down to that quarter of the medina where the butchers are to be found and to hand-pick the bird of your choice. Then you can either ask the butcher to kill it for you or take it home and do it yourself. As I am squeamish I prefer the former. I well remember seeing a lad of about ten holding the neck of a helpless chicken with his two hands and then twisting tightly. For a second I felt my heart stop! Blood spurted all over him and the ground while he whispered '*Bismillah*'. The cruelties man imposes in the name of God!

libyan chicken marinade

150ml (1/4 pint) olive oil
3 cloves garlic, finely chopped
Juice 1 lemon
2 teaspoons salt
1/2 teaspoon black pepper
1/2 teaspoon sweet basil

Mix all the ingredients together in a large bowl, add the chicken – whole, halved or in pieces – and mix well. Leave at room temperature for about 2 hours. Thread the chicken onto skewers and grill until tender turning frequently and basting with any remaining marinade.

moroccan chicken marinade

1 tablespoon paprika
1 teaspoon cumin
1/2 teaspoon chilli pepper
110g (4oz) butter, melted
1/2 teaspoon thyme
1/2 teaspoon thyme
1/2 teaspoon marjoram
1/2 teaspoon salt
1/4 teaspoon black pepper

Follow the directions for Libyan marinade above.

grilling a chicken

Tie the wing tips over the breasts and fasten the neck skin to the back with a skewer. Push the spit through the bird from the tail end towards the front – the spit should emerge between the branches of the wishbone. Tie the drumsticks and tail together.

You can of course cut the chicken into halves or into smaller pieces. If you are grilling halves push two skewers lengthways through each half. This makes them easier to turn without them slipping around the skewer.

To test if the chicken is cooked pierce a thigh with a fork. If the juices run clear and the meat is not pink then the chicken is ready.

kabab hamam

pigeon kabab

'Both the moon and the pigeon in the morning,
Her face above and through the jasmine flowers
Dominate the garden's beauty.
Her eyes, neither black nor blue
Sing a song of love.
Her lashes, wings that flutter in joy
Seducing all the flowers of the arbour.
Two roses dance a waltz;
You and I.'
'Pigeon in the Morning', Jardins de Marrakech

In most Middle Eastern and North African lands small birds (*assafeer*) are highly prized and popular. They are pickled or grilled on charcoal and eaten – bones and all! One of the most popular of these birds is the pigeon. Since they are not always so easily available in Britain (although squabs are available in the USA), I suggest you use poussins.

I also give two marinades for pigeon kebabs. Each is for six pigeons. First pluck them, remove all entrails and wash and dry thoroughly.

libyan-egyptian marinade

150ml (1/4 pint) oil
3 teaspoons cumin
2 teaspoons coriander
Juice 1 large onion or 1 onion, finely chopped
2 cloves garlic, finely chopped
1 teaspoon chilli pepper

Mix all the ingredients together in a large bowl, add the birds, turn several times to coat thoroughly and set aside for at least 2 hours.

Either thread the birds onto a spit passing it through the tail and towards the front or pass two skewers lengthways through each bird. Grill for 15-20 minutes, turning and basting frequently with any remaining marinade. Serve with lemon wedges, olives, pickles and a fresh salad.

a moroccan marinade

110g (4oz) butter, melted
Juice 1 large lemon
1 teaspoon salt
1/2 teaspoon black pepper
1 teaspoon cinnamon
1 teaspoon chopped chives
1 teaspoon chilli pepper
1 teaspoon coriander

Mix all the ingredients together. Thread the birds onto spit or skewers and brush all over with the butter mixture.

Grill for 15-20 minutes, turning frequently and brushing with the marinade. Serve as above.

bibi mhammar

grilled stuffed turkey

Try this marvellous dish from Algeria next Christmas or (why wait that long?) for your next party or picnic.

3.6-5.4kg (8-12lb) oven-ready turkey, giblets removed

stuffing
175g (6oz) couscous
110g (4oz) raisins
50g (2oz) pine kernels
25g (1oz) blanched almonds
1 teaspoon cinnamon
1/2 teaspoon ground nutmeg
1 teaspoon salt
50g (2oz) butter, melted

1 large onion, finely chopped
1 clove garlic, finely chopped
2 teaspoons chilli pepper
1/2 teaspoon ginger
300ml (1/2 pint) oil
600ml (1 pint) water
1 tablespoon salt

Prepare and steam the couscous as described on page 134. When cooked transfer the couscous to a large bowl. Add all the remaining stuffing ingredients and mix thoroughly.

Wash and dry the turkey inside and out. Pack the stuffing into the turkey and secure the opening. Truss the turkey by tying the wingtips over the breasts and fastening the neck skin to the back with a skewer. Push the spit through from tail end towards the front – the spit should emerge between the branches of the wishbone. Tie drumsticks and tail together.

Mix all the marinade ingredients together in a large bowl and brush it over the turkey regularly as it turns on the spit. Cook for 2-3 hours, basting and turning. Check if the turkey is done by piercing a thigh with a fork. If the juices run clear the bird is cooked.

Meanwhile, in a small pan bring any remaining marinade to the boil, lower the heat and simmer for 6-8 minutes. To serve remove the turkey from the spit and transfer to a large platter. Spoon out the stuffing and serve with the marinade. Accompany with olives, pickles etc. **Serves 8-10**

kabab-el-arnab

grilled rabbit

Still relatively little eaten in cities, rabbit – oven-roasted, grilled or cooked in a tajine – is popular in the countryside. Choose a young, white-fleshed rabbit for grilling. The older, fatter ones are excellent in stews and pies.

Ras-el-hanout (see Glossary) gives this dish its exotic flavour. Serve with rice or couscous, fresh salads and olives.

1-1.5 kg (2-3lb) rabbit, skinned and drawn and with liver reserved
3 cloves garlic, halved lengthways
450ml (3/4 pint) fresh orange juice
150ml (1/4 pint) olive oil
1 teaspoon dried mint
1 bay leaf, crumbled

1 level teaspoon ras-el-hanout (see Glossary)
3 tablespoons finely chopped parsley

sauce
75g (3oz) butter
2 cloves garlic, finely chopped
25g (1oz) raisins
25g (1oz) blanched almonds
Juice 1 lemon
1 teaspoon salt
1/4 teaspoon black pepper

Wash and dry the rabbit and, with the point of a sharp knife, make 6 incisions in the body and stud with the garlic halves. In a large bowl mix together 300ml (1/2 pint) of the orange juice, the oil, mint, bay leaf, ras-el-hanout and parsley. Add the rabbit, turning several times to coat thoroughly and refrigerate for 10-15 hours. Turn the rabbit occasionally during that time.

Remove the rabbit from the marinade and thread onto a spit or long skewers as with Grilled Chicken (page 125). Grill over a charcoal fire for 11/2-13/4 hours turning regularly.

Meanwhile melt the butter in a small pan, chop the rabbit's liver and add to the butter together with the garlic, raisins and almonds. Fry gently for 3-4 minutes stirring frequently. Remove from the heat and set aside for 5-10 minutes. When cool reduce to a smooth paste with a mortar and pestle or in a blender. Return the paste to the pan and gradually stir in the remaining orange juice, the lemon juice, salt and pepper. Bring to the boil, lower the heat and simmer for about 10 minutes, stirring constantly.

When the rabbit is cooked remove it from the spit and transfer to a large serving dish. Serve the sauce separately or pour it over the rabbit. **Serves 6**

kabab jarad

locust kabab

'Yesterday I came suddenly upon two youngsters, the Rais's slaves who at mid-day were devouring roasted locusts and drinking water (during Ramadan they were not permitted to do so), in the style of sumptuous feasting. I called out "Halloa! How now? Are you feasting or fasting?" They began laughing and then handed me some roasted locusts to bribe me not to blab.' Travels in the Great Desert of Sahara

'Such sights today are very rare, but in the Saharan interior, or for that matter the Yemen and central Saudi Arabia, the locust is still a part of the diet. The Tuareg eat locusts, snakes and lizards. They are pretty good eating – I tasted of this which I bought and liked it.' Travels

'All the Bedouins of Arabia are accustomed to eat locusts. I have seen at Medinah and Tayf locust shops where these animals were sold by measure. In Egypt and Nubia they are only eaten by the poorest beggars. The Arabs, in preparing locusts as an article of food, throw them alive into boiling water, with which a good deal of salt has been mixed; after a few minutes they are taken out and dried in the sun; the head, feet and wings are then torn off, the bodies are cleansed from the salt and perfectly dried; after which process whole sacks are filled with them by the Bedouins. They are sometimes eaten broiled in butter; and they often contribute materials for a breakfast when opened over unleavened bread mixed with butter.' Notes on the Bedouins and Wahabis

Here then, for your gratification, is a *Sahraoui* (people who live in or near the Sahara) recipe for grilled locusts.

110g (4oz) *smen* or butter
1 teaspoon ras-el-hanout (see Glossary)
About 1kg (2lb) locusts

to serve
Lemon wedges

Melt the *smen* or butter in a small pan and stir in the ras-el-hanout. Thread the locusts tightly onto thin wood or metal skewers and grill over charcoal embers for 20-30 minutes basting frequently with the butter mixture and turning regularly.

When cooked slide the locusts off the skewers and remove and discard heads, legs and wings. Squeeze lemon juice over the bodies and eat.

And may the Lord have mercy on us for treating the food of the very poor as a luxury!

l'hoot mechoui

fish kabab

'O Man, see and be silent; if you eat meat say it is fish.' Libyan proverb

The Mediterranean coastline of the Meghrib is rich with all kinds of fish and although little use is made of it in the vast interior, those who live near the waters have a rich choice to pick from. Whiting, mullet, sea bream, shad and mackerel are the most popular, but other fish such as cod, dogfish, sepia (cuttlefish), tuna, swordfish, mullet and sardines etc are also used.

A typical seaside restaurant will fry fresh fish in olive oil, garnish it with lemon juice and lemon wedges and serve with bread and fresh vegetables. Dogfish and swordfish are cut into smaller chunks and grilled over charcoal; whilst mackerel is either grilled whole or cut into smaller pieces and served with a marinade.

A simple and very popular marinade which is used throughout the Meghrib is two-thirds olive oil mixed with one-third lemon juice and seasoned with herbs or spices – use this mixture to baste the fish as it grills. The most popular Moroccan fish marinade, *chermoula* (see page 244), is equally suitable for grilled fish and is one that will suit almost any type of fish – whole, sliced or in chunks. However, there are some well-known fish dishes that do not use this marinade. One of these is the following which is from Tunisia. It is a very tasty dish, often served on a bed of couscous (see page 134).

6 medium mackerel, cleaned, gutted and with backbones removed
10-12 pickling onions
6 small, firm tomatoes
2 green peppers, seeded and cut into 2.5cm (1in) squares
Juice 2 lemons
60ml (2fl oz) olive oil
1/2 teaspoon black pepper
1/2 teaspoon paprika
1/2 teaspoon harissa (see Glossary)

Cut each mackerel into 5 slices and set aside. In a large, shallow dish mix all the remaining ingredients. Add the fish slices, turning each one in the marinade to coat well and then set aside to marinate at room temperature for at least 1 hour.

Thread the slices onto skewers, alternating them with onions, tomatoes and pepper squares. Grill over charcoal for 10-12 minutes, turning frequently and basting with any remaining marinade. Serve with couscous, salads and pickles. **Serves 6**

kabab mellou

red mullet with herbs

Another Tunisian favourite with its own aromatic marinade.

4 medium red mullet, cleaned, gutted and with eyes removed

marinade
150ml (1/4 pint) olive oil
Juice 1 large lemon
3 cloves garlic, crushed
4 tablespoons chopped fresh mint or 2 tablespoons dried mint
1 tablespoon chopped fresh basil or 1 1/2 teaspoons dried basil
1 tablespoon chopped fresh marjoram or 1 1/2 teaspoons dried marjoram

1 teaspoon salt
1/2 teaspoon black pepper
1/4 teaspoon ras-el-hanout (see Glossary)

garnish
Lemon wedges, olives, pickles and fresh vegetables

Mix all the marinade ingredients together in a large shallow dish, add the fish and rub the marinade into them with your hands. Set aside to marinate at room temperature for at least 1 hour, turning occasionally.

Place in an oiled double mesh grill and cook over charcoal for 10-15 minutes, basting and turning regularly. Serve with the garnishes and with fried or roast vegetables of your choice. **Serves 4**

kabab skoumbri bil kemoun

mackerel in cumin kabab

Another Tunisian favourite. The Tunisian kitchen is perhaps the richest of all in North Africa in fish-based dishes. It seems the Tunisian has devoted his genius to creating *breiks* and fish-based dishes of remarkable originality. Serve this kabab with rice and salad, or on its own with lemon wedges.

6 medium mackerel (or trout or grey mullet), cleaned, gutted, backbones and heads removed

marinade
90ml (3fl oz) olive oil
2 cloves garlic, crushed
1 teaspoon harissa (see Glossary)
60ml (2fl oz) lemon juice
1 1/2 tablespoons cumin
1/2 teaspoon paprika
1/2 teaspoon black pepper

Make two deep incisions on each side of each fish. Mix all the marinade ingredients together in a large shallow dish, add the fish and turn several times to coat thoroughly. Set aside to marinate at room temperature for at least 1 hour.

Thread the fish onto skewers or place in a well oiled double mesh grill and cook over charcoal for 10-12 minutes, turning and basting regularly with any remaining marinade. **Serves 6**

kesksou
— couscous —

Couscous (also written as *koskos*, *keuscass* and *koskosou*) is the name both of a grain made with semolina and flour and of a dish which is cooked in a utensil called a couscousier. This, traditionally made of earthenware or, as in Western Morocco, of alpha grass, has a base pierced with holes and is set on top of another pan. Today couscousiers are usually made of aluminium and are commercially produced. They can be bought in England from shops specialising in kitchen utensils.

Couscous is the national dish of the Meghrib and is of very ancient origin – pre-Islamic, pre-Arabic and undoubtedly pre-Punic. It is the food of the poor and the rich, of peasants and kings – the latter being a dying species. Couscous is to North Africa what rice is to China, potatoes to Russia, beans to Brazil, burghul (cracked wheat) to Armenia and, of course, spaghetti to Italy. Made with millet flour or rice flour it is served in large volcano-shaped mounds with vegetables and all kinds of meat, fruits, nuts and a sauce of harissa. Couscous is the classic Muslim, as well as Jewish, Sabbath (Friday to the former, Saturday to the latter) dish. It can be served as a one-course family meal or at the end of a ceremonial banquet, and almost always at all celebrations, religious festivals etc.

Today couscous grains are commercially prepared and they are very good indeed, but in the *bled* (countryside) they are still made at home. I suggest that for all your couscous dishes, as well as tajines etc, you use the ready-made couscous grains, but – and a mild but – just for interest or education (call it what you like) I give you below the way a vast number of Meghribi women still prepare their couscous grains.

home-made couscous grains

900g (2lb) fine semolina
450g (1lb) plain flour, sifted
Salt
Water

Place the semolina in a large bowl or on a large baking sheet and make a well in the centre. Pour a little water into the centre and then scoop the semolina over the water. Sprinkle 3 tablespoons of salt and 2 tablespoons of flour over the grains and mix lightly and quickly in one direction with the palms of your hands. This process forms the meal into tiny uncooked tapioca-sized grains. When some grains have formed sift the semolina through a large medium-meshed sieve. The fine grains which remain in the sieve are the couscous. Return the big lumps and the fine grains which have fallen through the sieve back into the bowl or onto the baking sheet. Reserve the prepared couscous.

Rework the remaining semolina in the same way using a sprinkling of water and 2 tablespoons of flour each time. Continue to sieve and rework until you have used up all the semolina. You may find that you do not need all the flour, but on no account use more than the recipe states.

When all the couscous grains have been prepared transfer them to the top of a couscousier or to a colander which will fit snugly over a large saucepan. Half fill the bottom part of the couscousier or the saucepan with water and bring to the boil. Place the couscous container on top, cover and steam for 30 minutes, stirring with a long-pronged fork occasionally.

Spread the grains out on a large board or cloth and leave to dry in a warm, airy place – preferably in the sun – for 24 hours. The grains are now ready to cook as described in the recipes below or you can store them in an airtight container for future use.

The size of couscous grains varies, depending on the sieve openings, from small (standard) to large and small pellet size. For the recipes in this book I suggest you use commercial couscous and the standard-sized grains. There are other types of grain: *bilboula* is made with barley while *badaz* (also known as *bilboula deddre*) is made of maize. In the Middle East Couscous Meghribi is made with burghul and flour. This latter is only used in a classic Syrian dish called *Banjan Sumakiyah* made with aubergines, chunks of meat, chickpeas, pepper and the Caucasian spice sumak.

It is couscous, however, that is used in or with virtually any dish from the Meghrib. How does one prepare the couscous grains? Simple – see below.

preparing couscous grains for eating

450g (1lb) couscous grains
1 teaspoon ginger
1 teaspoon cumin
1 teaspoon coriander
1 teaspoon chilli pepper
50g (2oz) *smen* or butter

Spread the couscous grains out on a baking sheet and sprinkle with warm salted water. Work lightly between your fingers so that each grain is separated, moistened and beginning to swell. Set aside for 15 minutes. Repeat this process twice more.

Half fill with water the bottom part of a couscousier or a large saucepan over which a colander will fit snugly. Add all the spices and bring to the boil. When the couscous is ready pour it into the top part of the couscousier. If you are using a colander first line it with a fine tea towel as the holes may be too large and the grains will fall through. Place on top of the pan with the water and cover. Lower the heat and simmer for 30 minutes fluffing the couscous up from time to time with a long-pronged fork.

Cut the *smen* or butter up into small pieces and stir into the couscous. Continue to steam for a further 12-15 minutes fluffing up with the fork occasionally to ensure that all the grains are evenly coated. Pile the couscous onto a serving dish and serve.

variation 1

You can use the following group of spices as an alternative to the above:
1/2 teaspoon black pepper
1 teaspoon cinnamon
1/2 teaspoon sweet basil

variation 2

In the mountain ranges of the High Atlas the villagers often add a few dates to the couscous grains. The dates they use are a black sweet variety called *tafilalt*. I suggest you use either fresh Israeli dates or any dried stoned dates. While steaming the grains simply incorporate 4 or 5 thickly sliced dates and cook as with the recipe above.

You can also add 50g (2oz) grated cheese (feta, Cheddar, Edam) to the grains while they are steaming.

qalib kesksou

oven-baked couscous

Here the couscous grains are first steamed and then mixed with an egg and tomato sauce and baked in the oven. This Libyan dish is ideal with all kinds of tajines as well as roast meats.

450g (1lb) couscous grains
150g (50g) *smen* or butter
6 eggs beaten
2 tablespoons tomato purée diluted in 4-5 tablespoons water
1/2 teaspoon ground nutmeg
1/2 teaspoon black pepper
1 teaspoon salt
75g (3oz) grated cheese (feta, haloumi, Cheddar, Edam)

Prepare the couscous grains as in Couscous for eating (page 134), but omit the spices. When the grains have been steaming for 30 minutes cut three-quarters of the butter into small pieces and stir into the couscous. Continue to steam for 5 minutes, fluffing up with a long-pronged fork occasionally to ensure the grains are evenly coated.

Grease an ovenproof baking dish with the remaining butter and transfer the couscous to the dish. Spread it out evenly. Place the beaten eggs, diluted tomato purée, nutmeg, pepper and salt into a bowl and mix well. Pour evenly over the couscous. Sprinkle the cheese over the top. Bake in an oven preheated to 325F, 160C, Gas Mark 3 for 25–30 minutes. Serve hot. **Serves 6**

Couscous grains are also used in sweets and desserts – a few of which have been included in the relevant chapters. This precious grain may not be to the liking of many Westerners for it tends to be rather rich (semolina in general is rather heavy), but to the North African it is a must, a way of life, God's gift to man.

If you wish to steam couscous grains to serve with some dish other than a couscous stew, or if you are going to prepare *Kesksou Ahmar* or *Qalib Kesksou* then follow the recipes above. If however you are going to cook the grains and stew at the same time then follow instructions in the recipe below. You can then adapt this for any recipe in the chapter.

kesksou bil khodra

vegetable couscous

'If you see ants on the staircase, know that there is couscous upstairs' Moroccan saying

This recipe for vegetable-based couscous is from Libya. It uses potatoes, carrots, courgettes and tomatoes in a rich tomato sauce.

I have included a few classic vegetable couscous dishes, but I suggest that you also try experimenting and improvising with your own favourite vegetables.

450g (1lb) couscous grains
50g (2oz) *smen* or butter

stew
2 tablespoons *smen* or 25g (1oz) butter
2 cloves garlic, crushed
2 teaspoons salt
1 teaspoon cumin
1/2 teaspoon black pepper
1/2 teaspoon ginger
2 bay leaves
2 tablespoons tomato purée
3-4 fresh chilli peppers
4-5 medium carrots, peeled, quartered lengthways and
cut into 5cm (2in) pieces
3 medium courgettes, topped and tailed, quartered lengthways and cut
into 5 cm (2in) pieces
3 large tomatoes, blanched, peeled and quartered
450g (1lb) potatoes, peeled and cut into 5cm (2in) pieces
Water

Spread the couscous grains out on a baking sheet and sprinkle with warm, salted water. Work lightly between your fingers so that each grain is separated, moistened and beginning to swell. Let the couscous rest for 15 minutes. Repeat this process twice more.

Melt the stew *smen* or butter in the bottom of the couscousier or in a large saucepan, add the garlic and fry for 1-2 minutes, stirring constantly. Add the salt, cumin, black pepper, ginger, bay leaves, tomato purée and stir well. Add the chilli peppers, carrots, courgettes, tomatoes and sufficient water to cover, and bring to the boil.

When the couscous grains are ready place them in the top of the couscousier, or into a colander, lined with a fine tea towel, which will fit snugly into the top of the saucepan. Place on top of the pan with the vegetables, cover and simmer for about 20 minutes. Make sure that the container holding the couscous grains does not touch the liquid or the grains will go lumpy. Fluff up with a long-pronged fork occasionally. At this point, add the potatoes to the other vegetables and mix gently.

Cut the 50g (2oz) *smen* or butter into pieces and add to the couscous grains. At this point you can, if you wish, further season the grains by sprinkling in a teaspoon of one or two of your favourite spices (cumin, ginger, chilli pepper, coriander etc). Continue to cook the vegetables for a further 20 minutes, or until the potatoes are tender. Do not overcook or the vegetables will disintegrate. Fluff up the couscous grains from time to time to ensure the butter and spices are evenly distributed. When cooked pile the couscous onto a large serving platter, make a well in the centre and pile the vegetables into the middle. Serve immediately, with harissa sauce if you wish (see page 292). **Serves 6**

kesksou ahmar

red couscous

This is a Tunisian favourite. It is usually prepared with leftover cooked couscous grains, but there is no reason why you shouldn't prepare it as an alternative to the above recipe and serve it as an accompaniment, or a pilav, for stews, tajines and meat dishes.

If you are using leftover couscous follow the recipe below. If not then you must first prepare the grains as with the recipe above and then continue.

90ml (3fl oz) oil
2 cloves garlic, crushed
1/2 teaspoon harissa (see Glossary), mixed with 2-3 tablespoons water
1 teaspoon paprika
1 teaspoon powdered caraway
1 teaspoon salt
90ml (3fl oz) water
Juice 1 lemon
450g (1lb) couscous grains, previously cooked

Heat the oil in a large saucepan, add the garlic, harissa mixture, paprika, caraway and salt, mix thoroughly, cover the pan and cook gently for 5 minutes. Add the water, lemon juice and couscous grains and mix thoroughly – the mixture should have a uniform colour. Cook for several minutes, stirring frequently, until thoroughly heated through. Transfer to a serving dish and serve immediately. **Serves 6**

kesksou agayine

tunisian vegetable couscous

450g (1lb) couscous grains
50g (2oz) *smen* or butter

stew

90ml (3fl oz) oil
1 onion, coarsely chopped
2 cloves garlic, crushed
3 tomatoes, blanched, peeled and chopped
110g (4oz) chickpeas, soaked overnight in cold water
4 carrots, peeled, quartered lengthways and cut into 5cm (2in) pieces
2 turnips, peeled and cut into 5cm (2in) pieces
3 courgettes, topped and tailed, quartered lengthways and
cut into 5cm (2in) pieces
2 teaspoons salt
1 teaspoon paprika
1/2 teaspoon black pepper
1/2 teaspoon harissa (see Glossary)
4 potatoes, peeled and cut into 5cm (2in) pieces
3 eggs, beaten

Prepare the couscous grains as described on page 134.

Heat the oil in the bottom of the couscousier or in a large saucepan, add the onion and fry until soft. Add the garlic and tomatoes and fry for 2-3 more minutes, stirring frequently. Add the drained chickpeas and half fill the pan with water. Bring to the boil, lower the heat, cover the pan and simmer for about 30 minutes. Add the carrots and continue to cook until the chickpeas are tender.

Add the turnips, courgettes, salt, paprika, pepper and harissa and simmer for 15 minutes. Start steaming the couscous with the turnips as it takes about 45 minutes. Add the potatoes and simmer for 10 minutes.

Gradually pour in the beaten eggs, stirring gently and continue to simmer for about 20 minutes or until the vegetables are tender. Do not overcook. Serve the couscous and the vegetables separately. **Serves 6**

kesksou bil hlib

couscous with milk

'A friend is better than milk' – said when one's own brother does not help one.

Fresh broad beans and cabbage are cooked in a milk sauce – rather bland when compared with most other couscous dishes. This is Algerian, but in Morocco chicken or chunks of meat are often added, and turnips and courgettes often replace the cabbage.

450g (1lb) couscous grains
50g (2oz) *smen* or butter

stew
350g (3/4lb) fresh, shelled broad beans
600ml (1 pint) water
1 teaspoon salt
50g (2oz) *smen* or butter
350g (3/4lb) cabbage, shredded
1/2 teaspoon black pepper
450ml (3/4 pint) milk

garnish
2 hard-boiled eggs, shelled and quartered lengthways

Prepare the couscous grains as described in Kesksou bil Khodra (page 136). As the vegetables will take about 45 minutes to cook, start steaming the grains when you begin to cook the beans. Remember to add the butter.

Place the beans, water and salt in the bottom of the couscousier or in a large saucepan and bring to the boil. Lower the heat and simmer for 15 minutes. Add the *smen* or butter, cabbage and black pepper and stir well. Simmer for a further 15 minutes. Add the milk, stir well and simmer very gently for a further 10 minutes. Taste and adjust seasoning if necessary.

Heap the couscous grains on a large heated platter and make a well in the centre. Spoon the vegetables into the middle and pour over a little of the sauce. Garnish with the boiled eggs. **Serves 6**

kesksou bidaoui

meat and seven vegetable couscous

Traditionally the seven vegetables would be turnips, carrots, cabbage, pumpkin, onions, chickpeas and broad beans. They can be cooked on their own as a vegetable dish, with meat as in this recipe or with chicken or offal. The choice is wide – as is yours.

450g (1lb) couscous grains
50g (2oz) butter

stew
450g (1lb) lamb or veal, cut into 5cm (2in) pieces
225g (8oz) cabbage, shredded thickly
3 carrots, peeled, quartered lengthways and cut into 5cm (2in) pieces
2 onions, thinly sliced
50g (2oz) butter
1/4 teaspoon saffron
1 1/2 teaspoons salt
1/2 teaspoon black pepper
2 tomatoes, blanched, peeled and quartered
225g (8oz) pumpkin, peeled and cut into 5cm (2in) pieces or 2 courgettes, cut into 5cm (2in) pieces
2 turnips, peeled and cut into 5cm (2in) pieces
1 large aubergine, cut into 5cm (2in) pieces
1 fresh chilli pepper
2 tablespoons finely chopped coriander or parsley

Prepare couscous grains as in *Kesksou bil Khodra* (page 136). Add the butter at the appropriate time.

Place the meat, cabbage, carrots, half the onions, the butter, saffron, salt and black pepper in the bottom of a couscousier or in a large saucepan. Half fill with water and bring to the boil. Lower the heat, cover and simmer for 45 minutes. For the last 15 minutes place the container with the couscous grains on the pan and start to steam them.

Now add the remaining ingredients to the stew, stir well and simmer for a further 30 minutes or until the vegetables are tender. Heap the couscous grains onto a large serving platter, make a well in the centre and fill with the meat and vegetables. Serve the extra sauce in a bowl. **Serves 6**

kesksou diala

A very popular couscous, better known as *Kesksou Bidaoui bil Khli*, replaces the meat with 450g (1lb) *khli*, covered in its own fat (see Glossary). Otherwise cook as for Kesksou Bidaoui (a dish traditionally prepared on the feast of Ashura). Often dry bones (*Azem Mujafaff* — see Glossary) are substituted for the meat or *khli*. Use 4-5 bones and 50g (2oz) butter.

kesksou medfouna

chicken offal couscous

This is a Moroccan recipe, but there are many local variations throughout North Africa. If chicken offal is not readily available you can substitute lamb or chicken meat, but you can buy offal in most good supermarkets (often frozen), or you can freeze them yourself over a period of time, whenever you have a chicken.

450g (1lb) couscous grains
50g (2oz) *smen* or butter

stew
900g (2lb) chicken offal (liver, giblets, gizzards, hearts) from 7-8 chickens
110g (4oz) *smen* or butter
3 large onions, coarsely chopped
1/2 teaspoon saffron diluted in 4-5 tablespoons water
1 teaspoon cinnamon
2 teaspoons salt
1 teaspoon black pepper
Water

garnish
Few tablespoons warm milk
1 tablespoon cinnamon
4-5 tablespoons caster sugar

Prepare the couscous grains as described in Kesksou bil Khodra (page 136). Add the butter. Wash and clean the offal and pat it dry.

Heat the butter in the bottom of a couscousier or in a large saucepan, add the onion and fry, stirring frequently until soft. Add the offal and fry for 2-3 minutes, stirring constantly. Stir in the spices and add sufficient water to cover the mixture by about 2.5cm (1in) and bring to the boil. At this point place the container with the couscous grains on top of the pan to steam and cover. Lower the heat and simmer for about 40 minutes or until the water has evaporated.

To serve arrange a layer of couscous over the bottom of a serving dish, spread the offal mixture evenly over it and then top with the rest of the couscous. Sprinkle with the warm milk and decorate with the cinnamon and sugar. **Serves 6**

kesksou k'dra tangeria

tangiers-style couscous

This is a speciality of Tangiers – 'the gateway to Morocco' and also to the vast African continent. It is a city of incredible beauty and history, founded (according to legend) by Antea and it became the chief town of Mauretania Tingitana after the fall of Carthage. It was, in turn, occupied by Rome, the Vandals, Byzantium and the Arabs who, in 711 AD under the leadership of Tarik ibn Ziyad, crossed over to conquer Spain. Then came the Portuguese, the Spanish the English and in 1923 Tangiers became an international zone. Today her steep streets (one of her most striking features), the numerous café-restaurants, churches and mosques as well as the famed Grand Socco and Little Socco (the two market places surrounded by dated hotels, small shops and eating houses fragrant with mint tea and kababs and where Rif Berber peasants bring their produce to sell) have made her a popular tourist haven.

Tangiers is undoubtedly still the most cosmopolitan city in North Africa, though she has lost a great deal of her past glory, sparkle and wealth – a product of international political and financial intrigues. Her many restaurants offer the tourists Spanish, Moroccan, French and what is loosely labelled 'international food', and her inhabitants are fortunate to live in what I found to be one of the most pleasant spots in the Meghrib.

This fragrant couscous is typical of a cuisine both simple yet extravagant – very much like the city and her inhabitants.

450g (1lb) couscous grains
50g (2oz) *smen* or butter

stew
1.5kg (3lb) lamb or beef, cut into 2.5-5cm (1-2in) pieces
6 tablespoons finely chopped parsley
1/4 teaspoon nutmeg
1/2 teaspoon ginger
1/4 teaspoon saffron diluted in 2 tablespoons water
1 teaspoon cinnamon
2 teaspoons salt
1 teaspoon black pepper

1/2 teaspoon curry powder
120ml (4fl oz) oil
900ml (1 1/2 pints) water
110g (4oz) raisins

sauce

2 tablespoons *smen* or 25g (1oz) butter
1 onion, thinly sliced
1/4 teaspoon saffron diluted in 6 tablespoons water or meat stock
110g (4oz) raisins
2 tablespoons blanched almonds
2 teaspoons cinnamon
1 teaspoon salt

Prepare couscous grains as described in Kesksou bil Khodra (page 136). Don't forget to add the butter.

Put all the stew ingredients except the water and raisins in the bottom of the couscousier or large saucepan, cover and cook over a medium heat for about 20 minutes, stirring occasionally. Add the water and bring to the boil. Cover the pan, lower the heat and simmer for about 1 hour or until the meat is tender. Add the raisins and simmer for a further 10-15 minutes. The couscous grains will take about 45 minutes to steam so place on top of the couscousier or saucepan at the appropriate time (about 30 minutes after the stew begins its simmer).

Meanwhile prepare the sauce by placing all its ingredients in a small saucepan and simmering for 10-15 minutes, stirring frequently. When ready to serve pile the couscous grains onto a large platter, make a well in the centre and fill with the meat. Spoon the sauce over the meat and then sprinkle a little meat sauce over the whole dish. Serve the remaining meat sauce separately. **Serves 6**

kesksou akhir al sana

– new year's eve couscous –

This dish is only prepared on New Year's Eve. It consists of 900g (2lb) shoulder of lamb cut into 7.5 cm (3in) pieces cooked in 1.2 l (2 pints) water seasoned with 50g (2oz) chopped fresh mint or 25g (1oz) dried mint. Serve with couscous grains.

kesksou bil djaj

algerian chicken couscous

'If you are a date tree, suffer fools to throw stones at you.' Berber saying

A tasty chicken stew with vegetables and dates which comes from Algeria. Serve with warm milk or, as is the custom in Libya and Egypt, with a bowl of fresh yogurt.

450g (1lb) couscous grains
50g (2oz) *smen* of butter

stew

2 tablespoons *smen* or 25g (1oz) butter
1 onion, finely chopped
1 tomato, blanched, peeled and chopped
2 teaspoons salt
1/2 teaspoon cinnamon
1/2 teaspoon black pepper
900ml (1 1/2 pints) water
110g (4oz) chickpeas, soaked in cold water overnight
3 carrots, peeled, quartered lengthways and cut into 5cm (2in) sticks
3 turnips, peeled and cut into 5cm (2in) pieces
3 medium courgettes, topped, tailed and cut into 5cm (2in) rounds
1 teaspoon harissa (see Glossary)
1 x 1.5kg (3lb) chicken, cut into pieces
175g (6oz) dried dates, stoned and halved

Prepare the couscous grains as described in Kesksou bil Khodra (page 136). Add the butter as usual.

Heat the stew *smen* or butter in the bottom of a couscousier or in a large saucepan, add the onion, and fry until soft. Add the tomato, salt, cinnamon and pepper and fry for a few minutes, stirring frequently. Add the water and drained chickpeas and bring to the boil. Cover the pan, lower the heat and simmer for about 30 minutes.

Add the vegetables, harissa and chicken pieces and bring to the boil. Add a little more water if you think it necessary. Lower the heat and place the container with the couscous grains on the top. Simmer for 30 minutes. Stir the dates into the stew and simmer for a further 15 minutes, by which time the chicken and vegetables should be cooked.

To serve pile the couscous onto a serving dish and make a well in the centre. Spoon the meat and vegetables into the centre and pour a little of the stock over the top. Serve the rest in a separate bowl.

kesksou bil frakh

– pigeon couscous –

Replace the chicken with 4 pigeons. Cook the halved pigeons with 2 large, chopped onions, 225g (8oz) soaked chickpeas, 175g (6oz) raisins, 2 tablespoons dried rosemary, 1/2 teaspoon cinnamon, 1/2 teaspoon cumin, 2 teaspoons salt, 1/2 teaspoon black pepper and 1.8 l (3 pints) water. Serve with couscous grains as in other recipes.

kesksou k'dra bil bjaj

chicken, honey and onion couscous

'He who loves honey should be patient of the stinging of the bees' Moroccan saying

From Morocco and, more specifically, from Casablanca – the setting of one of my favourite films! Dar al Bayda (the white house) is the Arab name for this vast modern city (2¹/₂ million inhabitants), which is the second largest city in Africa after Cairo. It is the commercial, industrial and hence social centre of Morocco, with excellent hotels and restaurants – many of which serve authentic Meghribi dishes such as the one below.

450g (1lb) couscous grains
50g (2oz) *smen* or butter

stew
1.5kg (3lb) chicken, cut into pieces
1.2 l (2 pints) water
25g (1oz) *smen* or butter
2 teaspoons salt
1 teaspoon black pepper
1/2 teaspoon saffron diluted in a few tablespoons of the water
5cm (2in) stick cinnamon

sauce
900g (2lb) onions, sliced into rings
110g (4oz) *smen* or butter
1 teaspoon cinnamon
1 teaspoon cinnamon
1/2 teaspoon salt
120ml (4fl oz) honey

Prepare the couscous grains as described in *Kesksou bil Khodra* (page 136). Add the butter as usual.

Place the chicken pieces, water, *smen* or butter, salt, black pepper, diluted saffron and cinnamon stick in the bottom of the couscousier or in a large saucepan and bring to the boil. Place the container with the couscous grains on the top and cover. Lower the heat and simmer for about 45 minutes or until the chicken pieces are tender.

Meanwhile place the sliced onions in a small saucepan, cover them with water and bring to the boil. Lower the heat and simmer for 5 minutes and then drain. Melt the *smen* or butter in a pan, add the cooked onion, and fry for 2-3 minutes stirring regularly. Add the remaining ingredients and cook for a further 5 minutes, still stirring regularly.

To serve, pile the couscous grains onto a large serving plate and make a well in the centre. Arrange the chicken in the middle and pour the honey sauce over them. Serve a bowl of hot chicken stock separately. **Serves 6**

kesksou bil hoot

fish couscous

Although fish is popular in Morocco and Algeria it is at its best in Tunisia where, thanks to a bountiful sea coast, there are found some of the finest North African fish recipes.

Below is a typical fish couscous recipe and I have also included a Libyan one where the fish is first fried and then added to the vegetables. Sometimes a rich fish stock is prepared by boiling fish tails and heads with all the vegetables and spices. The heads and tails are then removed and fish slices are added to the vegetables and cooked. This makes a very rich stew, not to everyone's liking. Almost any type of fish can be used – grouper, turbot, dogfish, swordfish, halibut, bonito etc – but the most popular are the red or grey mullet.

450g (1lb) couscous grains
50g (2oz) *smen* or butter

stew
120ml (4fl oz) oil
2 onions, finely chopped
1 clove garlic, finely chopped
1 teaspoon harissa (see Glossary), diluted in 2-3 tablespoons water
1/2 teaspoon black pepper
1/2 teaspoon cumin
1.5 l (21/2 pints) water
2 tomatoes, blanched, peeled and chopped
2 carrots, peeled and cut into 1cm (1/2in) rounds
2 turnips, peeled and cut into 5cm (2in) pieces

2 bay leaves

4 potatoes, peeled and cut into 2cm (3/4in) thick rounds

1.5kg (3lb) fish, cut into 6 thick slices

Prepare the couscous grains as described in Kesksou bil Khodra (page 136). Add the butter as usual.

Heat the oil in the bottom of a couscousier or in a large saucepan, add the onion, garlic, diluted harissa, black pepper and cumin and fry for 1-2 minutes. Add the water, tomatoes, carrots, turnips and bay leaves and bring to the boil. Place the container with the couscous grains on top of the pan and cover. Lower the heat and simmer for 20 minutes. Add the potato and fish slices and simmer for a further 20-25 minutes or until fish and vegetables are tender.

To serve, pile the couscous grains onto a large serving dish and make a well in the centre. Arrange the fish slices and vegetables in the middle and sprinkle with a little of the fish stock. Serve the rest separately. **Serves 6**

You could also fry 6 fish steaks in 2-3 tablespoons *smen* or butter until golden on both sides, then transfer to the couscousier to cook with vegetables and spices above.

Sometimes fishballs are prepared by mincing together fish, onion, celery and garlic and then mixing in an egg and some stale bread soaked in a little water. The mixture is shaped into walnut-sized balls and fried in oil until golden. Serve with vegetables and couscous grains.

tajines

'Lasa jiyid mer rehturban' – A good meal is known by its odour.

Tajine (also known as *touajen slaoui*) is the name of both an earthenware dish with a pointed lid and a style of cooking of ancient origins. The cooking is done in a taoua, a large copper casserole container used throughout North Africa, the Middle East and India, but the dish is served either individually in small tajines or in a larger one.

Basically tajine dishes are stews, usually of meat (lamb, mutton, also goat, rarely beef, sometimes chicken) but hardly ever fish – although there are exceptions. The meat is usually stewed with spices and herbs, with vegetables, with fruits, with nuts, but more usually with a combination of some or all of the above ingredients. The main characteristic of this form of cooking is to fill the taoua with a lot of water (much more than is usually used in western cooking), bring to the boil and then reduce the heat and simmer until the juices thicken.

There are hundreds of tajines and it is often difficult to differentiate what is merely a stew from one that is labelled tajine. Some dishes are simple, others are highly spiced and aromatic. Moroccans love to use saffron and cinnamon while Tunisians inevitably add a spoonful of hot harissa paste, giving their dishes a characteristic piquancy.

Tajines are usually served on their own. However, I suggest you accompany these flavoursome dishes with steamed couscous (page 134), red couscous (page 137), oven-baked couscous (page 135) or with a rice pilav (page 225). There is often no need for a vegetable accompaniment as many of the tajines incorporate vegetables, but once again you can be flexible. Roast or boiled potatoes would make an ideal accompaniment for several of the dishes.

You can diversify both the vegetables and the spice content of most of these tajines to your taste. There are no set rules.

One other characteristic of several of these tajines is that they are sweet-based – i.e. fruits, nuts, sugar and honey are often incorporated into the meat and vegetables. There is nothing unusual about this form of cooking. It was particularly popular in ancient times: the Persians and Romans used to mix meat with fruit, nuts and honey. Indeed today, as well as on the high Atlas ranges, on the even higher Caucasian and Persian Elbrus mountain ranges people have retained this 'sweet and savoury' style of cooking.

Finally a few words from the eleventh century Moorish poet Al Sumaisir (from *An Anthology of Moorish Poetry*) warning us not to overdo things.

'You gobble all and each
Your fancy bid you cram,
And then abuse the leech
And call his craft a sham.

The fruits of what you sow
You'll gather pretty quick;
The harvest is not slow –
Expect then to be sick.

Your belly is a pot
Collecting day by day
If's noisome food, with what
Dire illness to repay!'

tajine choua

sautéed meat tajine

I start the chapter with simple meat tajines flavoured only with herbs and spices. A particularly well-known example is this one from Algeria.

1.5kg (3lb) leg or shoulder of lamb, cut into 2.5cm (1in) cubes
2 onions, finely chopped
110g (4oz) *smen* or butter
2 teaspoons salt
1 teaspoon black pepper
1 teaspoon paprika
1/2 teaspoon ginger
1/2 teaspoon turmeric
Water

to serve
Lemon wedges

Place the meat, onions, half the *smen* or butter and all the spices in a large saucepan and fry over a low heat for about 10 minutes, stirring frequently. Add enough water to cover the mixture by about 5cm (2in) and bring to the boil. Lower the heat and simmer for 45-

60 minutes or until the meat is tender. Carefully remove the meat cubes with a slotted spoon and reserve. Continue cooking until the pan juices are reduced and smooth.

Meanwhile melt the remaining *smen* or butter in another pan, add the meat cubes and sauté for 3-4 minutes, stirring constantly until they are well coated and browned. Return to the juices, mix well and simmer for a further 4-5 minutes. Serve and eat with a little lemon juice squeezed over the top. **Serves 6**

tiab l'sane

meat, cumin and coriander tajine

Similar to the recipe above, this tajine is Moroccan – hence the generous use of coriander.

1.5kg (3lb) leg or shoulder of lamb, cut into 5cm (2in) cubes
2 onions, finely chopped
50g (2oz) *smen* or butter
1 teaspoon salt
1 teaspoon paprika
Water
1/2 teaspoon cumin
1¹/2 teaspoons coriander
60ml (2fl oz) vinegar

Place the meat, onions, *smen* or butter, salt and paprika in a large saucepan and sauté over a low heat for about 10 minutes, stirring frequently. Add enough water to cover by about 5cm (2in) and bring to the boil. Simmer for 45-60 minutes or until the meat is tender.

Add the cumin, coriander and vinegar, mix well and continue to simmer until the sauce thickens. Serve immediately. **Serves 6**

tajine mquali

meat, olives and lemon tajine

In this recipe, pickled lemon rind (see page 150) and preserved olives
(see Glossary) are combined with lamb chops. The saffron in this dish gives it an exquisite golden colour.

1.5kg (3lb) lamb chops, trimmed of fat, or shoulder of lamb cut
into 5cm (2in) cubes

1 small onion, whole
1 clove garlic, crushed
1 teaspoon ginger
1 teaspoon saffron diluted in 6-7 tablespoons water
50g (2oz) *smen* or butter
2 tablespoons oil
Water
1 teaspoon flour
1 pickled lemon zest, quartered (see page 250)
12 preserved olives (see Glossary)

Place the meat, onion, garlic, ginger, diluted saffron, *smen* or butter and oil in a large saucepan and sauté for about 10 minutes, stirring frequently. Add enough water to cover the ingredients by about 2.5cm (1in) and bring to the boil. Cover the pan, lower the heat and simmer for 45-60 minutes or until the meat is tender.

Remove the onion and blend to a pulp with a little of the pan juices. Stir in the flour until smooth and then return this mixture to the pan, stirring constantly until it boils. Add the lemon zest and preserved olives, raise the heat a little and cook until the sauce thickens. **Serves 6**

tajine kabab maghdour bil bayd

'betrayed' tajine with eggs

I have not been able to find out why this dish is called 'betrayed'. I suspect it has something to do with the fact that the meat traditionally used is cut out of joints used in kabab recipes. So the leftover bones with strips of meat are used with other cuts of meat (lamb or veal) from rib, shoulder etc. 'Betrayed' are, I surmise, those poor, wretched meats that did not quite make a kabab! The meats may have been betrayed but, I assure you, you will not be, as it is a simple and filling dish. Serve with rice or couscous.

1.5kg (3lb) meat, cut into 5cm (2in) pieces
1¹/2 teaspoons salt
1 teaspoon paprika
1 teaspoon cumin
1/2 teaspoon chilli pepper
50g (2oz) *smen* or butter
1 teaspoon flour
3-4 eggs

garnish
1 tablespoon finely chopped parsley or tarragon

Place the meat, salt, paprika, cumin, chilli pepper, *smen* or butter and enough water to cover the ingredients by about 2.5cm (1in) in a pan. Bring to the boil, cover the pan, lower the heat and simmer for about 45-60 minutes or until the meat is tender.

Place the flour in a small bowl with a few spoonfuls of the pan juices and mix to a smooth paste. Return to the pan and stir constantly until the mixture thickens.

Just before serving crack the eggs over the meat mixture and cook over a low heat until the whites are set, but the yolks still runny. Garnish and serve immediately.
Serves 6

tajine tfaiya

tajine with eggs and almonds

This delectable-looking dish is as exotic as it is simple to prepare.

The traditional recipe – one of the dishes that appear at weddings, circumcisions, anniversaries etc – makes an over-generous use of saffron (about 1½ tablespoons) which is all very well for the Meghribi housewife – she can purchase it at an incredibly cheap price. We can't, so I suggest we compromise and use turmeric – 'poor man's saffron' – so that the meat will still have that golden look about it.

In this version the almonds are cooked with the meat, but if you wish you can fry them until golden in a little oil and stir into the stew just before serving.

1.5kg (3lb) lamb, shoulder or leg and chops mixed
1½ teaspoons salt
½ teaspoon black pepper
2 onions, finely chopped
50g (2oz) *smen* or butter
½ teaspoon powdered saffron diluted in 3-4 tablespoons water
1 teaspoon turmeric
½ teaspoon coriander
110g (4oz) blanched almonds
3 hard-boiled eggs, halved

Cut the shoulder or leg of lamb into 5cm (2in) pieces and trim most of the fat from the chops. Place in a large saucepan with all the other ingredients except the eggs. Fry for about 10 minutes, stirring frequently. Add enough water to cover the meat by about 2.5cm (1in) and bring to the boil. Lower the heat, cover the pan and simmer for 45-60 minutes or until the meat is tender. Remove the lid, raise the heat and boil until the sauce has thickened.

To serve, transfer the meat to a large serving dish, decorate with the halved eggs and pour the sauce over the top. **Serves 6**

tajine mhaouete

chunks of meat with meatballs tajine

From Algeria this is a sophisticated dish of meat 'balls' or, to be more accurate, little 'sausages' which are first fried then added to the meat chunks and spices in the pan. It is from Oran, the birthplace of one of my favourite French writers, Albert Camus, who had this to say about his town in *La Peste*.

'The town itself, let us admit, is ugly. It has a smug, placid air and you need time to discover what it is that makes it different from so many business centres in other parts of the world. Now conjure up a picture, for instance, of a town without pigeons, without any trees or gardens. . . . During the summer the sun bakes the houses bone dry, sprinkles our walls with greyish dust, and you have no option but to survive those days of fire indoors, behind closed shutters.'

At least he had one consolation – he could drink pure orange juice, eat fresh fruit and of course *Tajine Mhaouete*, but I suppose that like most *colons* he refrained from such 'peasant' dishes!

900g (2lb) shoulder or leg of lamb, cut into 5cm (2in) chunks
3 tablespoons oil
1 tablespoon *smen* or 15g (1/2oz) butter
1 onion, finely chopped
1 tablespoon tomato purée diluted in 4-5 tablespoons water
1 teaspoon black pepper
1 teaspoon paprika
1/2 teaspoon harissa (optional)
2 tablespoons vinegar

minced meat
450g (1lb) minced lamb
2-3 cloves garlic, crushed
1 teaspoon cumin
1 teaspoon salt
1 egg, beaten
1 tablespoon flour

garnish
2 tablespoons finely chopped parsley
Lemon wedges

Place the meat chunks, oil, *smen* or butter, onion, diluted tomato purée, salt, pepper and paprika in a large saucepan and fry over a low heat for abut 10 minutes, stirring frequently. Add enough water to cover the meat by about 2.5cm (1in), stir in harissa and vinegar, and bring to the boil. Cover the pan, lower the heat and simmer for about 45 minutes.

Meanwhile prepare the meatballs by placing all the ingredients in a bowl and kneading until the mixture is smooth and well blended. Dampen your hands and form into walnut-sized balls. If you wish you can now roll them between your palms to form sausages about 7.5cm (3in) long. Heat a little oil in a large pan and fry the balls or sausages for 10-15 minutes, turning occasionally. Transfer with a slotted spoon to the stew and simmer for a further 5-10 minutes.

Arrange the meat chunks in the centre of a large serving dish, spoon the meatballs around the edge and pour the sauce over the top. Garnish with the parsley and lemon wedges. **Serves 6**

In the eleventh century the Andalusian poet Ibn al-Talla (from *An Anthology of Moorish Poetry*) sang the praises of an artichoke thus:

> *'The artichoke*
> *Lovely little daughter*
> *Born of earth and water.*
> *Still her excellence is*
> *Barred by the defences*
> *Avarice erects*
> *Hopeful hearts to vex . . .*
> *With her flesh so white*
> *Guarded in the height.*
> *Of her tower surging*
> *Like a Turkish virgin*
> *Bashfully she peers*
> *Through her veil of spears.'*

tajine karnoune

artichoke heart tajine

Because artichokes are so cheap in North Africa they are used generously. This recipe includes 12 which allows 2 per person, but for the sake of economy you can reduce this to 6 without affecting the overall flavour.

12 artichokes
1 lemon, halved
900g (2lb) shoulder or leg of lamb cut into 5cm (2in) chunks
1¹/₂ teaspoons salt
1 teaspoon ginger
¹/₂ teaspoon saffron diluted in 4-5 tablespoons water

½ teaspoon turmeric
90ml (3fl oz) oil
2 tablespoons finely chopped parsley
Zest of pickled lemon (see page 250)
8-10 preserved olives (see Glossary)

First prepare the artichokes. Take one and slice off the stem. Rub the cut edge with a lemon half, then pull back the lower leaves until they snap off. Remove all the outer leaves until you reach the greenish-white ones bending inwards. Place the artichoke on its side and cut off the remaining leaves just above the white heart. Rotating the base of the artichoke against the knife blade, trim off all the green leaf bases. Drop into a bowl of water into which you have squeezed the juice of half the lemon. Repeat with the remaining artichokes.

Place the meat, salt, ginger, diluted saffron, turmeric and oil into a pan and fry for about 10 minutes, stirring frequently. Add enough water to cover by about 5cm (2in) and bring to the boil. Lower the heat, cover the pan and simmer for 45-60 minutes or until the meat is tender. Remove the meat with a slotted spoon and reserve.

Add the artichoke hearts to the pan and add a little more water if there is not enough to cover them. Cover and simmer for 30-40 minutes or until tender. Add the lemon zest and pickled olives and return the meat to the pan. Simmer for a further 5-10 minutes or until the sauce has thickened. Spoon the stew into a large serving dish arranging the hearts on top of the meat. **Serves 6**

tajine karnoune bil limoun

lemon and artichoke tajine

An Algerian recipe. Once more, as artichokes are expensive here you can reduce the number used.

90ml (3fl oz) oil
2 onions, finely chopped
4 cloves garlic, crushed
900g (2lb) shoulder of lamb, cut into 5cm (2in) chunks
Zest of 1 pickled lemon (see page 250), cut into 2cm (¾in) pieces
1½ teaspoons salt
½ teaspoon black pepper
5cm (2in) cinnamon stick
12 artichokes, prepared (see above), and halved

Heat the oil in a large saucepan, add the onion and garlic and fry for 2-3 minutes, stirring frequently. Add the meat and continue to fry for a further 10 minutes still stirring regularly. Add the lemon zest, salt, black pepper, cinnamon stick and enough water to cover by about 5cm (2in). Bring to the boil, lower the heat, cover the pan and simmer for 30 minutes.

Add the halved artichokes and the potatoes, cover the pan and simmer for a further 30-40 minutes or until the meat and vegetables are tender. Discard the cinnamon stick and spoon the tajine into a large serving dish. Serve with couscous or a rice pilav.
Serves 6

Tajines are also prepared with Jerusalem artichokes (*Helianthus tuberosus*) – in Arabic *tartuf* or *tuffah el ard*. The Jerusalem artichoke has nothing whatsoever to do with the cultivated or wild artichoke (*Cynara scolymus*). It is the edible part of a North American plant which was cultivated by American Indians before the French introduced it to Europe (1616) and North Africa (early nineteenth century). If you wish you can substitute Jerusalem artichokes for those in the recipes above. To prepare them, scrub and peel and then cut into quarters. Drop immediately into cold water to prevent discolouring and then cook.

In Morocco the stems of wild thistles are also prepared as tajines, as indeed are the stems of wild artichokes. These are difficult to peel as the stems have thorns on them, but the taste is claimed to be very delicate.

tajine maderbel

aubergine tajine

This filling meal is from Algeria. The aubergines are fried separately and added to the meat mixture towards the end of the cooking time.

900g (2lb) aubergines, topped, tailed and cut crossways into
2.5cm (1in) slices
3 teaspoons salt
Oil
675g (1¹/₂lb) leg or shoulder of lamb, cut into 2.5cm (1in) cubes
4 cloves garlic
¹/₂ teaspoon black pepper
¹/₂ teaspoon powdered caraway
¹/₂ teaspoon cinnamon
¹/₄ teaspoon ginger
¹/₂ teaspoon turmeric
110g (4oz) chickpeas, soaked overnight in cold water
1 tablespoon vinegar or lemon juice

Sprinkle the aubergine slices with 2 teaspoons of the salt and set aside for 30 minutes. Rinse under cold running water and pat dry with kitchen paper.

Meanwhile heat 6 tablespoons oil in a large saucepan, add the meat, garlic, black pepper, caraway, cinnamon, ginger and turmeric and fry for about 10 minutes, stirring frequently. Add the drained chickpeas and enough water to cover by about 5cm (2in). Bring to the boil, lower the heat, cover the pan and simmer for 45-60 minutes or until the chickpeas are tender. Add a little more water if necessary.

Meanwhile heat about 150ml (1/4 pint) oil in a large frying pan and fry the aubergine slices, a few at a time, until golden on both sides. Remove with a slotted spoon, drain on kitchen paper and keep warm while you cook the remaining slices in the same way. Add a little more oil if necessary.

When the chickpeas are cooked stir remaining salt and the vinegar or lemon juice into the stew and add the fried aubergine slices. Cover the pan and simmer for a further 15 minutes or until the sauce is reduced. Serve immediately in a large dish with the meat in the centre decorated with the aubergine slices and topped with the chickpeas and sauce. **Serves 6**

tajine badendjel mehshi

stuffed aubergine tajine

This is a Tunisian way of preparing aubergines. The aubergine slices are stuffed with a meat and egg mixture, fried and then transferred to a pan and cooked in a sauce. Courgettes can be cooked in the same way. Serve with couscous or a rice pilav.

3 large aubergines, topped, tailed and cut crossways into 2cm (3/4in) thick slices
Salt

stuffing
275g (10oz) minced meat
4 tablespoons finely chopped parsley
2 cloves garlic, crushed
1/2 teaspoon black pepper
2 hard-boiled eggs, finely chopped
1 egg

for frying
150ml (1/4 pint) oil
50g (2oz) flour
1 large egg, well beaten

sauce
2 cloves garlic, crushed
1/2 teaspoon paprika
1/4 teaspoon chilli pepper
1/2 teaspoon cumin
600ml (1 pint) water

Make one deep incision in each aubergine slice, sprinkle with salt and set aside for 30 minutes. Rinse under running water and pat dry.

Meanwhile place all the stuffing ingredients, plus 1 teaspoon salt, together in a bowl and knead until well blended and smooth. Take 1 teaspoon of the filling and place it in the incision in one of the slices. Spread what will not fit into the slit over one of the flat surfaces of the slice and press hard to make it stick. Continue until you have used up all the ingredients.

Heat the oil in a large pan and, one at a time, dip a few of the slices first in the flour and then in the beaten egg. Fry in the oil, turning once until golden on both sides. Remove with a slotted spoon and drain on kitchen paper. Fry all the remaining slices, and any meatballs, in the same way. When all the slices are cooked pour any remaining oil into a large saucepan, add all the sauce ingredients, plus 1 teaspoon salt, and bring to the boil. Carefully arrange the slices in the pan, lower the heat, cover the pan and simmer for 30 minutes. Serve hot. **Serves 6**

tajine lham bil loubia khadra

green bean and meat tajine

'Every bean finds its blind measurer' Algerian proverb

A delicious and easy to prepare tajine, from Rabat in Morocco.

900g (2lb) shoulder or leg of lamb, cut into 2.5cm (1in) slices
1¹/2 teaspoons salt
1/2 teaspoon saffron diluted in 4-5 tablespoons water
1/2 teaspoon turmeric
1 teaspoon ginger
2 teaspoons paprika
1/2 teaspoon cumin
60ml (2fl oz) oil
675g (1¹/2lb) French beans, topped, tailed, stringed and halved
Juice 1 lemon

Place the meat slices in a large saucepan with the salt, diluted saffron, turmeric, ginger, paprika, cumin and oil. Fry for about 10 minutes, stirring frequently. Add enough water to cover by about 2.5cm (1in) and bring to the boil. Lower the heat, cover the pan and simmer for 45 minutes or until tender.

Meanwhile rinse the beans and place in a pan of lightly salted boiling water. Simmer for 5 minutes and then drain.

When the meat is cooked add the beans and lemon juice and stir well. Simmer for a further 5-10 minutes, with the lid off, until the beans are tender and the sauce has thickened. Spoon into a large dish and serve hot. **Serves 6**

tajine kanaria

cardoon tajine

The cardoon is beloved of the Berbers of the Atlas mountains. It is (like the globe artichoke) a thistle, the leaf of which is eaten – as are the flower heads sometimes. This very Moroccan tajine, with the almost obligatory lemon zest and olives, is well worth the effort – if you can find the cardoons.

3 heads of cardoons – about 1.75-2kg (4lb)
Bowl of water with 1 tablespoon lemon juice or vinegar
900g (2lb) shoulder or leg of lamb, cut into 5cm (2in) pieces
2 teaspoons salt
1 clove garlic, finely chopped
110g (4oz) chickpeas, soaked overnight in cold water
6 tablespoons oil
1/2 teaspoon saffron diluted in 4-5 tablespoons water
1/2 teaspoon turmeric
1 teaspoon ginger
Zest 1 pickled lemon, cut into 2cm (3/4in) pieces (page 250)
10-12 pickled olives (see Glossary)
Juice 1 lemon
1 teaspoon flour

First prepare the cardoons. String and trim them after having removed the tips. Next separate the stalk and heart, cutting them so that you do not strip away the skin and string. Carefully remove all tough parts of the vegetable. Cut into 5cm (2in) pieces taking off the inner smooth skin each time as you go along. Drop the pieces immediately into the bowl of acidulated water. Cut the tips of the cardoons into two and prepare these as with the stems. Add to the bowl.

Take the meat, salt, garlic, drained chickpeas, oil, diluted saffron, turmeric and ginger and fry for about 10 minutes, stirring frequently. Add enough water to cover by about 5cm (2in) and bring to the boil. Simmer for 15 minutes. Add the cardoons, except for the tips, and, if necessary, enough water to completely cover them – to delay the discolouring (which happens even during the cooking process). Bring to the boil, lower the heat, cover the pan and simmer for 30 minutes. Add the tips and continue to cook for a further 30 minutes or until the meat and chickpeas are tender.

Stir in the lemon zest, pickled olives and lemon juice. Mix the flour to a paste with some of the hot stock and then stir into the pan. Simmer until the sauce thickens. Spoon into a large dish and serve hot. **Serves 6**

tajine zrodiya

carrot and meat tajine

This simple recipe is from the Tripoli area of Libya. If possible use small, young carrots.

900g (2lb) leg or shoulder of lamb cut into 5cm (2in) pieces or
1.5kg (3lb) chicken cut into serving pieces
3 spring onions, thinly sliced
4 tablespoons *smen* or 50g (2oz) butter
1/2 teaspoon black pepper
1/2 teaspoon cinnamon
1 teaspoon hilba (see Glossary)
1/2 teaspoon ginger
11/2 teaspoons salt
900g (2lb) young carrots, scraped clean
3 tablespoons finely chopped coriander or parsley

garnish
6-8 olives
2 tablespoons lemon juice

Place all the ingredients except the carrots and coriander or parsley in a large saucepan and fry for about 10 minutes, stirring frequently. Add enough water to cover by 5cm (2in) and bring to the boil. Lower the heat, cover the pan and simmer for about 30 minutes. Add the carrots, re-cover the pan and simmer for a further 20-30 minutes or until the meat and vegetables are cooked.

Remove the lid, stir in the coriander or parsley and simmer vigorously until the sauce is reduced and has thickened a little. Sprinkle with the olives and lemon juice. Serve in the Libyan style with a rice pilav or spaghetti. **Serves 6**

tajine lham bil brouklou

cauliflower and meat tajine

A delicious and attractive tajine. The cauliflower is cooked and served whole.

900g (2lb) shoulder of lamb cut into 5cm (2in) pieces or
lamb chops trimmed of fat
1¹/₂ teaspoons salt
¹/₂ teaspoon saffron diluted in 4-5 tablespoons water
5-6 tablespoons oil
1 teaspoon ginger
1 large cauliflower
2 teaspoons flour
1 teaspoon paprika
¹/₂ teaspoon chilli pepper
¹/₂ teaspoon cumin
Juice 1 large lemon

garnish
Lemon wedges

Put the meat in a large saucepan with the salt, diluted saffron, oil and ginger and fry for about 10 minutes, stirring frequently. Add enough water to cover by about 2.5cm (1in) and bring to the boil. Lower the heat, cover the pan and simmer for about 45 minutes or until tender.

Meanwhile trim the cauliflower of all blemishes. Cut out most of the stalk then rinse and drain. Make 1 teaspoon of the flour to a smooth paste with a little water. Bring a large pan of lightly salted water to the boil, add the cauliflower and paste and simmer until the stalk is tender. Drain and reserve.

When the meat is cooked remove with a slotted spoon and reserve. Stir the paprika, chilli pepper, cumin and lemon juice into the pan juices. Make remaining teaspoon of flour into a paste with 4 tablespoons water. Add to the pan, and simmer for 1-2 minutes. Return the meat and cauliflower to the pan, keeping them separate. Cover and simmer for 10 minutes basting the cauliflower with the sauce regularly.

To serve, arrange the meat on a serving dish, place the cauliflower on top and pour the sauce over. Serve with the lemon wedges. **Serves 6**

tajine bil kromb

Meat and cabbage tajine. Use the same quantities as above, but replace the cauliflower with a 1.5kg (3lb) firm round cabbage. Trim off discoloured and wilted leaves and

bouraniyat el-kousa

courgette and meat tajine

This and many similarly named *bouraniyat* dishes are reputed to be named after Bourane – the daughter of Hasan ibn Sahl and the wife of the great Kalif al-Mamoun (813-833 AD). This, as with many other Arab and Meghribi myths, is pure tosh! *Bouraniyat* are named after the daughter of King Khosrow Parviz of Persia. She was called Poorandokh and she flourished some 300 years before her Arab counterpart. She was so fond of yogurt and yogurt-based dishes that several are still named after her. The Middle Eastern *borani* or *porani* has travelled to the East as *biriani* and to the West as *bouraniyat*. Interestingly enough the main ingredient that distinguishes a stew from a *borani* – yogurt – does not appear at all in the Meghribi cuisine.

This is a simple dish, also sometimes known as *Bouraniyat-al-Anabu*, from Algeria, and it is equally good with aubergines. Traditionally the vegetables are fried in the fat from the tail of the Mediterranean sheep (these can weigh up to 10kg or about 22lbs)! I suggest you use *smen*, ghee or butter.

900g (1lb) lamb or beef, cut into 2.5cm (1in) pieces
1 teaspoon ginger
1/2 teaspoon saffron diluted in 4-5 tablespoons water
1/2 teaspoon turmeric
1/2 teaspoon chilli pepper
900ml (11/2 pints) water
1 onion, thinly sliced
3 tablespoons finely chopped parsley
2 tablespoons finely chopped fresh coriander
110g (4oz) *smen*, ghee or butter
900g (2lb) courgettes, topped, tailed and cut into 1cm (1/2in) rounds
2 teaspoons salt
1 teaspoon black pepper

Place the meat, ginger, diluted saffron, turmeric, chilli pepper and water in a pan and bring to the boil. Lower the heat, cover the pan and simmer for 15 minutes. Now add the onion slices, parsley and coriander, stir, cover and simmer for a further 20-30 minutes.

Meanwhile heat the fat in a large frying pan and fry the courgette slices, a few at a time, until golden on both sides. Remove with a slotted spoon, drain and keep warm while you fry the remaining slices in the same way.

When the meat is nearly cooked add the courgette slices to the pan. Sprinkle with the salt and pepper, cover and simmer for a further 10 minutes. **Serves 6**

k'dra bil zaatar

This Moroccan tajine traditionally uses a marrow locally called *gara harcha*, but any rough-skinned variety will do, and courgettes are ideal. Cook as above but omit chilli pepper, chopped parsley and coriander, and substitute 2 tablespoons of *zaatar* – wild marjoram or oregano, or wild thyme or headed thyme or even garden thyme. In Arabic *zaatar* implies any of these and a few more! I suggest you stick to oregano.

You could also add 450g (1lb) okra to the above tajine to give extra flavour and interest.

tajine mlokhia

okra tajine

Okra – ladies' fingers or gumbo – is a native of tropical Africa.
Although widely used in Middle Eastern, African and Indian cuisines it is still relatively unknown in Europe.

Okra is generally known as *bamia* or *tamya*. In Morocco it is also called *mlokhia* – not to be confused with *mulukhiyah* which is the national dish of Egypt, made with the leaves of *Corchorus olitorius* (Jew's mallow or Malta Jute – a spinach-like vegetable). In Tunisia okra is also known as *guanaouia*.

Fresh okra can be bought in this country for only a few weeks of the year, but dried or tinned okra is readily available at all Indian shops as well as large supermarkets. Buy small, young okra with very little fuzz. Trim the stems, but never cut into the pods.

900g (2lb) lamb cut into 5cm (2in) pieces or chicken pieces
1 large onion, finely chopped
2 teaspoons salt
1/2 teaspoon black pepper
1/2 teaspoon powdered caraway
1/2 teaspoon saffron diluted in 4-5 tablespoons water
1/2 teaspoon turmeric
1 teaspoon paprika
75g (3oz) *smen* or butter
3 medium courgettes, topped, tailed and cut into 2cm (3/4in) rounds
450g (1lb) okra, stems trimmed

Place the meat or chicken pieces in a large saucepan with the onion, 1½ teaspoons salt, black pepper, caraway, diluted saffron, turmeric, paprika and *smen* or butter. Fry gently for about 10 minutes, stirring frequently. Add enough water to cover by 2.5cm (1in) and bring to the boil. Lower the heat, cover the pan and simmer for 45-60 minutes or until the meat or chicken is tender. When done, remove with a slotted spoon and reserve.

Place the sliced courgettes in the pan and, if necessary, add just enough water to cover. Stir well and bring to the boil. Lower the heat, cover the pan and simmer for 10-15 minutes or until tender. Remove the slices with a slotted spoon and reserve. Raise the heat and simmer until the sauce has a creamy thickness.

Meanwhile place the okra in another saucepan, sprinkle with remaining salt, add 5-6 tablespoons of the hot sauce from the meat pan and a little water and bring to the boil. Cover the pan and simmer for about 15 minutes or until tender. Remove cover and simmer until the sauce is reduced.

Return the meat or chicken and the courgette slices to the creamy sauce, stir well and simmer for a few minutes. To serve spoon the meat and courgettes into a serving dish, arrange the okra over the top and pour over any remaining sauce. **Serves 6**

tajine guanaouia bil bataa

This tajine with okra uses duck as well. Use a 1.5-2kg (3-4lb) duck, cut off any excess neck skin and remove the clusters of fat from the inside of the body and discard. Cut into serving pieces. This is a Tunisian favourite and Tunisians use a lot of garlic – I suggest 4 cloves, finely chopped. Otherwise follow the recipe above omitting the saffron and turmeric and substituting 2 tablespoons of tomato purée. Serve with couscous grains.

tajine mlokhia bil batata

okra and potato tajine

A rich and nourishing Moroccan dish.

900g (2lb) lamb chops trimmed of fat or shoulder of lamb cut into 5cm (2in)
pieces
2 teaspoons salt
1 teaspoon ginger
1/2 teaspoon turmeric
1 teaspoon paprika
1/2 teaspoon chilli pepper (optional)
90ml (3fl oz) oil
450g (1lb) tomatoes, blanched, peeled and chopped
450g (1lb) potatoes, peeled and cut into 2.5cm (1in) pieces
3-4 tablespoons finely chopped parsley
1 teaspoon coriander
450g (1lb) okra, stems trimmed

Place the meat in a large saucepan with 1 1/2 teaspoons of the salt, the ginger, saffron, turmeric, paprika, chilli pepper and oil. Fry gently for 10 minutes, stirring frequently. Add enough water to cover by about 2.5cm (1in) and bring to the boil. Lower the heat, cover the pan and simmer for 45-60 minutes or until the meat is tender. Remove the meat with a slotted spoon and reserve.

Put the tomatoes and potatoes in the pan with the parsley and coriander and stir well. If necessary add a little more water and bring to the boil. Lower the heat, cover the pan and cook, stirring occasionally until the potatoes are cooked.

Meanwhile place the okra in another pan, sprinkle with remaining salt, add 5-6 tablespoons of the meat pan juices and a little water. Bring to the boil, cover the pan and cook for about 15 minutes or until tender. Return the meat to its, pan stir well and simmer for a few minutes. Spoon the mixture into a large dish and top with the okra. Pour any pan juices over the top. **Serves 6**

tajine mlokhia bil sfardjel

okra and quince tajine

A fascinating and tasty dish that uses quince – an uncommon fruit, at least
in Britain. The quince, with a yellow-green colour, is the size of an apple, but the
shape of a pear, and is widely used in North Africa – as well as in the Caucasus.
Its tart flavour means it is seldom eaten raw, but is excellent in stews.
It is best known in Britain and the US for the jam.

Try this dish around September and October when the fruit is in season.
The recipe comes from Algeria, but it is popular, in one form or another,
throughout the Meghrib.

900g (2lb) lamb, cut into 5cm (2in) pieces
1 onion, finely chopped
1/4 teaspoon cinnamon
2 tablespoons *smen* or butter
1/4 teaspoon turmeric
1/2 teaspoon black pepper
110g (4oz) chickpeas, soaked overnight in cold water
3-4 large quinces
2 teaspoons salt
450g (1lb) okra, stems trimmed

Place the meat in a large saucepan with the onion, cinnamon, *smen* or butter, turmeric and black pepper. Fry for about 10 minutes, stirring frequently. Add the drained chickpeas and enough water to cover by about 5cm (2in). Bring to the boil, lower the heat, cover the pan and simmer for about 45-60 minutes or until the meat and chickpeas are cooked.

Meanwhile peel, core and quarter the quinces and place immediately in a bowl of cold water to prevent discolouring. When the meat is cooked remove it with a slotted spoon and reserve. Add the quartered quinces and 1¹/2 teaspoons of salt to the pan, mix well, add just a little more water if necessary, cover the pan and simmer for 10 minutes. Stir the meat back into the mixture and remove the pan from the heat until the okra is cooked.

Meanwhile place the okra in another pan, sprinkle with remaining salt, add 5-6 tablespoons of the meat pan juices and a little water and bring to the boil. Cover the pan and simmer for about 15 minutes or until tender.

Return the meat pan to the heat and cook for a few more minutes. To serve pour the meat and quinces into a serving dish and top with the okra. If you would like a slightly thicker sauce, stir 1 teaspoon of flour into the okra pan juices and simmer for a further 5 minutes before pouring over the tajine.

tajine zaitun

meat and olive tajine

'Thou art like olives; it is needful to beat thee' Libyan proverb

Olives play a very important role in the Meghribi cuisine, much more so than in any of the other olive-growing Mediterranean cuisines, including Greece and Turkey where, although the oil of the fruit is widely used, the fruit is not.

This recipe is from Tunisia and uses large, black, stoned olives.

1.5kg (3lb) lamb or beef, cut into 7.5cm (3in) pieces
2 tablespoons *smen* or 25g (1oz) butter
4 tablespoons oil
2 large onions, coarsely chopped
3 cloves garlic, crushed
3 tablespoons tomato purée diluted in 150ml (¹/4 pt) water
1.2 l (2 pints) water
3 bay leaves
4 tablespoons finely chopped parsley
1¹/2 teaspoons salt
¹/2 teaspoon black pepper
¹/2 teaspoon crushed fennel seeds
350g (12oz) black olives, stoned
1 tablespoon flour

Place the meat in a large saucepan with the *smen* or butter, oil, onion and garlic. Fry for about 10 minutes, stirring frequently. Add all the remaining ingredients, except the olives and flour, and bring to the boil. Lower the heat, cover the pan and simmer for

45-60 minutes or until the meat is tender.

Meanwhile place the olives in another pan, cover with water and bring to the boil. Simmer for 5-7 minutes then remove and drain.

When the meat is cooked add the olives, stir well and simmer for a few minutes. Mix the flour with a little water and stir into the stew. Cook for a further minute or two or until the sauce has a creamy consistency. Turn into a large serving dish and serve hot. **Serves 6**

tajine be zaitun m'amman

tajine with stuffed olives and meat

Green olives are stuffed with a meat mixture and cooked with meat or chicken pieces. An imaginative and tasty recipe from Algeria.

900g (2lb) lamb cut into 5cm (2in) pieces or 1.5kg (3lb) chicken pieces
1 tablespoon *smen* or 15g (1/2oz) butter
1 onion, finely chopped
1/2 teaspoon saffron diluted in 4-5 tablespoons water
1 teaspoon salt
1/2 teaspoon black pepper
1/4 teaspoon cinnamon
250g (9oz) green olives, stoned

stuffing
175g (6oz) meat, minced twice
1 egg
2 tablespoons finely chopped parsley
1/2 teaspoon salt
1/4 teaspoon black pepper
1/4 teaspoon cinnamon

to serve
Juice 1 lemon

Place the meat in a large saucepan with the *smen* or butter, onion, diluted saffron, salt, black pepper and cinnamon. Fry for about 10 minutes, stirring frequently. Add enough water to cover by about 2.5cm (1in) and bring to the boil. Lower the heat, cover the pan and simmer for 30 minutes.

Meanwhile place the olives in another pan, cover with water and bring to the boil. Simmer for 5-7 minutes and then drain and reserve. Prepare the stuffing by mixing all the ingredients together until well blended and smooth. Fill each olive with some of this mixture. Make marble-sized balls with any remaining stuffing.

When the meat or chicken has been cooking for about 30 minutes add the stuffed olives and meatballs, cover the pan and simmer for a further 15-20 minutes. Just before serving stir in the lemon juice, and simmer for a further 2-3 minutes. Transfer the stew to a large serving dish and accompany with rice or couscous. **Serves 6**

kdra bsal bil louz

onion and almond tajine

'Live in a palace and eat of its onions' Libyan saying

This is one of those rich dishes that are often labelled 'exotic'. In fact it is a simple meal of meat, onion and almonds coloured with saffron.
A Moroccan housewife would use 1 tablespoon of the latter spice, but I suggest that you use a little turmeric for financial reasons! The name *kdra* simply suggests a dish cooked with *smen* or butter.

You can substitute the almonds with chickpeas that have been soaked overnight.

900g (2lb) shoulder of lamb cut into 5cm (2in) pieces
6 lamb chops, trimmed of excess fat
75g (3oz) *smen* or butter
900g (2lb) onions, thinly sliced
2 teaspoons salt
1/2 teaspoon black pepper
1/2 teaspoon saffron diluted in 4-5 tablespoons water
1/2 teaspoon turmeric
1 teaspoon paprika
175g (6oz) blanched almonds
3-4 tablespoons finely chopped parsley

Place the meats in a large saucepan with the *smen* or butter, half the onion and salt, the black pepper, diluted saffron, turmeric and paprika. Fry for about 10 minutes, stirring frequently. Add the almonds and enough water to cover by about 5cm (2in) and bring to the boil. Lower the heat, cover the pan and simmer for 45-60 minutes or until the meat is tender.

Remove the meat with a slotted spoon and reserve. Add the remaining onion and salt and the parsley to the pan, mix well and simmer, uncovered, for about 15 minutes or until the sauce is reduced and thickened. Return the meats, mix well and simmer for a further 5 minutes. Arrange the meats in a large dish and pour the onion-almond sauce over the top. Serve with couscous or bread as is the Moroccan custom.
Serves 6

tajine bil hoot

fish tajine

This Libyan fish recipe is cooked in the oven so is not a true tajine,
but a fish casserole. But you may well ask what a 'true' tajine is as there are scores
of tajine-labelled dishes which are also baked in the oven.
There is no answer except that when cooked the food is transferred to a large
earthenware tajine dish to be served.

For this dish almost any fish will do. Favourite North African ones include marou,
mullet, ombrine, daurade, pagre, angel shark, shad, bass or hannasha.
Since most of these are rather difficult to find I suggest you use fish steaks of your
choice! My favourite is halibut.

This is a tasty and filling meal. Serve it with rice or couscous.

6 halibut steaks
4 tablespoons finely chopped parsley
1 stick celery plus leaves, cut into 2.5cm (1in) pieces
2 cloves garlic, crushed
1/2 teaspoon cumin
1 teaspoon salt
2 medium onions, cut into rings
3 potatoes, peeled and cut into 1/2cm (1/4in) rounds
4 tomatoes, cut into thick rounds
1/2 teaspoon oregano
4 tablespoons oil
1 tablespoon tomato purée diluted in 4-5 tablespoons water
Juice 1 lemon
4 tablespoons water
3 whole fresh chilli peppers

Arrange the fish steaks in the base of a lightly greased casserole dish. Mix together the parsley, chopped celery, garlic, cumin and salt. Sprinkle this mixture evenly over the fish. Arrange the onion rings and potato and tomato slices over the fish and sprinkle with the oregano.

In a small saucepan mix together the oil, diluted tomato purée, lemon juice and water and bring to the boil. Pour over the fish and place the casserole in an oven preheated to 35OF, 18OC, Gas Mark 4. Bake for about 30-40 minutes or until the fish and potatoes are cooked. Carefully transfer the fish slices to a large dish, spoon the vegetables over them and pour in the sauce. **Serves 6**

tajine kefta min hoot

tunisian fish ball tajine

900g (2lb) white fish (cod, whiting etc)
3 tablespoons finely chopped parsley
3 cloves garlic, crushed
2 medium onions, finely chopped
1$^1/_2$ teaspoons salt
$^1/_2$ teaspoon black pepper
$^1/_2$ teaspoon harissa (see Glossary)
110g (4oz) stale bread, cut into slices and soaked in water
1 egg
Oil

sauce
2 cloves garlic, crushed
1 teaspoon salt
$^1/_4$ teaspoon black pepper
$^1/_2$ teaspoon harissa (optional, see Glossary)
2 tablespoons tomato purée
450ml ($^3/_4$ pint) water

Remove any skin and bones from the fish and discard. Chop or finely flake the flesh and place in a large bowl with the parsley, garlic, onion, salt, pepper, harissa and bread slices which have been squeezed as dry as possible. Mix together thoroughly, add the egg and knead until smooth. Taking 1 tablespoonful at a time form the mixture into balls and then gently flatten between your palms. Continue until you have used up all the mixture.

Heat some oil in a large frying pan, add a few of the fish balls and fry for 3-4 minutes, turning once. The fish balls must be only partially cooked at this stage. Remove with a slotted spoon and reserve while you fry the remaining fish balls in the same way.

Spoon about 4 tablespoons of the frying oil into a large saucepan, add the sauce ingredients and bring to the boil. Arrange the fish balls carefully in the pan and simmer for 15-20 minutes. Carefully transfer to a large dish. **Serves 6**

tajine mrouzia

great festival tajine

'If your friend is honey don't eat it all' Moroccan proverb

This is the tajine of Aid el-Kebir or the Sacrificial Feast – also known as Sheep Festival – when every Muslim who can afford to, sacrifices a lamb or sheep. The meat for this dish is usually chosen from saddle or shoulder of lamb. It is a rich, colourful dish of almonds, raisins, honey and spices.

1 tablespoon ras-el-hanout (see Glossary)
1 teaspoon ginger
1/2 teaspoon saffron diluted in 4-5 tablespoons water
1/2 teaspoon black pepper
1.5kg (3lb) shoulder or best end of neck, cut into 7.5cm (3in) pieces
1 1/2 teaspoons salt
75g (3oz) butter
175g (6oz) blanched almonds
1 onion, finely chopped
225g (8oz) raisins, soaked in cold water for 15 minutes
90ml (3fl oz) honey
1 teaspoon cinnamon

In a small bowl mix together the ras-el-hanout, ginger, diluted saffron, black pepper and 6 tablespoons of water. Brush the meat pieces with half of this mixture. Arrange the meat in the bottom of a large saucepan, add the salt, butter, almonds and onion and enough water to cover by 5cm (2in). Bring to the boil, lower the heat, cover the pan and simmer for 45 minutes, stirring occasionally.

Meanwhile drain the raisins and leave to soak in the rest of the spice mixture. After 45 minutes add the raisin and spice mixture to the pan together with the honey and cinnamon. Stir well and simmer for another 15 minutes or until the meat is cooked. If the sauce is too runny boil briskly for a few minutes. Pour into a large dish. **Serves 6**

tajine djaj bil assel

chicken, prune and honey tajine

Tajines are prepared with all kinds of fruits, fresh or dried, and some of the most popular are apples, dates, pears, prunes and quinces.
This recipe from Morocco is rich, colourful and extremely tasty. Serve with bread or rice and a bowl of fresh salad.

1.5-1.7kg (3-4lb) chicken, cut into serving pieces (reserve the giblets)
1 teaspoon salt
1/2 teaspoon black pepper
1/4 teaspoon saffron
1 teaspoon turmeric
5cm (2in) cinnamon stick
1 onion, finely chopped
50g (2oz) *smen* or butter
225g (8oz) prunes
60ml (2fl oz) honey
75g (3oz) blanched almonds
1 tablespoon sesame seeds, lightly toasted under the grill

Place the chicken pieces in a large saucepan. Chop the chicken liver and heart and add to the pan. Add the salt, pepper, saffron, turmeric, cinnamon stick, onion, butter and 600ml (1 pint) water. Bring to the boil, lower the heat, cover the pan and simmer for 45-60 minutes or until the chicken is tender. Add the prunes and simmer for a further 15 minutes. Stir in the honey and simmer, uncovered for a further 5-10 minutes.

Meanwhile fry the almonds in a little oil until golden and remove with a slotted spoon and reserve. Transfer the tajine to a large serving dish and sprinkle with the almonds and sesame seeds. **Serves 6**

tajine djaj bil tmar

Another of those exotic Moroccan sweet and savoury dishes. Similar to the recipe above, but use fresh dates instead of the prunes. Fresh dates can now be bought from many good greengrocers.

It is advisable to add the dates to the pan just 10 minutes before the end of the cooking time so that they remain whole. The fresh dates can be substituted with dried ones in which case I suggest you soak them for 1 hour before cooking.

chbah sefra

meat and almond croquette tajine

From Constantine in Algeria this is a very refined dish with almond croquettes dipped in egg, fried and then cooked in the pan. There are many such dishes – almost all from Algeria. This dish often view with one from Tlemcen in which the powdered almonds are mixed with the eggs and cinnamon and cooked in the oven as an omelette. It is then shredded into thin lozenges which are used to garnish the meat pieces.

900g (2lb) leg or shoulder of lamb, cut into 5cm (2in) pieces
2 tablespoons *smen* or 25g (1oz) butter
1 onion, finely chopped
5cm (2in) cinnamon stick
1 teaspoon salt
50g (2oz) sugar
1 tablespoon rosewater

almond paste
275g (10oz) ground almonds
110g (4oz) icing sugar
1/2 teaspoon cinnamon
4 eggs, separated
Oil for frying

Place the meat in a large saucepan with the *smen* or butter, onion, cinnamon stick and salt. Add enough water to cover by 2.5cm (1in) and bring to the boil. Lower the heat, cover the pan and simmer for about 45-60 minutes or until the meat is tender.

Meanwhile mix the ground almonds, icing sugar and cinnamon together in a bowl. Add the egg yolks and mix thoroughly with a fork. Take 1 tablespoon of this mixture and roll into a ball. Press gently between your palms to flatten to 1cm (1/2in) thickness and set aside. Prepare all the mixture in the same way. Beat the egg whites with a fork.

Heat some oil in a large frying pan. Dip each ball into the egg white and fry in the hot oil for 1 minute, turning once. Remove with a slotted spoon and drain on kitchen paper. Continue until you have fried all the balls in the same way. Now repeat this process once more dipping each ball in the egg whites and frying for 1 minute.

When the meat is cooked remove the pieces with a slotted spoon and reserve in a warm place. Stir the sugar and rosewater into the sauce and simmer for 5 minutes. Carefully add the croquettes, bring to a quick boil and then remove from the heat. Arrange the meat in the centre of a large serving plate, decorate with the croquettes and pour the sauce over the top. **Serves 6**

saba al-arousa

bride's finger tajine

From Algeria, this recipe is similar to the one above. Use the same quantities of ingredients for the meat mixture, but include 1/2 teaspoon saffron diluted in 4-5 tablespoons water. Cook as above. Instead of the almond croquettes, the almond mixture is enclosed in paper-thin pastry.

350g (12oz) ground almonds
110g (4oz) icing sugar
1/2 teaspoon cinnamon
6 tablespoons orange blossom water
12 sheets dioul or ouarka (see Glossary) or 6 sheets filo pastry
Oil for frying
50g (2oz) blanched almonds

Place the ground almonds, icing sugar, cinnamon and orange blossom water in a bowl and mix to a firm paste.

If you are using the dioul or *ouarka* cut the pastry sheets in half. Arrange 1 tablespoon of the mixture in a ridge across the short edge nearest to you. Fold the 2 long edges inwards over the ends of the mixture and then roll up to form a cigar shape. If using filo pastry cut each sheet into 4 rectangles and fill as above. When the fingers are ready heat some oil in a large frying pan and fry them, a few at a time, until golden. Remove with a slotted spoon, drain on kitchen paper and reserve while the remaining fingers are fried. Drop the blanched almonds into the remaining oil and fry until golden. Remove with a slotted spoon and drain.

Arrange the meat pieces in the centre of a large serving dish, pour the sauce over them and then arrange the fingers around the dish and sprinkle the fried almonds over the top. Serve immediately. **Serves 6**

tajine-el-bargoug

tajine with dried fruits

Bargoug are prunes, which are used in this recipe with apricots and raisins.
A Moroccan favourite, this dish can be cooked with pigeons or poussins as well as
with beef and the traditional lamb. In Algeria this dish is also known as
Tajine-al-Ays. Serve with rice or bread and salad.

900g (2lb) leg or shoulder of lamb cut into 5cm (2in) pieces
1 onion, finely chopped
4 tablespoons *smen* or 50g (2oz) butter
1/2 teaspoon salt
1/2 teaspoon black pepper
1/2 teaspoon cinnamon
4 cloves
1/2 teaspoon cumin
1/4 teaspoon ginger
225g (8oz) stoned prunes
110g (4oz) raisins
110g (4oz) dried apricots, halved
110g (4oz) blanched almonds
50g (2oz) sugar
4 tablespoons orange blossom water

Place the meat in a large saucepan with the onion, *smen* or butter, salt, black pepper, cinnamon, cloves, cumin and ginger and fry for about 10 minutes, stirring frequently. Add 1.2 l (2 pints) water and bring to the boil. Lower the heat, cover the pan and simmer for 45-60 minutes or until the meat is tender.

Meanwhile place the prunes, raisins and apricots in a saucepan with 600ml (1 pint) of water. Bring to the boil, lower the heat and simmer for 15 minutes.

When the meat is cooked add the fruits and their cooking liquid to the tajine. Stir in the almonds, sugar and orange blossom water and simmer, uncovered, for a further 20 minutes, stirring regularly. Serve the meat in the centre of a large dish with the fruit and almond sauce poured over the top. **Serves 6**

tajine teffah

meat and apple tajine

'A stone from the hand of a friend is an apple' Moroccan proverb

This Tunisian recipe is for an apple tajine, but you can use firm slightly unripe pears and quinces. You can also substitute beef or chicken for the lamb.

900g (2lb) lamb or beef, cut into 5cm (2in) pieces
2 tablespoons *smen* or 25g (1oz) butter
1 onion, whole
1 teaspoon salt
5cm (2in) cinnamon stick
1/2 teaspoon saffron diluted in 4-5 tablespoons water
900g (2lb) cooking apples
Juice 1 lemon
3 tablespoons icing sugar
4 tablespoons orange blossom water

Place the meat pieces in a large saucepan with the *smen* or butter, onion, salt, cinnamon stick and diluted saffron. Add enough water to cover by about 2.5cm (1in) and bring to the boil. Lower the heat, cover the pan and simmer for about 45-60 minutes or until tender.

Meanwhile peel, core and quarter the apples and place in a large bowl of cold water with the lemon juice.

When the meat is cooked remove and discard the onion. Stir in the sugar and orange blossom water and arrange the quartered apples in the pan. Cover the pan and simmer for a further 5-10 minutes or until the apple is tender. Do not overcook or the fruit will disintegrate. Arrange the meat in a large dish, top with apple pieces and pour the sauce over the top. **Serves 6**

When a tree does not give much fruit a mouse is often sacrificed close to it and buried at the foot of the tree. A pailful of boiling water is then poured over the grave in the hope that the water will carry away the blood of the mouse to the most distant roots. The idea is that since the mouse is very prolific and productive it will thus give its power to the tree.

With vines cats and dogs are often sacrificed.

When an orange or an apple tree bears fruit for the first time three oranges or apples are left on the topmost branches when the fruit is gathered. The idea is to encourage the tree to go on producing.

If a tree (or any other form of plant life) flowers out of season people say that the tree was dreaming that spring had already arrived.

— everyday dishes —

'Kul uwakel d-daif alu t'tun mhayiyef' – Eat and give the guests to eat, even though you are starving.

There is a generosity of spirit amongst the people of North Africa that is totally lacking with Europeans in general. Every year we may collect millions of pounds to help the poor of the world, the so-called 'third world' – a classification inaugurated by us which begs the simple question, 'Third in what?' Material or spiritual accomplishments? We donate out of guilt and, having cleansed our consciences, wash our hands and try to forget.

And yet, we are the real poor of this world. We do not know, or love our neighbours. We do not care about the poverty prevailing in our society. We pay our taxes, shrug our shoulders and exclaim 'let the authorities do the job'. We would never starve so that our guests could eat. Well, would you? When did you last invite your neighbours – I do not mean relations or close family friends, but the folk across the road or even complete strangers – to come and share in your happiness? I only recall one incident of such spontaneity – during the Coronation when street parties were held and neighbours, friends and, yes indeed, even strangers passing by, were invited to drink a toast to Her Majesty.

This 'group feeling', a favourite subject of the Meghribi historian, Ibn Khaldun, has virtually died out in the West, and only in times of dire need does it seem to arouse itself. Otherwise we just mind our own business and go our own selfish ways.

'We alighted at an encampment of Bedouins, and entered the sheik's tent, though he was absent; and the Arabs had a long and fierce dispute among themselves, to decide who should have the honour of furnishing us a supper, and a breakfast the next morning. He who first sees a stranger from afar, and exclaims "Here comes my guest", has the right of entertaining him, whatever tent he may alight at. A lamb was killed for me, which was an act of great hospitality; for those Bedouin are poor, and a lamb was worth upwards of a Spanish dollar – a sum that would afford a supply of butter and bread to the family for a whole week.' Travels in Syria and the Holy Land

❧

A Moroccan adage goes like this:

'The mother is the tent, the father the main support,
the children the fixing pegs,
the family are the palms,
the tribe the oasis.
But the guests are the angels putting in to rest.'

One need not slaughter a lamb to feed a guest. Simple, everyday fare will suffice. The recipes in this chapter are such simple everyday dishes, delicious stews often prepared in winter, or economical and tasty dishes making use of everyday ingredients such as fresh vegetables, dried meat, sausages, eggs, bones etc.

The chapter is subdivided into meat and vegetable stews and stuffed vegetables, then meat, poultry and fish dishes. I have also included several offal-based dishes since they are extremely popular in the Meghrib.

The first few recipes make use of *khli* (dried meat) which is described in the Glossary. It is a must with everyone, rich or poor, throughout the Meghrib.

ads be qar wa khli

lentils with pumpkin and khli

You can use courgettes or marrow in place of the pumpkin and also substitute other beans for the lentils.

2 onions, thinly sliced
150g (5oz) *khli* (see Glossary)
2 tablespoons *khli* fat, *smen* or 25g (1oz) butter
1 tablespoon paprika
2 whole chilli peppers
1 teaspoon salt
1.8 l (3 pints) water
225g (8oz) lentils, rinsed
675g (1¹/₂lb) pumpkin, peeled and cut into 5cm (2in) slices
2 tomatoes, blanched, peeled and finely chopped

Place the onions, *khli*, fat, paprika, chilli peppers, salt and water in a large saucepan and bring to the boil. Simmer for 5 minutes, stirring occasionally. Add the lentils, cover the pan and cook for 20 minutes.

Remove the pieces of *khli* with a slotted spoon and set aside to drain. Add the pumpkin and tomatoes to the pan, cover and cook for a further 20 minutes or until pumpkin and lentils are tender.

Return the pieces of *khli* to the pan and cook for a further 5 minutes, adding a little more water if necessary. Taste and add more salt if necessary – it is wise to only add a little at the beginning as the *khli* is salted. Serve immediately with a rice or couscous accompaniment. **Serves 6**

tomatich wa batata be khli

tomatoes and potatoes with khli

1.75kg (4lb) tomatoes, blanched, peeled and chopped
1 teaspoon salt
1 large onion, chopped
150g (5oz) *khli* (see Glossary)
3 tablespoons *khli* fat, *smen* or 40g (1¹/2 oz) butter
1 tablespoon paprika
1 teaspoon chilli pepper
450g (1lb) potatoes, peeled and cut into 2.5cm (1in) pieces
5-6 tablespoons water
¹/2 teaspoon salt
¹/4 teaspoon powdered or crushed caraway
2 tablespoons finely chopped parsley

Put the tomatoes in a large saucepan and cook over a moderate heat for 10 minutes. Add the salt, onion, *khli*, fat, paprika and chilli pepper, stir well and cook for a further 20 minutes, stirring frequently. Carefully remove the *khli* with a slotted spoon and reserve.

Meanwhile place the potato pieces in another saucepan with the water, salt, caraway and 3-4 tablespoons of the tomato mixture. Cook over a moderate heat, stirring frequently to prevent sticking, until the potatoes are tender.

When the tomato mixture has thickened, stir in the parsley, *khli* and cooked potatoes and simmer for a further 5 minutes. Remove from the heat and serve immediately. **Serves 6**

You could replace the potatoes with an equivalent amount of quinces – quartered and cored, but not peeled. You can also use cooking apples or prepare and cook okra with the tomatoes and *khli*.

mezqueldi

onion with khli

Since *khli* is a basic ingredient in North African cooking it has many recipes to its credit. This is a particularly popular one from the Atlas mountain villages.

2.25kg (5lb) onions, peeled and cut into rings
150g (5oz) *khli* (see Glossary)
3 tablespoons *khli* fat, *smen* or 40g (1¹/₂oz) butter
1 tablespoon paprika
1¹/2 teaspoons chilli powder or 2 whole dried chillies, crushed
2 teaspoons salt
1 teaspoon cumin
Juice 1 lemon
2 tablespoons finely chopped parsley

Place the onion rings in a large saucepan, add enough water to cover and bring to the boil. Simmer for 3-4 minutes and then drain. Return the onions to the pan and add all the remaining ingredients. Stir well, lower the heat and simmer for 15-20 minutes or until the onions and *khli* are cooked. Remove from the heat and serve immediately with bread and mint tea. **Serves 6**

In the small snack bars that are found in every back street a particularly popular, quick and cheap dish is *khli* with eggs. The *khli* is cut into 5cm (2in) pieces and cooked for 10 minutes in its own fat. An egg or two are cracked over it and when the whites are set they are sprinkled with salt, paprika and black pepper and served with a bowl of salad and bread.

Khli goes very well with lemons and olives as well. Cook as above and add to the spices 1 teaspoon each of cumin and chilli pepper, 2 tablespoons chopped parsley, 6-8 stoned olives and the juice of 2 lemons – very tasty and cheap.

Before we arrive at the meat and vegetable dishes mention should be made of the vast and rich 'offal' tradition of the North African cuisines. Throughout the ages innards have been an important part of man's diet. Unfortunately, in this age of abundance (i.e. abundance for some, but not for all) innards are often neglected. The abundance of beef, pork, lamb etc has been taken for granted and with it there has been a great deal of waste. However, in other parts of the world as well as in North Africa offal still plays a major role in the people's diet. Head, brains, tongue, heart, liver, feet, tails etc are prepared in many a wonderful way to enhance and enrich the everyday food. Some of these have already appeared in other chapters. Here I have included a few more that I regard as well worth preparing for three reasons – they are very tasty, they are easy to prepare and, in this age of cost consciousness, they are cheap. The animal involved is usually lamb, although others are sometimes used.

bouzellouf masli

lamb's head

Lamb's head is by far the most popular offal throughout North Africa and the Middle East. In the old days whole fire-roasted lamb's heads were sold by butchers and small itinerant salesmen calling out aloud over the din of camels, asses and their two-legged cousins '*Ya bouzellouf muchwi*' or, in the Middle East of my childhood, '*Kela, kela, kela-al-kharouf*'. Today, search as you may, roasted lamb's heads are difficult to purchase ready cooked, but I have been assured by many Algerian, Moroccan and particularly Libyan friends that lamb's head and the rest of the animal's parts are still popular and highly prized. This includes the exalted sheep's eyes which, I hasten to add, I have never eaten although I am assured by those more adventurous than I that they do have an exquisite flavour of their own!

Order the lamb's head from your butcher and ask him to cut it in half and to remove the snout altogether as it is very difficult to clean.

This is an Algerian recipe. The original suggests that you use 8-10 cloves garlic, but I have reduced this to 4 although you can increase the number it you like.

2 lamb's heads (ask the butcher to remove eyes, ears and snout)
150ml (1/4 pint) oil
Juice 1 lemon
300ml (1/2 pint) water
1 teaspoon harissa (see Glossary)
4 cloves garlic, crushed
1 teaspoon cumin
1/2 teaspoon coriander
1/2 teaspoon crushed or powdered caraway
1 teaspoon paprika
1/4 teaspoon nutmeg
1 teaspoon salt
1/2 teaspoon black pepper

garnish
2 tablespoons finely chopped parsley
Lemon wedges
3-4 tomatoes, sliced
10-12 olives

First clean the halved heads by singeing off any remaining hairs and then rinsing thoroughly. Place in a large saucepan or bowl, cover with water and leave to soak for 30 minutes. Drain and rinse again. Arrange the halved heads in a large ovenproof casserole.

Mix all the remaining ingredients together and pour over the heads. Cover the casserole and place in an oven preheated to 325F, 160C, Gas Mark 3. Bake for about 1¹/2 hours, basting frequently.

To serve arrange the heads on a large serving plate. Scoop out the brains and cut off the meat. Sprinkle with the parsley and garnish the plate with the lemon wedges, tomatoes and olives. Serve with bread and other fresh vegetables. **Serves 4-6**

tajine bil mokh wa tomatich

brains tajine with tomatoes

Try this tasty dish from Tunisia and don't ever believe the Arab saying 'too much sheep's brain makes you sheepish too'. Accompany with fresh salad.

2 calf or lamb brains
150ml (¹/4 pint) oil
4 tablespoons finely chopped parsley
4 cloves garlic, crushed
Juice 1 lemon
2 teaspoons salt
¹/2 teaspoon black pepper
50g (2oz) flour
2 eggs, beaten
1 heaped tablespoon tomato purée diluted in 450ml (³/4 pint) water

garnish
Lemon wedges
Sliced tomatoes, cucumber and radishes

Clean and wash the brains as described in Mokh Megli (page 184). In a bowl mix together 2 tablespoons of the oil, the parsley, half the crushed garlic, the lemon juice and half the salt and pepper. Slice the brains, add to the mixture, turn to coat and leave to marinate for 30 minutes.

Heat the remaining oil in a frying pan. Taking 1 slice of brain at a time coat it first with flour and then dip in the beaten egg. Fry until golden, remove with a fork and reserve until all the brain slices are fried.

Pour any remaining oil into a saucepan and stir in the rest of the garlic, salt and pepper and the diluted tomato purée. Bring to the boil, lower the heat and simmer for 5 minutes. Add the fried brain slices, cover the pan and simmer for 12-15 minutes. To serve transfer to a large dish and decorate with the various garnishes. **Serves 4-6**

lisen mahchia be zaitun

tongue stuffed with olives

This is a regal dish. A calf tongue is filled with minced meat, olives and hard-boiled eggs and then cooked in a sauce flavoured with herbs and spices. Preparing this dish needs a little more time and care than usual, but is well worth the effort. Serve with rice, couscous or fresh salads of your choice.

You can replace the minced meat with 150g (5oz) of salted capers. Some people also like to add peas or beans to the sauce for the last 10-15 minutes of the cooking time. It's also difficult to find calf tongue here: use a small ox tongue.

1 small ox tongue – about 1.5kg (2-3lb)
1 tablespoon lemon juice or vinegar
110g (4oz) minced beef
2 tablespoons finely chopped parsley
4 cloves garlic, crushed
2 teaspoons salt
1/2 teaspoon black pepper
1 egg, beaten
4 hard-boiled eggs
1.8 l (3 pints) water
3 tablespoons tomato purée
175g (6oz) green olives, stoned
2 bay leaves
1 1/2 teaspoons thyme

Place the tongue in a large bowl, cover with water and add lemon juice or vinegar. Stir and set aside for 30 minutes. Remove, brush and rinse the tongue thoroughly. Now very carefully slide the blade of a sharp knife inside the thick end of the tongue without piercing the skin, and remove some of the flesh to make a good-sized pocket. Chop the flesh and add to the minced meat.

Put the minced meat mixture into a large bowl and add the parsley and half of the garlic, salt and black pepper. Add the beaten egg and knead until smooth. Now carefully slide 1 tablespoon of this mixture as far as possible into the tongue. Next slide in a hard-boiled egg, then another tablespoon of the meat mixture, another egg and so on until you have used up all the eggs and meat and the tongue is filled. Carefully sew up the tongue opening with a needle and thread.

Place the tongue in a large saucepan, cover with the water and bring to the boil. Lower the heat and simmer for 2 hours. Remove the tongue and, when cool enough to handle, skin it. This done, return the tongue to the pan, add the remaining garlic, salt and pepper and the tomato purée, drained olives, bay leaves and thyme. Cover the pan and simmer for a further 1 hour, by which time the sauce should have a creamy consistency.

To serve remove the tongue and place in a serving dish. Discard the thread and slice. Pour the sauce over the top. **Serves 4-6**

krom bi l'ham marhi

sautéed cabbage with minced meat

This is a delicious dish – and simple and economical! Serve with couscous, rice and/or a fresh salad and pickles.

1 large, firm cabbage
5 tablespoons oil or 70g (2^{1}/$_{2}$oz) butter
450g (1lb) minced meat
1 teaspoon salt
1 teaspoon paprika
^{1}/$_{2}$ teaspoon black pepper
3 cloves garlic, crushed

Quarter the cabbage and cut out the hard core. Separate the leaves. Bring a large pan of lightly salted water to the boil, add the leaves and blanch for 5 minutes. Drain the cabbage and, when cool enough to handle, squeeze out as much of the water as possible. Chop the cabbage roughly.

Meanwhile heat 1 tablespoon of the oil or 15g (^{1}/$_{2}$oz) of the butter in a saucepan, add the meat, salt, paprika and black pepper and fry, stirring frequently, for about 20-30 minutes or until cooked.

Heat the remaining butter or oil in a large frying pan or casserole, add the garlic and fry for 1 minute. Add the chopped cabbage and fry, stirring occasionally until the cabbage browns. Add the cooked meat and mix well. Leave to cook for a further 5 minutes, taste and adjust seasoning if necessary. Serve immediately. **Serves 6**

tajine batata

baked potatoes

'A cuckold, and he sups on potatoes' – potato without meat is considered the poorest of food.

I have to include this delicious potato dish because since the day I first prepared it I have loved it, and now often prepare it for friends and family. The recipe is from Southern Algeria.

6 cloves garlic
1 small leg of lamb
1.5-1.75kg (3–4lb) potatoes
1 large onion, chopped
4 tablespoons finely chopped parsley
1^1/$_2$ teaspoons salt
^{1}/$_2$ teaspoon black pepper
110g (4oz) butter, melted
2 large tomatoes, blanched
300ml (^{1}/$_2$ pint) water

Peel the garlic and cut 3 of the cloves into half lengthways. With a sharp, pointed knife make 6 shallow incisions into the meat and slide a piece of garlic into each one. Place the meat in a large buttered baking dish and cook for 1 hour in an oven preheated to 350F, 180C, Gas Mark 4.

Meanwhile peel the potatoes and cut each one lengthways into 4 slices. Place in a saucepan, cover with water, bring to the boil and simmer for 3 minutes. Drain. Place the onion and parsley in a large bowl, add the potato slices, salt, pepper and melted butter and mix well until all the potato slices are coated with butter.

Remove the baking dish from the oven and arrange the potato mixture around the meat. Chop the tomatoes and scatter over the potatoes. Pour in the water and return the dish to the oven. Bake for another hour or until the meat is tender and the potatoes are browned. Remove the meat to a large serving dish, slice, and spoon the potatoes around it. Serve immediately. **Serves 6**

— mahchi —

Under this heading I have grouped together a few (out of the many) vegetable dishes that are stuffed with rice, meat, nuts, fruits etc.

This is very old fare, not necessarily North African. Stuffed vegetables appear throughout the Middle East (Turks and Armenians being the past masters) as well as in certain southern Mediterranean lands like Greece, Bulgaria and Italy.

Quite a few vegetable stuffings are similar to those of the Middle East and the very obvious ones I have discarded. Undoubtedly it is Libyan cuisine that has the widest repertoire because of her historically long association with Ottoman Turkey and her proximity to Egypt. On the other hand the Moroccan cuisine has few examples of this method of cooking.

It is interesting to note that cold stuffed vegetables such as the famed stuffed vine leaves of Turkey, Armenia and Syria do not exist in the Meghrib where all stuffed vegetables are served warm.

badendjel mahchi 1

stuffed aubergines

6 large aubergines or 8 large courgettes

meat filling
90ml (3fl oz) oil
1 large onion, finely chopped
4 cloves garlic, crushed
2 tablespoons finely chopped parsley
225g (8oz) minced meat
4 eggs
2 teaspoons salt
1 teaspoon black pepper
450ml (3/4 pint) water

Cut the stalks off the vegetables and cut each one in half lengthways. With an apple-corer or a spoon carefully remove and reserve most of the flesh leaving a shell about 1cm (1/2in) thick. Take care not to make any holes in the shells. Leave to soak in lightly salted water for 30 minutes and then rinse thoroughly and drain.

Chop the reserved flesh and place in a saucepan with 2 tablespoons of the oil, the onion, half the garlic, the parsley, minced meat, 2 of the whole eggs (in their shells), and half the salt and black pepper. Add 300ml (1/2 pint) of the water, cover the pan and cook for about 30 minutes or until the meat is cooked and most of the water has evaporated. Stir the mixture occasionally to break up the meat. Remove the eggs, shell and chop. Add the chopped eggs to the meat, break the 2 remaining eggs over the mixture and mix thoroughly with a wooden spoon. Set aside to rest.

Pat the vegetable halves dry and then fill with the egg and meat mixture. Place the remaining oil, garlic, salt, pepper and water in a baking dish large enough to take the halved vegetables side by side. When the vegetables are arranged in the dish cover and bake in an oven preheated to 330F, 180C, Gas Mark 4 for abut 1 hour or until meat and vegetables are cooked. Uncover and cook for a further 10 minutes to brown the tops.

Transfer the stuffed aubergines to a large serving dish and pour any remaining pan juices over the top. If you wish you can sprinkle a little chopped parsley, tarragon or mint over the top. Serve with rice, couscous, vegetables or salads of your choice.
Serves 6

Aubergines tend to soak up a great deal more oil than courgettes so use a little less if using the latter.

badendjel mahchi 2

stuffed aubergines

6 aubergines or 8 large courgettes

meat and rice filling
350g (12oz) minced meat
3 tablespoons finely chopped parsley
2 cloves garlic, crushed
75g (3oz) long-grain rice, rinsed thoroughly and drained
2 teaspoons salt
1 teaspoon black pepper
1/2 teaspoon nutmeg
1 egg
4 tablespoons oil
300ml (1/2 pint) water
110g (4oz) breadcrumbs

Prepare the aubergines as described above. Chop the reserved flesh and place in a large bowl with the meat, parsley, garlic, rice, half the salt and black pepper and the nutmeg. Break the egg in and knead until the mixture is smooth.

Fill the halved vegetables with the meat and rice mixture and arrange side by side in a large baking dish. Place the oil, water and remaining salt and pepper in a small saucepan and bring to the boil. Pour evenly over the vegetables. Spread the breadcrumbs thickly over the top, cover the dish and place in an oven preheated to 350F, 180C, Gas Mark 4. Bake for about 1 hour or until meat and vegetables are cooked. Uncover and bake for a further 10 minutes to brown the breadcrumbs. Serve with cooked vegetables or salad. **Serves 6**

zaitun mahchi

stuffed olives

This is a Tunisian speciality. Meatballs are covered with halved olives, coated in
flour and eggs and then fried before being cooked in a tomato-based sauce.
It is an ingenious and tasty dish which, although a little time-consuming,
is well worth the effort.

450g (1lb) large halved or broken green olives, stoned and soaked in tepid water
for 20 minutes
2 hard-boiled eggs
450g (1lb) minced meat
4 cloves garlic, crushed
3 tablespoons finely chopped parsley
2 teaspoons salt
1 teaspoon black pepper
2 eggs
About 150ml (1/4 pint) oil for frying
50g (2oz) flour
2 tablespoons tomato purée diluted in 6 tablespoons water
450ml (3/4 pint) water

garnish
1 tablespoon finely chopped fresh mint or 1 teaspoon dried mint

Drain the soaked olives and pat dry with kitchen paper. Shell the hard-boiled eggs,
chop them finely and place in a bowl with the meat, half the garlic, the parsley and half
the salt and pepper. Break 1 egg into the mixture and knead until smooth. Keeping
your hands damp form the mixture into small walnut-sized balls. Now put some olive
halves around each ball pressing them gently so that they stick to the meat. Arrange
on a plate.

When all the balls are prepared heat the oil in a large, deep frying pan. Beat the
remaining egg in a small bowl. Taking one stuffed olive ball at a time roll them in the
flour to coat thoroughly and then dip in the beaten egg. Drop carefully into the oil and
fry gently, turning occasionally until cooked through and golden. Remove with a
slotted spoon and reserve while you cook the remaining balls in the same way.

Add to the frying pan the diluted tomato purée, the remaining garlic, salt and
pepper and the water. Bring to the boil and simmer for 5 minutes. Return the balls to
the pan, cover, lower the heat and simmer for a further 30 minutes. Transfer to a dish
and garnish with the mint. Serve with rice, couscous, spaghetti or macaroni. **Serves 6**

doulmah karnoune

stuffed artichokes

'Yet another artichoke dish' you may exclaim! Why not? They are so cheap in the Meghrib that (or so I am assured) they are fed to the animals! We, of course, have to pay a fair amount for each of these prickly globes therefore I suggest you make the most of this clever and flavourful dish from Tunisia.

6 large artichokes
225g (8oz) minced meat
6 tablespoons finely chopped parsley
3 cloves garlic, finely chopped
2 hard-boiled eggs, shelled and chopped
2 teaspoons salt
1 teaspoon black pepper
1 teaspoon paprika
1 egg
4 tablespoons oil
Juice 1 lemon
2 bay leaves
1/2 teaspoon basil
600ml (1 pint) water

Prepare the artichokes as described in Chalda Karnoune (page 51), leaving the halved vegetables to soak in acidulated water.

Place the minced meat, parsley, half the garlic, the chopped eggs and half the salt, pepper and paprika in a bowl. Break the egg over the mixture and knead until smooth. Place the oil in a large saucepan with the lemon juice, bay leaves, basil and remaining garlic, salt, pepper and paprika. Bring to the boil, lower the heat and leave to simmer while you stuff the artichokes.

Pat the artichoke halves dry and then fill each one with some of the meat mixture. Arrange them carefully in the saucepan, cover and simmer for about 40 minutes or until cooked. Add a little more water if necessary. Transfer to a large dish and serve hot. **Serves 6**

basal mahchi 1

stuffed onions

'What causes neither pain nor sorrow, yet makes us weep?' – The onion.

The onion was a favourite vegetable of the Prophet hence perhaps its great popularity with all Muslims. Indeed, I am assured by some Polish friends that Polish Muslims (yes, there are some in the land of 'more popish than the Pope' Catholicism) have a particular liking for this indispensable vegetable.
The North Africans, like their cousins in the Middle East, eat onions raw like a fruit.

Onions are not only fried and cooked in stews, but also stuffed with other vegetables, meat and nuts. I have included here two such recipes, both from Libya. The first is a speciality from the north-west of the country – the Charian region where most Libyan Berbers still live and practise their ancient customs and speak their language.

4 large onions, peeled

filling
300g (10oz) minced meat
4 cloves garlic, crushed
2 eggs
1 teaspoon paprika
1 teaspoon salt
1/2 teaspoon black pepper
1/2 teaspoon *baharat* (see Glossary)
50g (2oz) fine semolina

sauce
60ml (2fl oz) oil
1 1/2 tablespoons tomato purée
600ml (1 pint) water
Juice 1 large lemon
1/2 teaspoon salt
1/2 teaspoon black pepper
1/2 teaspoon *hilba* (see Glossary)

With a sharp knife cut lengthways into the centre of each onion. Place them into a large saucepan, cover with water and bring to the boil. Simmer for 10-12 minutes, remove and leave until cool enough to handle. Taking one onion at a time carefully separate each layer and set aside.

Meanwhile place the meat in a bowl with half the garlic and all the remaining filling ingredients. Knead until smooth.

Prepare the sauce by heating the oil in a large saucepan and frying the remaining garlic for 1 minute. Stir in all the remaining ingredients and bring to the boil. Lower the heat and simmer while you stuff the onion layers.

Take a dessertspoonful of the meat mixture, place it inside one of the layers and roll it up. Set aside while you use up the remaining meat and onion layers. If you have any meat left over roll it into small balls. Carefully arrange the stuffed leaves in the sauce and add any meatballs. Simmer for 30-45 minutes or until the onion and meat are tender and the sauce has thickened. Serve immediately with rice, couscous or macaroni. **Serves 6**

basal mahchi 2

stuffed onions

This recipe is from the Benghazi region of the country and is related to similar Middle Eastern mahchis.

6 large onions, peeled

filling
175g (6oz) minced meat
25g (1oz) chopped almonds
25g (1oz) raisins
1 teaspoon salt
1/2 teaspoon black pepper
110g (4oz) breadcrumbs
3 tablespoons finely chopped parsley
25g (1oz) butter
300ml (1/2 pint) yogurt
1 egg

Place the onions in a large saucepan, cover with water and bring to the boil. Simmer for 10-12 minutes and then drain and set aside until cool enough to handle. Carefully slice 1/2cm (1/4in) from each root end and, using an apple corer hollow out the centre of each onion leaving a shell about 1cm (1/2in) thick. You may find that the inner rings slip out quite easily. Chop the removed onion layers and place in a large bowl. Add the meat, almonds, raisins, salt, pepper, breadcrumbs and 2 tablespoons of the parsley. Mix well.

Fill the onions with this mixture and arrange them side by side in a large, greased ovenproof dish. Dot the onions with the butter. Place in an oven preheated to 350F, 180C, Gas Mark 4 and bake for 1 hour.

Mix the yogurt and egg together thoroughly. Remove the dish with the onions and pour the yogurt sauce over the onions. Return the dish to the oven for 10 minutes and then remove and serve immediately garnished with the remaining parsley. Serve with bread, salads, pickles etc. **Serves 6**

yabrat doulmah

stuffed leaves

Leaves such as vine, cabbage, spinach and sometimes fig or apricot are filled with mixtures of meat, rice and nuts, or simply rice and then cooked in tomato or yogurt-based sauces. This is a Middle Eastern favourite and probably passed to North Africa via the Ottoman Turks. Indeed the very name is of Turkish origin.

I give a standard filling from Libya with which you can also stuff other vegetables, such as aubergines, courgettes, green peppers, potatoes, tomatoes and even cucumbers.

1-1.5kg (2-3lb) firm white cabbage
(or vine leaves. Buy in 450g or 1lb packets from many Continental stores)

filling
450g (1lb) minced lamb
175g (6oz) long-grain rice, washed thoroughly under cold water and drained or
175g (6oz) coarse couscous grains, rinsed
1 small onion, finely chopped
1 large tomato, blanched, peeled and chopped
1 teaspoon salt
1/2 teaspoon black pepper
1/2 teaspoon cinnamon
1/2 teaspoon dried mint

sauce
25g (1oz) butter
1 clove garlic, crushed
1 tablespoon tomato purée
600ml (1 pint) water
1 teaspoon salt
1/2 teaspoon black pepper

to serve
Lemon wedges

To prepare the cabbage leave it whole, but cut out as much of the thick core as possible. Bring a large saucepan two-thirds filled with lightly salted water to the boil. Add the cabbage and simmer for 7-8 minutes. Remove the cabbage to a large plate and, when cool enough to handle, carefully peel away the outer leaves, taking care not to tear them, and place in a colander to cool. When it becomes difficult to remove the leaves, return the cabbage to the water and boil for a few more minutes. Continue removing the leaves in this way until you have all you need. Reserve the small inner leaves. Meanwhile place all the filling ingredients in a large bowl and knead thoroughly.

To fill a leaf place one on a board, veins uppermost and cut out the hard stem. With the cut end towards you place 1 tablespoon – exact amount depends on the size of the leaf – near the cut end. Fold the cut end over the filling and then fold the 2 sides in over the filling towards the centre. Roll the leaf up towards the tip to form a cigar-shaped parcel. Continue in this way until you have used up all the filling and leaves. Use any remaining leaves to cover the base of a large saucepan. Pack the parcels carefully into the pan in layers. Place a plate over the leaves to cover as many as possible and hold down with a small weight – this prevents the leaves from unwrapping while cooking.

To prepare the sauce melt the butter in a small pan, add the garlic and fry for 1 minute. Stir in all the remaining ingredients and bring to the boil. Pour over the stuffed leaves and simmer over a medium heat for about 1 hour. Add a little more water if necessary. To serve, lift the stuffed leaves carefully out of the pan and arrange in a serving dish. Pour any remaining sauce over them and garnish with the lemon wedges.

Serves 6

— tfina —

Tfina is the North African name given to the Jewish dish better known as *cholent, sholent* or *shalet*, which is prepared for the Sabbath lunch. The ritual of *tfina* (or *cholent*) was an important part of Jewish life throughout the centuries of dispersion whether in Central Europe, the Middle East or North Africa. The name comes from the Arabic '*dfi ne*' (to bury, inter) for the cooking pot was buried in the ashes of a wooden fire.

There was, of course, a substantial minority of Jews in the Meghrib before the proclamation of the State of Israel and the consequent migration of Jews to the land of their ancestors, or to France. There are still a few thousand Jews in Morocco and Tunisia.

As is often the case the Jews have left behind their 'food' and out of the many *tfina* dishes I have chosen two to show the brilliant use of local vegetables and fruits. The first recipe is from the island of Djerba – better known to historians as Homer's Island of the Lotus Eaters – off the coast of Tunisia.

tfina djerbaliya

djerba-style sabbath stew

This is a rich stew of meat, spices and fruits. Serve it with couscous or rice and a fresh salad.

50g (2oz) butter
675g (1¹/₂lb) stewing beef, cut into 5cm (2in) cubes
675g (1¹/₂lb) lamb, cut into 5cm (2in) cubes
2 cloves garlic, crushed
2 large onions, thinly sliced
1 green pepper, thinly sliced
1¹/₂ teaspoons salt
¹/₂ teaspoon black pepper
¹/₂ teaspoon chilli pepper
¹/₂ teaspoon cumin
¹/₄ teaspoon allspice
110g (4oz) chickpeas, soaked overnight in cold water and drained
1.2 l (2 pints) water
50g (2oz) dried apricots, soaked overnight, drained and chopped
110g (4oz) prunes, soaked overnight, drained, stoned and chopped
50g (2oz) sultanas or raisins

Melt the butter in a large frying pan, add the meat cubes, a few at a time, and fry until evenly browned. Remove with a slotted spoon and place in an ovenproof casserole. Add the garlic, onions and green pepper to the frying pan and cook, stirring frequently until the onions are soft. Remove with a slotted spoon and place in the casserole.

Sprinkle the seasoning and spices into the casserole and then add the chickpeas and water. Stir well and bring to the boil. Cover and place in an oven preheated to 325F, 160C, Gas Mark 3 and braise for 1 hour. Stir in the dried fruits and cook for a further hour or until the meat and chickpeas are tender. Remove and serve. **Serves 6**

Moroccan Jews have a favourite *tfina* (*dafina* in Moroccan dialect) made with beef, chickpeas, potatoes, beef trotters and tongue. Sometimes the chickpeas are replaced by rice or whole wheat – *Dafina Arrisha*.

Tunisian Jews like to cook their meat with spinach, beef trotters, fresh mint and haricot beans – *Tfina Pkaila*.

tfina aadame soussiya

sousse-style passover tfina

There is very little one can say about this dish. It is overwhelming, a true classic of the Jewish and Meghribi cuisines. I could go on, but no need. A quick glance at the list of ingredients and you will understand my understatement! This magnificent dish is in a class of its own.

Traditionally the sausage – *osbana* – was made of chopped tripe and veal lungs mixed with spinach, rice, herbs and spices and then used to fill beef entrails. This process is long and difficult and the easy way out is to use either Mergues sausages (see Glossary) or any commercial sausages – beef if you wish to be authentic.

Matzo bread (or biscuits) can be bought from any Jewish or Continental store.

This dish is cooked long and slowly and, as it is a celebration meal, the proportions are for 10-12 people.

900g (2lb) spinach, tough stems and leaves discarded,
thoroughly washed and drained
2 artichokes, prepared as in Tajine Karnoune (page 154)
1 small cabbage, quartered, cored and coarse outer leaves discarded
2 onions, chopped
2 leeks, green tops discarded, halved lengthways, cut into 2.5cm (1in) pieces,
and rinsed very thoroughly
1 bulb fennel, quartered
4 carrots, peeled and cut into 2.5cm (1in) pieces
3 turnips, peeled and cut into 2.5cm (1in) pieces
4 sticks celery, cut into 2.5cm (1in) pieces
2 courgettes, cut into 2.5cm (1in) rounds
1 cardoon (optional)
1 khercher or wild cardoon (optional)
900g (2lb) broad beans
450g (1lb) peas
150ml (1/4 pint) oil
900ml (11/2 pints) water
6 cloves garlic, crushed
6 tablespoons finely chopped parsley
3 teaspoons salt
5cm (2in) cinnamon stick
1 teaspoon black pepper
1/2 teaspoon ginger
1/2 teaspoon ground cloves

1/2 teaspoon grated nutmeg
1.5kg (3lb) leg or shoulder of lamb
10-12 Mergues or other sausages (see above)
About 10 fresh mint leaves or 2 teaspoons dried mint
6 matzo breads (or biscuits)
3 large potatoes, peeled and cut into 2.5cm (1in) pieces

Chop the spinach and place in a very large saucepan. Slice the artichoke hearts thinly and add to the pan. Coarsely chop the cabbage and place in the pan with the prepared onions, leeks, fennel, carrots, turnips, celery, courgettes, cardoon, khercher, broad beans and peas. Add the oil, water, garlic, parsley, seasoning and spices. Place over a moderate heat and bring to the boil. If you find that the saucepan cannot hold all of the vegetables, put the pan over the heat when it is three-quarters full and slowly add the remaining vegetables as the contents reduce during the cooking. Stir the mixture well, lower the heat and cover the pan. After 15 minutes place the meat on top of the vegetables, cover and cook over a low heat for 1½ hours.

Meanwhile place the sausages in a pan, cover with water and bring to the boil. Lower the heat and simmer for 15 minutes. Remove from the heat.

After 1½ hours remove the lamb and set aside. Chop the fresh mint or crumble the dried mint and stir into the vegetables. Cover pan and cook over a low heat for a further 1½ hours. Add a little more water if necessary. Crumble the matzo breads and add to the pan together with the cubed potatoes. Mix well. Place the meat and sausages on top of the vegetables and pour the sausage stock into the pan. Cover and simmer for a further hour.

To serve transfer the meat and sausages to a large serving dish and carve the meat at the table. Pour the vegetables into a large tureen and serve immediately. Serve with couscous – the traditional accompaniment to all tfina dishes. **Serves 10-12**

Another Jewish culinary peculiarity is to add several whole eggs to the pot near the end of the cooking time. Since *tfinas* were traditionally served for Saturday lunch, the food was kept simmering very gently for hours on end and the eggs would harden to a glossary brown colour inside and out exuding a delicate odour and flavour.

Overheard in the large souk of Sousse – 'I always do the family shopping. Naturally, my wife carries my purchases home.'

— meatballs —

'The oven precedes the mosque' Arab saying

The range of meatballs is vast, varied and mostly regional. The meat is usually minced twice and then used to make kababs (pages 116-131) or shaped into various-sized balls. They are then either cooked in stews, fried, flattened like a hamburger and grilled or – as in the Libyan *siniya* – put into the bottom of a casserole, topped with whole chilli peppers and halved tomatoes, baked in the oven and then cut into squares or lozenges and served with rice and salad.

I include here two more meatball mixtures that are standard (another one, normally used for all minced meat kababs whether ball, sausage or 'hamburger'-shaped, was given under Kababs – see page 119).

kabab magli

fried meatballs

3 slices white bread, crusts removed
900g (2lb) fairly lean lamb or beef, minced twice
2 eggs
1 clove garlic, crushed
1 teaspoon cinnamon or allspice
1¹/2 teaspoons salt
1/2 teaspoon black pepper
Oil for frying

Soak the bread in water, then squeeze out as much water as possible and crumble into a large bowl. Add all the remaining ingredients except the oil and knead until the mixture is very smooth. Keeping your hands damp roll the mixture into small marble-sized balls.

Heat some oil in a large pan and fry the balls, a few at a time, until they are cooked through and golden. Remove with a slotted spoon and drain. Serve hot or cold with salad and/or pickles. **Serves 6**

kafta bil roz fi tabikh

meat and rice balls in sauce

450g (1lb) lamb or beef, minced twice
75g (3oz) long-grain rice, washed thoroughly under cold water and drained
1 egg
2 cloves garlic, crushed
1 teaspoon salt
1/4 teaspoon cinnamon
1/4 teaspoon cumin
1/4 teaspoon black pepper
1/2 teaspoon paprika

600ml (1 pint) water
1 onion, grated
1 teaspoon salt
1/2 teaspoon chilli pepper
1/2 teaspoon saffron diluted in 4–5 tablespoons water
25g (1oz) *smen* or butter
2 tablespoons finely chopped parsley
Juice 1 small lemon

Place all the meatball ingredients in a large bowl and knead until smooth. Keeping your hands damp shape the mixture into walnut-sized balls.

Put all the sauce ingredients except the parsley and lemon juice into a large saucepan and bring to the boil. Add the meatballs, cover the pan, lower the heat and cook for 45 minutes. Stir in the parsley and lemon juice and cook, uncovered for a further 5 minutes. Serve with rice or couscous.

These meatballs can also be cooked in a tomato sauce, and chickpeas are sometimes added to the sauce to augment the meal.

m'chimeche

chop and meatball stew

A rich dish from Algeria and Tunisia where the meatballs are apricot-sized and each has an almond in the centre. There is another classic dish called *Mkhiouakh* in which the meat is shaped into balls as large as peaches.

2 tablespoons *smen* or 25g (1oz) butter
1 onion, finely chopped
6 lamb chops
75g (3oz) chickpeas, soaked overnight in cold water and drained
2 teaspoons salt
1 teaspoon black pepper
1 teaspoon cinnamon
900ml (1 1/2 pints) water
450g (1lb) minced lamb or beef
2 eggs, separated
About 12 blanched almonds
Oil for frying

Heat the fat in a large saucepan, add the onion and fry until soft. Add the chops, chickpeas, half the salt, pepper and cinnamon, and the water. Bring to the boil, cover the pan, lower the heat and simmer for 45 minutes.

Meanwhile place the minced meat, remaining cinnamon, salt and black pepper, and egg whites in a large bowl and knead until smooth. Keeping your hands damp form the mixture into apricot-sized balls. Enclose one blanched almond in the centre of each ball. After 45 minutes add the meatballs to the pan and simmer for a further 30 minutes, adding more water if necessary. Remove the meatballs with a slotted spoon and leave to drain. If necessary continue to cook the chops and chickpeas until the latter are tender.

Heat some oil in a large frying pan. Beat the egg yolks, dip the meatballs into them and fry gently, turning occasionally until evenly golden. To serve arrange the chops and meatballs in a large serving dish and pour the sauce over them. **Serves 6**

maadnoussiya

chunks of meat in parsley coating

This recipe is from Algeria. Chunks of meat are cooked in a sauce then coated in an egg, parsley and chopped almond mixture and fried in oil.

900g (2lb) lean lamb or beef, cut into 3.5cm (1¹/2in) cubes
2 tablespoons *smen* or 25g (1oz) butter
2 spring onions, chopped
1 teaspoon cinnamon
1 teaspoon salt
1 teaspoon black pepper
1.2 l (2 pints) water
50g (2oz) chickpeas, soaked overnight in cold water and drained
4 eggs
6 tablespoons finely chopped parsley
50g (2oz) finely chopped almonds
Oil for frying
4 tablespoons flour

Put the meat, fat, onions and half the spices in a large saucepan and fry over a medium heat for about 10 minutes, stirring frequently. Add the water and chickpeas and bring to the boil. Cover the pan and simmer for about 1 hour or until the meat and chickpeas are tender. Add a little more water if necessary. When the meat is cooked remove the cubes with a fork and drain on kitchen paper.

Meanwhile place the eggs, parsley, almonds and remaining spices in a bowl and beat well. Heat some oil in a large frying pan. Roll each piece of meat in the flour and then dip into the egg-parsley mixture. Place carefully in the oil and fry for about 4-5 minutes, turning several times until evenly golden. Keep hot while you fry all the meat in the same way. To serve arrange the meat in a serving dish and pour the hot sauce over the top. Serve with rice or couscous and with salad, pickles and olives. **Serves 6**

ktef ghalmi

roast shoulder of lamb

Lamb and goat, as well as being grilled on charcoal and wood, are often just as successfully roasted in the oven. The meat is first basted with herbs and spices, then deposited in a large baking tray with vegetables and cooked in the oven.

You can also use leg of lamb. Ask your butcher to bone the joint for you.

1.75-2.25kg (4-5lb) shoulder or leg of lamb, boned

baste 1 (from algeria)

6 cloves garlic, halved
1 teaspoon salt
1 teaspoon black pepper
110g (4oz) butter, melted
2 large ripe tomatoes, chopped

With the point of a sharp knife make 12 incisions into the meat and insert a halved clove of garlic, in each. Mix the salt and pepper together and rub all over the surface of the joint. Brush the meat thoroughly with the melted butter and set aside for 15 minutes.

Scatter the chopped tomatoes in the bottom of a baking tray and place the joint in the centre. Pour the rest of the butter over the top. Place in an oven preheated to 325F, 160C, Gas Mark 3 and roast for 2-3 hours, basting frequently with the pan juices. Serve the meat accompanied by the pan juices in a sauceboat. **Serves 6**

baste 2 (from morocco)

1 small onion, finely chopped
4 cloves garlic, chopped
1 teaspoon dried mint
3 tablespoons finely chopped parsley
2 cardamom pods (optional)
2 teaspoons salt
1 teaspoon cumin
1/2 teaspoon black pepper
1 teaspoon paprika
150ml (1/4 pint) oil
600ml (1 pint) water, boiling

With the point of a sharp knife make several shallow incisions over the surface of the joint. Place all the ingredients except the oil and water in a mortar and pound to a paste. Rub this paste over the surface of the meat and into the incisions. Place in a baking tray and pour in the oil and water. Cover.

Place in an oven preheated to 325F, 160C, Gas Mark 3 and roast for 2-3 hours, turning several times. Serve on a large dish with the stock as a sauce. **Serves 6**

Other spices and herbs such as saffron, ginger, coriander, tarragon etc can be used in the bastes.

Vegetables are often cooked with the meat. Among the most popular are artichoke hearts, peeled and quartered potatoes, quartered onions, quartered tomatoes, sliced courgettes or aubergines etc.

kharouf mahchi bil kesksou

lamb stuffed with couscous

And this is another classic from Morocco, where folk say that 'The sheep thinks only of the knife, while the butcher only of the meat', and also that 'every sheep hangs by its own tail'.

1.75-2.25kg (4-5lb) shoulder, leg or rack of lamb with breast, boned

stuffing
175g (6oz) couscous grains
2 tablespoons orange blossom water
50g (2oz) sugar
50g (2oz) raisins
50g (2oz) butter, melted
2 teaspoons cinnamon
50g (2oz) almonds, toasted or fried in oil, and ground

baste
2 teaspoons salt
1 teaspoon black pepper
1/2 teaspoon saffron diluted in 4-5 tablespoons water
1 large onion, finely chopped
110g (4oz) butter, melted
2 1/2 teaspoons cinnamon
900ml (1 1/2 pints) water, boiling
4 tablespoons thick honey

Mix all the stuffing ingredients together in a bowl and then stuff the joint of your choice. If using shoulder or leg roll up the joint and tie with string. If using breast sew up the opening and then roll up and secure. Place the joint in a large baking tin.

Mix all the baste ingredients together except 2 teaspoons of the cinnamon, the water and honey, and rub over the meat. Pour in the water, cover the tin and place in an oven preheated to 325F, 160C, Gas Mark 3. Roast for 2-3 hours, turning the meat occasionally.

About 20 minutes before serving remove the tin from the oven, spoon the honey over the meat and sprinkle with the remaining cinnamon. Return to the oven and cook for a further 15 minutes uncovered.

Transfer the meat to a serving dish and leave to stand for 5 minutes before carving. To serve remove the string, spoon out the stuffing and carve the meat. Serve the pan juices separately.

You can replace the almonds with pine kernels or walnuts and you can also add finely chopped fresh tarragon, basil or mint to the baste.

— poultry and game —

'In the name of Allah,' whispers the shopkeeper just before cutting the throat of a chicken whose blood bursts forth splattering his shirt, the ground and passers-by. I have seen Europeans aghast at this sight, with a few women almost in tears. Cruel perhaps, if one is – as we are – protected by all the required niceties of a civilised society where the killing is done in clean abattoirs – clinically, methodically, and with no thanks to God!

But in Africa man is nearer to his Maker and his Maker's creatures. Death may be cruel and public, but it is respected and appreciated nevertheless. In the mornings car and donkey loads of poultry (chickens, turkeys, pigeon etc) find their way to the markets where, in makeshift cages, they are put on display for sale. One picks up the chicken of one's choice, feels it, judges its weight, and then nods approval. The throat is then cut with the praise of God on one's lips.

After lamb, chicken is the most popular meat in the Meghrib where one thousand and one ways have been evolved for its preparation. Chicken are roasted, grilled, boiled, cooked in tajines and couscous dishes, stuffed, minced etc, etc, etc. But by far the nicest method is to grill them either whole or in smaller portions. The fire must be charcoal, so that the wood aroma mingles with that of the bird and its marinade. Chicken, duck and many smaller birds are thus prepared. The North Africans have no qualms about cooking anything – blackbird, bulbul, turtle dove, quail, thrush, plover, partridge. All is fair game as long as 'he who eats the fowl of others, fattens his own'.

djej mquali

chicken with coriander and mint

From Morocco. The chicken can either be cooked whole or jointed and can be prepared on top of the oven or in it. I prefer it baked.

2 cloves garlic, crushed
4 tablespoons finely chopped fresh coriander leaves
4 tablespoons finely chopped fresh mint leaves
4 tablespoons oil
1 tablespoon paprika
1/2 teaspoon saffron diluted in 2 tablespoons water
1/2 teaspoon oregano
1 teaspoon cumin
2 teaspoons salt
1/2 teaspoon black pepper
1.75-2.25kg (4-5lb) chicken, whole or jointed (reserve giblets)
1 whole onion
300ml (1/2 pint) water
10 preserved olives (see Glossary)
Zest 1 pickled lemon, cut into quarters (see page 250)

Place the first 10 ingredients in a bowl and mix well. Rub all over the chicken, inside as well as outside if using a whole chicken. Place the chicken in a saucepan or flameproof casserole. Chop the giblets and add to the pan together with the whole onion. Pour in the water and bring to the boil. At this point either cover the pan, lower the heat and simmer for 1 hour or cover the casserole and place in an oven preheated to 375F, 190C, Gas Mark 5 and cook for 1 hour. Baste the chicken with its own juices occasionally and add a little more water if necessary.

Add the olives and lemon zest and cook for a further 10 minutes.

Remove the giblets and onion and either blend in a liquidiser or pass through a sieve. Return this mixture to the sauce in the pan and cook for a further 5 minutes. Serve with rice or couscous and vegetables of your choice. **Serves 6**

marga djej bil louze

chicken in almond sauce

'When the chicken feathers are of gold it is foolish to make a broth of the hen'
Algerian saying

4 tablespoons oil
1 onion, finely chopped
1.75-2.25kg (4-5lb) chicken cut into serving pieces
1 teaspoon salt
1/2 teaspoon black pepper
1/2 teaspoon cinnamon
1/2 teaspoon ginger
2 cloves
1/2 teaspoon saffron diluted in 4-5 tablespoons water
450ml (3/4 pint) water
75g (3oz) blanched almonds
50g (2oz) raisins

Heat half the oil in a large frying pan, add the onion, and fry until soft and turning golden. Remove with a slotted spoon and transfer to a large saucepan. Add the remaining oil and the chicken pieces to the frying pan and sauté the chicken, turning occasionally, until evenly golden. Transfer to the saucepan.

Add all the spices, including the diluted saffron, to the remaining oil and fry for 1-2 minutes, stirring constantly. Stir in the water and then pour the contents of the frying pan over the chicken pieces. Cover the pan and bring to the boil. Lower the heat and simmer for 45 minutes. Add the almonds and raisins and cook for a further 15-20 minutes. Serve with rice. **Serves 6**

badendjel bil djej

chicken with aubergines

Aubergines and chicken go very well together as this Algerian speciality
will testify. It is a simple dish which is best served with a rice pilav and vegetables
of your choice.

1.75-2.25kg (4-5lb) chicken, cut into serving pieces
3 tablespoons oil
2 cloves garlic, thinly sliced

1/2 teaspoon saffron diluted in 2 tablespoons water
11/2 teaspoons salt
1 teaspoon black pepper
1/2 teaspoon ginger
900g (2lb) aubergines, peeled and cut lengthways into 1/2cm (1/4in) thick slices
3 tablespoons finely chopped parsley or tarragon

Place the chicken pieces in a large saucepan. Mix the oil, garlic, saffron, salt, pepper and ginger together, pour over the chicken pieces and rub in.

Arrange the aubergine slices around the chicken and then add enough water to cover. Bring to the boil, lower the heat, cover the pan and simmer for about 1 hour or until chicken and aubergines are tender. Remove from the heat and stir in the parsley or tarragon. Serve with rice, couscous or pasta. **Serves 6**

Moroccans like to fry the aubergine slices in oil first. They then add them to the chicken pan halfway through the cooking time. They also stir in the juice of 1 lemon and 1 teaspoon ginger mixed to a smooth paste with a few tablespoons of the sauce.

A local Moroccan variation from Marrakech removes the fried aubergines from the saucepan when they are cooked, transfers them to a frying pan and mashes them to a pulp with 3 tablespoons of lemon juice. Fry for 10 minutes, stirring constantly. Arrange the chicken pieces in a serving dish and spoon the aubergine pulp over them. You can also prepare this dish with courgettes or carrots.

djej bil zaitun

chicken with olives

There are several versions of this dish. This one, from Algeria, uses *meslalla* or crushed olives, which are stoned green olives. Serve with rice or cooked vegetables.

3 tablespoons *smen* or 40g (11/2oz) butter
1.75-2.25kg (4-5lb) chicken, cut into serving pieces
1 onion, finely chopped
1 clove garlic, crushed
1 teaspoon ginger
1 tablespoon paprika
1 teaspoon cumin
1 teaspoon salt
1 tablespoon flour
450ml (3/4 pint) water
450g (1lb) stoned green olives, soaked for 1 hour in cold water
2 tablespoons finely chopped fresh mint or parsley
Juice 1 lemon

Melt the *smen* or butter in a large saucepan and add the chicken pieces. Sprinkle the onion, garlic, ginger, paprika, cumin and salt over the chicken. Cook over a low heat for about 15 minutes, stirring frequently.

Mix the flour to a smooth paste with some of the water and add to the pan with the remaining water. Stir well and bring to the boil. Lower the heat, cover the pan and simmer for about 45 minutes, stirring occasionally.

Stir in the olives, mint or parsley and the lemon juice, cover and simmer for a further 15-20 minutes or until the chicken is tender. To serve, arrange the chicken pieces in a large dish and pour the sauce over the top. **Serves 6**

djej soury

chicken cooked in eggs

A tasty and exotic dish, also known as *Djej M'kadem*, from Fez. It is typical of the rich Andalusian school of cooking. Serve with rice, couscous or noodles of your choice.

40g (1½oz) butter or *smen*
1 large onion, finely chopped
1.75-2.25kg (4-5lb) chicken, cut into serving pieces (reserve giblets)
5cm (2in) stick cinnamon
½ teaspoon saffron diluted in 4-5 tablespoons water
½ teaspoon salt
450ml (¾ pint) water
Juice 1 large lemon
3 tablespoons finely chopped parsley

egg mixture
8 eggs
1 level teaspoon cinnamon
½ teaspoon paprika
¼ teaspoon cumin
1 teaspoon salt

garnish
1 tablespoon finely chopped fresh thyme or 1 teaspoon dried thyme

Heat the butter or *smen* in a large saucepan, add the onion and fry until soft. Add the chicken pieces and fry for 4-5 minutes, turning occasionally. Add the cinnamon stick, diluted saffron, salt and water and bring to the boil. Lower the heat, cover the pan and simmer for 45 minutes. Remove the lid, add the lemon juice and cook for a further 15-

20 minutes or until the sauce is reduced. Remove the cinnamon stick and stir in the parsley. Pour over and reserve most of the sauce.

Break the eggs into a bowl, add remaining ingredients and beat well. Pour this mixture over the chicken pieces, cover the pan and cook for a further 15 minutes. Transfer the chicken mixture to a large dish, reheat reserved sauce, pour over mixture and garnish with the thyme. Serve immediately.

djaj bil bargoug wa assel

chicken with prunes and honey

'He who has nothing to do will make a hen hatch' Tunisian proverb

Brilliantly colourful, another Andalusian-inspired dish from Fez – although popular throughout Morocco and parts of Western Africa. Serve with rice or roast potatoes and a bowl of fresh salad.

40g (1¹/₂oz) butter or *smen*
1 large onion, finely chopped
1.75-2.25kg (4-5lb) chicken, cut into serving pieces
1 teaspoon salt
¹/₂ teaspoon black pepper
5cm (2in) cinnamon stick
600ml (1 pint) water
225g (¹/₂lb) prunes, soaked for several hours in cold water
3 tablespoons honey
1 teaspoon cinnamon
75g (3oz) blanched almonds, toasted until golden

garnish
1 tablespoon sesame seeds, toasted until golden

Heat the fat in a large saucepan, add the onion and fry until soft. Add the chicken pieces and fry for 4-5 minutes, turning occasionally. Add the salt, pepper, cinnamon stick and water, and bring to the boil. Stir well, lower the heat, cover the pan and simmer for about 1 hour, stirring occasionally.

Meanwhile place the prunes in a small saucepan with 150ml (¹/₄ pint) of the soaking water. Bring to the boil and simmer for 10 minutes. Add the honey and cinnamon, mix well and simmer for 5 minutes. When the chicken is cooked transfer this prune-honey mixture to the large saucepan. Add the toasted almonds, stir well and simmer for a further 5-10 minutes.

To serve arrange the chicken pieces in a large dish, pour the sauce over them and scatter with the toasted sesame seeds. **Serves 6**

djaj maamer

stuffed chicken

On special occasions chicken, turkey, partridge and other birds are stuffed with couscous or rice and with nuts, fruits and meat. The chicken can be roasted with water and butter as below, or with honey and cinnamon, or with vegetables.

I have given two stuffings below, one from Morocco and one from Tunisia.

1.75-2.25kg (4-5lb) chicken, washed inside and out and dried thoroughly

couscous stuffing

110g (4oz) couscous grains
50g (2oz) raisins, soaked in water for 15 minutes
25g (1oz) blanched almonds
25g (1oz) pine kernels (or extra almonds)
3 stoned dates, thinly sliced
1/2 teaspoon cinnamon
1/2 teaspoon nutmeg
1 teaspoon salt
1 tablespoon sugar

baste
25g (1oz) butter or *smen*, melted
120ml (4fl oz) water

Spread couscous grains out on a baking sheet and sprinkle with warm salted water. Work lightly between your fingers so that each grain is separated, moistened and beginning to swell. Set aside for 15 minutes. Repeat this process twice more. Half-fill the bottom part of a couscousier or a large saucepan over which a colander will fit snugly. Bring to the boil. Place the couscous into the top part of the couscousier. If using a colander line it first with a fine tea towel as the holes may be too large and the grains will fall through. Place on top of the simmering water and steam for 20 minutes, stirring occasionally until the grains are soft.

Transfer the grains to a large bowl and add the remaining stuffing ingredients. Mix well and fill the chicken cavity. Tie up the opening or secure with toothpicks. If there is any stuffing left over heat it up and serve with the chicken.

Place the chicken in a large ovenproof dish and brush with the melted butter. Pour the water into the dish and roast in an oven preheated to 350F, 180C, Gas Mark 4 for about 2 hours or until tender. Baste frequently.

rice stuffing

40g (1¹/₂oz) butter or *smen*
Liver and heart of the chicken, coarsely chopped
1¹/2 teaspoons salt
1/2 teaspoon black pepper
1 small onion, finely chopped
2 tomatoes, blanched, peeled and chopped
110g (4oz) long grain rice, washed thoroughly under cold water and drained
2 tablespoons finely chopped parsley
1/2 teaspoon cinnamon
250ml (8fl oz) water

Melt the butter in a saucepan, add the liver and heart, salt and pepper and fry for 3 minutes, stirring frequently. Remove liver and heart pieces with a slotted spoon and reserve. Add onion to the pan and fry until soft. Stir in the tomatoes and simmer for 2-3 minutes. Stir in rice, parsley and cinnamon and cook for a further 3 minutes, stirring frequently. Stir in the reserved liver and heart and the water and bring to the boil. Lower the heat and simmer for about 15 minutes or until the liquid has been absorbed. Leave to cool and then stuff the chicken as described above. **Serves 4-6**

Apart from the simple butter and water baste mentioned above you can season the water with 2 bay leaves, salt and black pepper and 1/2 teaspoon harissa (see Glossary).

Vegetables such as onions, potatoes, tomatoes, courgettes, carrots etc can be added to the water and roasted along with the chicken.

You could try this particularly 'Fezian' baste where salt, pepper, 1/2 teaspoon saffron, a cinnamon stick, 50g (2oz) butter and 1 finely chopped onion are added to the water in the pan. This mixture is used to baste the chicken frequently. Towards the end of the cooking time add 3 tablespoons honey and 1 tablespoon cinnamon to the sauce, stir well and baste the chicken.

hlou bil mechmach

hlou with apricots

Tunisians have a penchant for foods of contrast – sweet and sour, light and dark. They are also very fond of dishes called *hlou* ('sweet' in Arabic). These are usually prepared with fruits or vegetables and are served with couscous. However, I have tried these *hlou* with roast chicken and the result has always been excellent. It can be served separately or poured over the chicken.

This is by far my favourite *hlou*. You can use fresh or dried apricots, but the latter must be soaked in water overnight.

225g (8oz) fresh apricots or 110g (4oz) dried apricots
90ml (3fl oz) oil
50g (2oz) sugar
1 onion, finely chopped
225g (8oz) pumpkin, finely chopped
600ml (1 pint) water
1 tablespoon lemon juice

If using fresh apricots cut them in half and remove the stones. If using dried ones cut into smaller pieces.

Place the oil and sugar in a saucepan and cook over a moderate heat, stirring constantly with a wooden spoon until the sugar has nearly caramelised. Add the chopped onion and cook for 2-3 minutes, stirring constantly. Add the pumpkin and half the water, cover the pan and cook for 10 minutes. Remove the lid and mash the pumpkin with a fork.

Stir in the apricots, lemon juice and remaining water and mix thoroughly. Cover the pan and cook over a low heat for about 30 minutes, stirring occasionally. The mixture should have the consistency of jam. Now you can either serve it hot or cold with couscous or semolina, serve it as an accompaniment to all kinds of roasts and even kababs, or carve the chicken and pour the hlou over it.

The apricots can be replaced by greengages, plums or dried chestnuts (the latter soaked overnight). 1 large quince or 2 cooking apples or pears can also be used instead of the apricots.

The essential hlou ingredients are the pumpkin and sugar.

You can add extra flavour with cloves or cinnamon.

haman mahchi

stuffed pigeon

'Don't marry an old woman even though you will eat with her young pigeons and lamb's meat' – i.e. only the best – Moorish proverb

Other small birds can be stuffed and cooked in the same way – partridge (*farkh hadjal*), quail (*soumanate*), and of course the beautiful turtle dove (*tirghallate*).

Since pigeons are sometimes difficult to find in our part of the world I often use poussins instead. However, if by chance (or stealth) you happen to come upon 6 plump, tender young pigeons then prepare them in the following manner!

Remove entrails by making a lengthways incision in each breast, roll in salt and rinse very thoroughly, inside and out, with cold running water. Drain. Stuff each bird with some of the couscous or rice stuffings described on pages 210-211, but do not pack the filling too tightly or the flesh may burst open during cooking. Sew up the openings or secure with toothpicks.

50g (2oz) *smen* or butter
1 teaspoon salt
1/2 teaspoon black pepper
1/2 teaspoon saffron
1 large onion, finely chopped
110g (4oz) mushrooms, thinly sliced
5cm (2in) cinnamon stick
600ml (1 pint) water
4 tablespoons honey
1 teaspoon ras-el-hanout (set Glossary)

Melt the *smen* or butter in a large casserole dish and arrange the birds in it. Add the salt, pepper, saffron, onion, mushrooms, cinnamon, and water.

Bring to the boil, cover the pan and simmer for 45 minutes. Stir in the honey and ras-el-hanout, cover the pan and simmer for a further 15 minutes until the sauce thickens and the birds are a golden colour. Arrange in a large serving dish and pour the sauce over the top. Makes a superb dish for a dinner party. **Serves 6**

arnab bil tomatich

rabbit with tomato sauce

This is a delicious recipe from Algeria.

2 tablespoons oil
2 tablespoons *smen* or 25g (1oz) butter
1 onion, finely chopped
2 cloves garlic, finely chopped
1-1.5kg (2-3lb) rabbit, skinned, drawn and cut into small pieces
1 teaspoon salt
1/2 teaspoon black pepper
1/2 teaspoon harissa (see Glossary)
2 bay leaves
1/2 teaspoon cumin
600ml (1 pint) water
450g (1lb) ripe tomatoes, blanched, peeled and chopped
1 tablespoon tomato purée diluted in 15ml (1/4 pint) water

Heat the oil and *smen* or butter in a large saucepan, add the onion and garlic and fry until soft. Add the rabbit pieces, stir, cover and fry for 15-20 minutes, stirring frequently. Stir in the salt, pepper, harissa, bay leaves, cumin and water and bring to the boil. Lower the heat, cover the pan and simmer for 40 minutes.

Stir the chopped tomatoes and diluted tomato purée into the casserole and simmer for a further 20-30 minutes or until the sauce has thickened and the rabbit is tender. Serve with steamed rice or pasta. **Serves 4-6**

arnab mrouzia

This Moroccan way of cooking rabbit or hare has a sauce seasoned with 1 teaspoon each of black pepper, cinnamon, saffron and ras-el-hanout (see Glossary). It is cooked with 110g (4oz) butter, 110g (4oz) blanched almonds, 1 finely chopped onion and 900ml (1½ pints) water. Ten minutes before serving 4 tablespoons of honey and 110g (4oz) raisins are stirred into the sauce.

l'hoot — fish

'The best way to cook fish,' said a Moroccan chef who ran an Italian trattoria-pizzeria in Liverpool, 'is to fry them in oil or grill them over charcoal.' Jean-Jacques (real name Ahmed-Ali) disapproved of all that 'tomato, cream and mayonnaise nonsense. Europeans, my friend, do not like fish so they kill its flavour and aroma with countless ingredients. Now you take shad . . .'

Shad is the fish of Morocco, found in the rivers and brooks fed from the Atlas mountains. It has a delicate flesh, but numerous bones. Shad must be eaten very fresh, as it is the way all along the Moroccan coastline and in Fez from where the two recipes below originate.

l'hoot bil chermoula fezie

shad, fez-style

Chermoula is a classic Moroccan sauce/marinade dating, according to some, from the days of the Romans, and is similar to a Roman fish dish described by Apicius. Other fish are equally successful with the sauce. (See page 244 for another *chermoula* sauce.)

2 tablespoons chopped fresh coriander
1/2 teaspoon salt
2 cloves garlic
250ml (8fl oz) water
2 teaspoons paprika
1 teaspoon cumin

1/4 teaspoon chilli pepper
2 tablespoons oil
90ml (3fl oz) vinegar or lemon juice
1.5-1.75kg (3-4lb) whole fish (shad, sea bream, mullet) or 6 thick steaks

to fry
Oil
50g (2oz) flour

Place the coriander, salt, garlic and half the water in a blender and liquidise. Pour into a large dish and stir in the rest of the water and the paprika, cumin, chilli pepper, oil and vinegar or lemon juice.

If using a whole fish first clean the inside of the fish. Being careful not to damage the roe (the Moroccans love the female shad because of the roe). The fishmonger will of course clean the fish for you if you prefer. Remove the head and tail and cut the fish in half lengthways. Divide the halves into 5cm (2in) thick slices. Rinse thoroughly under cold running water and pat dry with kitchen paper. If using fish steaks simply rinse and dry them. Transfer the fish slices to the sauce, turn to coat well, cover and set aside to marinate for at least 2 hours.

Heat some oil in a large frying pan. Remove the fish slices from the marinade and, a few at a time, dredge them in the flour and fry until cooked and golden brown. Serve hot or cold. **Serves 6**

A variation from Meknez makes fritters from the *chermoula* marinade which are then served with the fish. Marinate and fry the fish as above and keep warm while you prepare the fritters. Beat 2 eggs into the marinade and add 15g (1/2oz) fresh yeast or 8g (1/4oz) dried yeast dissolved in 4 tablespoons warm water. Mix in about 75g (3oz) plain flour and beat until you have a thin batter. Cover with a tea towel and leave for 30-45 minutes. Heat fresh oil in the frying pan and add a few tablespoons of batter to it. Fry them for a few minutes, turning once until set and golden. Remove, drain and keep warm while you fry the remaining batter. Serve these fritters with the fish – the taste is wonderful.

shabouka bil tmar

shad stuffed with stuffed dates

This is one of the great specialities of Fez – a brilliant admixture of Spain and the Meghrib. Salmon or bonito make good substitutes for the shad and you can use prunes instead of dates, and rice instead of couscous. Some people like to add 2-3 dried figs to the stuffing.

Served with roast vegetables and a fresh salad, it makes an excellent choice for a dinner party.

1.75-2.25kg (4-5lb) shad or salmon, gutted and washed inside and out
with salted water
75g (3oz) couscous or cooked long-grain rice
50g (2oz) blanched almonds, finely chopped
1 teaspoon sugar
1/2 teaspoon cinnamon
3/4 teaspoon ginger
40g (1½oz) butter or *smen*
1/4 teaspoon black pepper
110g (4oz) fresh dates (or dried)
110g (4oz) fresh figs (or dried)
300ml (½ pint) water
1/2 teaspoon salt
1 teaspoon chilli pepper
1 small onion, finely chopped

garnish
Cinnamon

If using couscous steam it according to the instructions for *Djaj Maamer* (page 210). Place the cooked couscous or rice in a bowl, add the almonds, sugar, 1/2 teaspoon cinnamon, ginger, butter and black pepper, knead well.

If using dried dates and figs drop them into boiling water for 2 minutes then remove, drain and leave to cool. Carefully fill the dates and figs with the couscous or rice mixture. Then fill the fish with the stuffed dates and figs. Sew up the opening or secure with toothpicks.

Generously butter a large baking dish and lay the fish in it. Pour in the water and sprinkle with the salt, chilli pepper, remaining ginger and onion. Place in an oven preheated to 330F, 180C, Gas Mark 4 and bake for 1-1½ hours or until the fish is crisp and golden and the water has evaporated. Remove from the oven and transfer to a large serving dish. Undo the belly and scoop some of the filling out onto the plate. Dust with a little cinnamon and serve. **Serves at least 8**

al-toune bil tomatich

tuna in tomato sauce

Below are two methods of preparing this dish. One is from Western Morocco (Casablanca and Rabat) and the other is from Northern Algeria and Tunisia. The versions are interesting for they reflect the Berber style and its westernised alternative.

You can prepare other kinds of fish – cod, haddock, whiting etc – in the same way.

1-1.5kg (2-3lb) tuna, either whole or cut into steaks

moroccan method

Chermoula sauce (see page 244)
900g (2lb) tomatoes, blanched, peeled and coarsely chopped
3 tablespoons finely chopped parsley
Zest 1 pickled lemon (see Glossary), thinly sliced
10-12 olives

If you have bought a whole fish, gut it and slice off head and tail. Wash thoroughly inside and out and then cut into thick slices. Prepare the *chermoula* sauce and pour into a large dish. Add the fish slices and turn to coat well. Cover and marinate for at least 2 hours.

Meanwhile place the tomatoes in a pan and cook over a moderate heat, stirring frequently until they are reduced to a purée. Stir in the parsley, lemon zest and olives and cook for a further 5 minutes.

Arrange the fish in a large ovenproof casserole and pour over any remaining *chermoula* marinade and the tomato sauce. Cover and bake in an oven preheated to 350F, 180C, Gas Mark 4 for about 45 minutes or until the fish is tender. Serve hot or cold. **Serves 6**

algerian method

175g (6oz) green olives
6 tablespoons oil
2 cloves garlic, crushed
3 tablespoons tomato purée
600ml (1 pint) water
1 teaspoon salt
1/4 teaspoon black pepper
1/2 teaspoon cumin

Place the olives in a small pan, cover with water and bring to the boil. Remove from the heat immediately and drain.

Heat the oil in a large frying pan or saucepan, add the garlic and fry for 1 minute. Stir in the olives, tomato purée, water, salt, pepper and cumin and bring to the boil. Cover the pan and simmer for 5 minutes. Add the pieces of fish, cover the pan and simmer for about 25-30 minutes or until the fish is tender. If necessary add a little more water, but not too much as the sauce should be thick. Arrange the fish steaks in a large serving dish and pour the sauce over the top. **Serves 6**

kelb el bhar chetitta

dogfish in hot sauce

'Fish follow their river' – People will support their own family or tribe.
Berber expression

The simplest description of *chetitta* is that it is hot or piquant. It is a sauce made with harissa or dried hot chillies and is a favourite of Algerians and Tunisians. Tuna is also often cooked in this way, as are bonito, grey mullet, sea bass – indeed most fish.

1-1.5kg (2-3lb) dogfish, cleaned and cut into 6 equal portions or 6 dogfish steaks
6 tablespoons oil
1 clove garlic, finely chopped
1 teaspoon paprika
1 teaspoon salt
1 teaspoon cumin
1/2 teaspoon coriander
1/2 teaspoon harissa (see Glossary)
450ml (3/4 pint) water
2 ripe tomatoes, blanched, peeled and chopped

Rinse the fish slices thoroughly, drain and pat dry with kitchen towels.

Mix the oil, garlic, paprika, salt, cumin, coriander, black pepper, harissa and 6 tablespoons of the water together in a bowl and then pour into a large frying pan. Bring to the boil and simmer for 2-3 minutes. Add the fish slices and pour in the rest of the water, with the chopped tomatoes.

Cover the pan and simmer for 25-30 minutes or until the fish is tender. Serve with rice, couscous or noodles and a salad of your choice.

bousif bil louze

swordfish with almonds

Fish and almonds go very well together and there are numerous North African recipes to verify this fact. This Tunisian recipe is one of many.

6 swordfish steaks, about 225g (8oz) each
1 teaspoon salt
1/2 teaspoon chilli pepper
75g (3oz) *smen* or butter

75g (3oz) slivered almonds
Juice 2 large lemons

Mix the salt and chilli pepper together and rub generously all over the steaks. Melt the *smen* or butter in a large frying pan, add the almonds and fry gently for 2-3 minutes, stirring frequently until evenly golden. Remove with a slotted spoon and reserve.

Add the fish steaks to the pan and fry for about 4 minutes on either side until evenly browned. Sprinkle the almonds over the fish, add the lemon juice to the pan, cover and cook gently for 10-12 minutes.

Transfer the fish steaks to a large serving dish, pour the almond- sauce over them and serve with rice or couscous and salads of your choice. **Serves 6**

l'hoot be-louz

fish stuffed with almond paste

A Moroccan recipe makes a paste of almonds and stuffs the fish with it. Almost any type of whole fish will do especially shad, trout, sea bass or mackerel.

1.5-1.75kg (3-3^1/$_2$lb) whole large fish or 6 medium sized fish, gutted and rinsed inside and out

almond paste
225g (8oz) blanched whole almonds, toasted until golden
110g (4oz) sugar
1 teaspoon cinnamon
1 tablespoon orange blossom water
2 tablespoons water
2 tablespoons oil

sauce
1 large onion, finely chopped
^{1}/$_2$ teaspoon saffron, diluted in 5 tablespoons water
1^1/$_2$ teaspoons salt
^{1}/$_2$ teaspoon black pepper
50g (2oz) butter, melted

To prepare the paste first grind the almonds and sugar in a blender. Place in a bowl, add the cinnamon, orange blossom water, water and oil and mix thoroughly. Carefully fill the cavity of the fish with half the paste. Secure opening(s) with wooden toothpicks and arrange the fish in a large greased ovenproof casserole.

Surround the fish with the chopped onion, pour over the diluted saffron and sprinkle with the salt and pepper. Spread the remaining paste all over the fish and pour the melted butter evenly over the top. Bake in an oven preheated to 350F, 180C, Gas Mark 4 for about 30-45 minutes or until the fish is cooked. Serve with salads and cooked vegetables of your choice. **Serves 6**

kannari bouri

grey mullet with egg stuffing

This is a beautiful-looking dish from Tunisia. It is fit for a banquet – or at least a mini banquet – for 10-12 people. The fish is first cooked in spices then divided in half, filled with an egg yolk mixture, re-shaped, covered with scale-shaped egg whites and refrigerated. There is a great deal of European influence in the preparation of this dish – and very good it is too.

1 grey mullet, about 2-2.5kg (4^1/$_2$-5^1/$_2$lb), scaled, gutted and rinsed thoroughly
750ml (1^1/$_4$ pints) water
4 tablespoons oil
4 cloves garlic, crushed
Juice 2 lemons
3-4 sprigs mint tied up with cotton
2 teaspoons salt
^{1}/$_2$ teaspoon black pepper
^{1}/$_2$ teaspoon paprika
^{1}/$_2$ teaspoon coriander
175g (6oz) stale bread, sliced, crusts removed
10 hard-boiled eggs
1 black olive

garnish
Lemon slices and parsley sprigs

Place the water, oil, garlic, lemon juice and mint in a fish kettle, or other pan large enough to take the whole fish, and bring to the boil. Carefully lay the fish in it, lower the heat, cover and simmer for 20 minutes. Remove the fish gently and set aside to drain and cool. Pour the fish stock into a basin, discard the mint, stir in the salt, pepper, paprika and coriander, and place the bread slices in the stock.

Cut the eggs in half crossways and set the whites carefully aside. Place the egg yolks in a large bowl, add the soaked bread slices and mix well to form a smooth paste – add a little more of the fish stock if necessary.

Carefully remove and discard the skin and fins of the mullet. Cut the fish open lengthways and carefully remove the backbone and all the small bones. Spread one-third of the egg paste over the inside of one-half of the fish. Put the other half back on top to look like a whole fish again. Spread the rest of the stuffing over the top to completely cover.

Cut the egg whites into thin slices and arrange them on the fish to look like scales. Draw the head of the fish with egg white slices and add a black olive for the eye. Garnish the dish with lemon slices and parsley sprigs and then refrigerate for at least 1 hour before serving. To serve cut into slices. Serve either as an appetiser or as a second course with fresh salads and pickles.

sardine osbane

stuffed sardines

'What brought the basil to the Solanum, what brought the red mullet to the Sardine?'
– If a low-bred person quarrels with a high-bred one, the latter says this to the former Moroccan proverb

The Algerian and particularly Tunisian fish repertoire is extremely rich with sardine-based recipes. They are boiled, fried, baked, cooked with fruits, rice, vegetables etc and they are stuffed – as in this recipe – with bread, parsley and mashed sardines and then coated with flour and egg and fried.

1.5kg (3lb) fresh sardines or other small fish
175g (6oz) stale bread, crusts removed
300ml (1/2 pint) milk
1 egg
3 tablespoons finely chopped parsley
2 cloves garlic, crushed
1 teaspoon salt
1/2 teaspoon black pepper

to fry
Oil
50g (2oz) flour
1 egg, beaten

garnish
1/2 teaspoon each ground coriander, caraway and paprika,
mixed together
Lemon wedges

Scale the fish and then, one at a time, slit along the belly and remove the entrails. Cut off the head, Continue the slit until you can lay the fish flat. Pull out the backbone. When you have prepared all the sardines rinse them thoroughly, inside and out, under cold running water, drain and then pat dry.

To prepare the stuffing place the bread in a bowl and pour the milk over it. When as much as possible has been absorbed squeeze out all the excess moisture and place the bread in a mixing bowl. Add the egg, parsley, garlic, salt, pepper and 2 of the sardines. Knead the mixture until well blended and smooth. Lay out 1 sardine and spread a layer of the stuffing over it. Fold the fish over to form its original shape. Do the same with remaining fish.

Heat some oil in a large frying pan. Taking a few at a time dredge the sardines in the flour, dip in the beaten egg and fry for several minutes, turning once or twice until golden. Remove, drain and keep hot while you fry the remaining fish in the same way. Arrange the fish on a large dish, sprinkle with the mixed spices, garnish with the lemon wedges and serve immediately. **Serves 6**

soles b-chakchouka

sole cooked à la chakchouka

An Algerian way of cooking sole with a rich vegetable base. Serve with a fresh salad or roast vegetables of your choice.

4 tablespoons oil
2 onions, finely chopped
3 large tomatoes, blanched, peeled and chopped
2 green peppers, seeded and finely chopped
1 teaspoon salt
1/2 teaspoon black pepper
Juice 1 lemon
1/2 teaspoon oregano
110g (4oz) butter
110g (4oz) flour
6 medium sole, washed, drained and dried

garnish
1 teaspoon paprika
2 tablespoons finely chopped parsley

Heat the oil in a large saucepan, add the onions and fry until soft. Add the tomatoes, green peppers, salt, black pepper, lemon juice and oregano and mix well. Simmer over a low heat for about 10 minutes.

Meanwhile heat the butter in a large frying pan and spread the flour over a large plate. Dredge the sole, one or two at a time depending on size of pan, in the flour and place in the frying pan. Fry for 4-5 minutes, turning once, until cooked and golden. Keep warm while you fry the remaining fish in the same way.

To serve spoon the vegetable mixture over the base of a large serving dish and arrange the fish over the top. Sprinkle with the paprika and parsley. Just before serving heat the butter in which the fish has been fried until bubbly and pour over the fish. **Serves 6**

shoubia-bil-roz

sepia with rice

Sepia are better known in this country as cuttlefish. This is a classic Algerian dish from Oran and is similar to the Italian *Riso con le seppie*, but minus the wine and the small sac containing a yellowish liquid which is discarded with the ink.

1.5kg (3lb) sepia (cuttlefish)
4 tablespoons oil
1 clove garlic
1/2 teaspoon cumin
1 teaspoon paprika
1 teaspoon salt
1/2 teaspoon black pepper
1/4 teaspoon harissa (see Glossary)
1 bay leaf
1 tablespoon tomato purée diluted in 150ml (1/4 pint) water
900ml (11/2 pints) water
350g (12oz) long-grain rice, rinsed thoroughly under
cold running water and drained

Clean and wash the fish in hot water. With the point of a sharp knife make a long incision down the back of the fish and remove the insides including the sacs containing the ink, the bones and also remove the eyes. Wash again with hot water and drain in a colander. Dry the fish and cut into strips. Place in a large pan with the oil, garlic, cumin, paprika, salt, black pepper, harissa and bay leaf. Fry gently for 30 minutes, stirring occasionally. Add the diluted tomato purée and simmer for a further 10 minutes.

Add the water and bring to the boil. Lower the heat and simmer for 45 minutes. When the fish is tender add the rice, stir well and cook for 15-20 minutes or until rice is cooked and liquid absorbed. Serve hot. **Serves 6**

— rice, noodles and breads —

Couscous is the staple grain of the Meghrib, particularly in Morocco and Algeria, then rice comes a poor second, followed by pastas of varying shapes and sizes. Rice of course is the staple grain of the Arabs and pastas are of European origin – at least those that are sold and used today in Libya and Tunisia.

roz — rice

There are very few rice-based dishes in the Meghrib and what is available is at its best in Libya. I have discarded all European-based rice dishes such as paellas or risottos which are sold in many hotels and restaurants and are often served in middle-class Meghribi homes.

roz klaya

plain rice pilav

This first recipe is for a plain and simple rice pilav in the Middle Eastern style of cooking which is sometimes substituted for couscous grains.

50g (2oz) *smen* or butter or 120ml (4fl oz) oil
350g (12oz) long-grain rice, washed thoroughly under cold running water and drained
1 teaspoon salt
850ml (28fl oz) boiling water

Melt the fat in a large saucepan, add the rice and fry, stirring constantly, until lightly browned. Stir in the salt and boiling water. Allow the mixture to boil vigorously for 3-4 minutes and then lower the heat, cover the pan and simmer for 20 minutes or until the liquid is absorbed.

Turn off the heat, cover the pan with a tea towel and place the lid firmly on top. Leave to 'rest' for 10-15 minutes. Carefully fluff up the rice with a long-pronged fork taking care not to break the grains. Serve as an accompaniment to all kinds of tajines, stews and roast dishes. **Serves 6**

Often 175g (6oz) vermicelli, broken into 5-7.5cm (2-3in) pieces, is added to the pan at the frying stage.

In Roz bil Djelbana, the rice is cooked with peas, artichokes and herbs and spices – thyme, saffron, parsley, bay leaf, salt and black pepper.

roz bil sardine

rice pilav with sardines

This is a particularly tasty rice dish from the Algerian coastline. You need fresh sardines and these can be found in good fishmongers and even a few large supermarkets. Other small fish are equally successful.

120ml (4fl oz) oil
2 onions, coarsely chopped
1 teaspoon salt
1/2 teaspoon black pepper
1/2 teaspoon chilli pepper
1/2 teaspoon paprika
1/4 teaspoon cumin
675g (1¹/2lb) tomatoes, blanched, peeled and chopped
2 bay leaves
300ml (1/2 pint) water
900g (2lb) fresh sardines or other small fish, cleaned and boned
Roz Klaya (as above, but with 3 cloves for extra flavour)

garnish
1 tablespoon finely chopped parsley or tarragon
Lemon wedges

Heat the oil in a large saucepan, add the onions and the spices and fry, stirring constantly until the onions are soft. Add the tomatoes, bay leaves and water and bring to the boil. Lower the heat and simmer for 5 minutes. Place the washed and cleaned sardines in the pan, turn carefully in the sauce and simmer for 20-25 minutes or until the fish are tender.

Meanwhile prepare the rice pilav. When the rice has rested and the fish are cooked spread the rice over a large serving dish, pour the fish sauce over the top and serve immediately garnished with the parsley and lemon wedges. **Serves 6**

roz mubowakh

libyan steamed rice

This dish, also known as *Roz Merga Hamra*, is as popular in Tunisia as it is in Libya from where this recipe comes.

It is prepared, as with couscous grains, in the top half of a couscousier although you can also use a colander which fits snugly onto the top of a saucepan. You can use all kinds of vegetables as well as the ones suggested below. Tunisians like to garnish this dish, with grated cheese (Parmesan or Cheddar).

5 tablespoons oil
900g (2lb) lamb, beef or veal, cut into 5cm (2in) cubes
1 medium onion finely chopped
2 cloves garlic, finely chopped
1 teaspoon paprika

1/2 teaspoon harissa (see Glossary)
1/2 teaspoon baharat (see Glossary)
11/2 teaspoons salt
1/2 teaspoon black pepper
2 large tomatoes, blanched, peeled and chopped
1 tablespoon tomato purée diluted in 5-6 tablespoons water
2-3 carrots, peeled and cut into 1cm (1/2in) rounds
1.2 l (2 pints) water
2 bay leaves
350g (12oz) long-grain rice rinsed thoroughly under cold running water
2 medium courgettes, cut into 1cm (1/2in) rounds
2 potatoes, peeled and cut into 5cm (2in) pieces
50g (2oz) butter

garnish
2-3 tablespoons grated cheese (optional)

Heat the oil in a large saucepan or in the bottom of a couscousier. Add the meat, onion and garlic and fry for about 5 minutes, stirring frequently. Add the paprika, harissa, baharat, salt, pepper, tomatoes and diluted tomato purée. Mix well and fry for 2-3 minutes. Add the carrots, water and bay leaves and bring to the boil.

Meanwhile run some hot water through the rice and place it either in a colander, lined with muslin, which will fit into the top of the saucepan, or into the top of the couscousier. Place on top of the stew and cover. Lower the heat and simmer for about 45 minutes, stirring the rice from time to time.

Add the courgettes and potatoes to the stew. Cut the butter into small pieces and stir into the rice. Continue to cook the stew and steam the rice, stirring the latter frequently for a further 15-20 minutes or until meat, vegetables and rice are tender. To serve spread the rice over a large serving plate, arrange the meat and vegetable mixture on top and sprinkle with the cheese if you wish. **Serves 6**

roz-bil-dagla

rice with dates

'The date palm must have its feet in water and its head in fire' Tunisian saying

There are various versions of this rice pilav, beloved of the Bedouins who prepare it in large quantities for special occasions such as weddings, circumcisions and feast days – especially *Ashoura*, the time of the year when the rich are supposed to give away a tenth of their wealth to the poor. This act is called *Zakat* – the third obligation of a good Muslim.

This rice dish often substitutes for the more traditional one of couscous or *berkoukes* (large grain semolina). It is popular throughout the Arabic-speaking world from Iraq and the Gulf States to Morocco and Mauritania. It is simple to prepare, delightful in appearance and 'different'.

rice pilav
Roz Klaya (page 225)

garnish
50g (2oz) *smen* or butter
50g (2oz) blanched almonds
75g (3oz) stoned dates, chopped
50g (2oz) raisins
1/4 teaspoon ras-el-hanout (see Glossary)
1 teaspoon orange blossom water or rosewater

Prepare the rice pilav following the instructions for Roz Klaya (page 225).

While the rice is resting, melt half the *smen* or butter in a large pan, add the almonds and fry, stirring constantly, until they turn a light golden. Add the remaining *smen* or butter and the dates, raisins and ras-el-hanout. Continue to fry for 3-4 minutes, stirring constantly.

Remove the pan from the heat, stir in the orange blossom water or rosewater. To serve spread the rice over a large serving plate and arrange the nuts and fruit over the top. Serve with all kinds of stews, roasts and grills. **Serves 6**

reuchta — noodles

Noodles, spaghetti, macaroni etc are popular in Libya and Tunisia, due primarily to the Italian influence. This does not mean, of course, that the North Africans were not familiar with pastas – they had been since the days of Rome. It simply means that with the advent of the Italian cultural and political influence in that region early in this century, noodles made rapid strides into the ethnic cuisines.

The housewives in rural areas prepare their own pasta, but more and more now buy the commercial versions. Indeed, Libya is famed for her locally manufactured pastas – originally developed by Italian entrepreneurs. I have given a recipe for preparing home-made noodles in the Glossary. If you wish to cook the authentic way try it, otherwise I suggest you use a commercially prepared version.

reuchta mubowakha

steamed noodles

This is a Libyan recipe from Tripoli. The noodles are steamed over a stew instead of being cooked in water. You can use spaghetti or macaroni instead of *reuchta*.

1 heaped tablespoon *smen* or 20g (³/₄oz) butter
1 large onion, coarsely chopped
900g (2lb) meat (lamb, goat or beef), cut into 5cm (2in) pieces
2 large tomatoes, blanched, peeled and coarsely chopped
2 tablespoons tomato purée diluted in 5 tablespoons water
1.5 l (2¹/₂ pints) water
175g (6oz) chickpeas, soaked overnight in cold water
1 teaspoon salt
1/2 teaspoon paprika
1/2 teaspoon black pepper
1/2 teaspoon baharat (see Glossary)
1/2 teaspoon saffron diluted in 3-4 tablespoons water
450g (1lb) reuchta, spaghetti or macaroni

Melt the *smen* or butter in the bottom half of a couscousier or in a large saucepan. Add the onion and fry, stirring frequently, until soft. Add the meat, chopped tomatoes and diluted tomato purée and cook for a further 5 minutes. Add the water, drained chickpeas and all the spices and stir well. Bring to the boil.

Break the reuchta, spaghetti or noodles into 5cm (2in) lengths and place in the top of the couscousier or into a large muslin-lined colander which fits into the top of the saucepan. Pour a little of the pan sauce over them and stir. Cover and place on top of the stew. Lower the heat and simmer for 20 minutes. Now remove 1 or 2 ladlefuls of the sauce and pour evenly over the pasta, stirring it well so that all the pieces are moistened.

Re-cover and continue to cook for a further 40 minutes or until the meat and chickpeas are tender. During this time moisten the pasta with a little sauce about every 10 minutes. Add a little more water to the stew if necessary. To serve spread the noodles, in a large serving dish and pour the meat and chickpea mixture over them.
Serves 6

You can of course prepare the noodles in the usual way by boiling in water for about 7 minutes, but steaming does give them the flavour of the stew.

reuchta bil khodra

vegetables with noodles

This tasty recipe from Kairawan, Tunisia, is usually served in winter as a thick rich soup. It makes use of cardoons which are very popular throughout the Meghrib, especially with Moroccans. For cleaning and preparing cardoons see *Tajine Kanaria* (page 161). As they are almost impossible to find in this country I suggest you use celery or fennel instead.

5 tablespoons oil
1 onion, finely chopped
900g (2lb) meat, lamb or veal, cut into 5cm (2in) pieces
1$\frac{1}{2}$ teaspoons salt
$\frac{1}{2}$ teaspoon black pepper
$\frac{1}{2}$ teaspoon powdered caraway
$\frac{1}{2}$ teaspoon paprika
1 tablespoon tomato purée diluted in 4 tablespoons water
1.2 l (2 pints) water
2 carrots, peeled and cut into 1cm ($\frac{1}{2}$in) rounds
2 turnips, peeled and cut into 1cm ($\frac{1}{2}$in) cubes
2 courgettes, cut into 2cm ($\frac{3}{4}$in) rounds
450g (1lb) cardoons (or celery or fennel)
450g (1lb) reuchta, spaghetti or macaroni, broken into 2.5-5cm (1-2in) pieces

Heat the oil in a large pan, add the onion and fry, stirring frequently, until soft. Add the meat and spices and fry for a further 2-3 minutes. Add the diluted tomato purée and water and bring to the boil. Lower the heat and simmer for about 40 minutes.

Add the prepared vegetables and simmer for a further 15 minutes. Add a little more water if necessary. Stir in the noodles and simmer for another 10 minutes or until the meat, vegetables and pasta are tender. Serve in individual bowls. **Serves 6**

A little story that makes every Libyan laugh to his heart's content (if not his stomach's!).

One day a Libyan goes to Tunisia on business and is invited to have supper in his host's house. The table is laid, but the host makes an apology. '*Coul el khodar gawe elnadar*' (eating vegetables will improve your eyesight).

The Libyan, who had already noticed that, although the table was rich with all kinds of vegetables, it lacked his, and most Libyans', favourite rice or couscous grains, answers '*Atene el name wen shaalah nama*' (give me grains and let me go blind).

Here, of course, a Libyan will burst into tearful laughter. Apart from the clever rhyming (poetically speaking), practically speaking these lines express a very fundamental point. Tunisia is rich in vegetables and Libya in grains.

dairy produce

'He who blows upon buttermilk will long for it' – Said of a person who has complained of his work, given it up and then longs to return – Moorish saying

Milk is a scarce commodity in the Meghrib, hence there is an obvious shortage of dairy produce, particularly of butter and cheese which are not only difficult to find, but also very expensive.

An interesting point about North Africa is the virtual non-existence of that great Middle Eastern favourite – yogurt. Surprising as it may seem, yogurt is not of Berber or Arab origin. It was created millennia ago by the Aryan tribes who lived on the shores of the Black Sea and in the Caucasus. The Arabs acquired their knowledge of yogurt from the Persians whose ancestors first developed the fermentation of the 'food of the gods'. However, the Meghribian does have curdled milk, though it is different from natural yogurt. It is made in a most interesting way and I give its description here for interest since both the ingredients and the implements are difficult to find in Europe.

The North Africans curdle their milk with artichoke beard which is dried and preserved in sterilised jars. Sometimes fig juice is used. A tablespoon of crushed artichoke beard is dropped into a bowl and covered with lukewarm water. Milk is heated (but not boiled) and flavoured with orange blossom water and sugar. The artichoke beard is then pressed through fine muslin and the juice is mixed with the milk. The milk is then poured into a bowl, covered with a tea towel, put into a warm place (near the hearth) and left to rest for 1-2 hours. Then the bowl is transferred to a cold place until ready to be served.

lben

berber whey

A more interesting way of preparing curds and whey is this, called *lben* – which is Arabic for yogurt (*laban*). This whey is usually prepared in a very special earthenware jar called a khabia, a large pot with a wooden lid through which a long, round stick is pushed.

First the milk is curdled in an earthenware dish which is covered and left for 3-4 days. Then it is transferred to a chkoua. This is a goatskin container which is hung, by both ends, from tree branches. It is swung to and fro for days on end. Indeed it is a tradition that passers-by give a gentle push to the chkoua to keep the fermentation going. A tradition that is still, interestingly enough, kept by the Tartars of Central Asia who prepare a similar drink called kumiss. This movement of the goatskin separates the particles of fat with which butter is made from the milk.

The *lben* is sieved into a jar while the curdled milk will be poured into the *khabia* and stirred with the wooden stick. After some time small lumps of fat will appear on the surface of the lid indicating that the lben is done.

It is served on its own or with a main dish. Often, in the kasbah, people can be seen drinking a glass of white liquid – it is *lben*, not yogurt or milk.

The Berbers also have a strong tradition of drying balls of milk under the sun which they then use in the winter by diluting them with water and either drinking it or adding it to stews.

Cheese is called *jbane*. There is little of it around. One version is similar to the Middle Eastern *labna* (cream cheese) and it is eaten with sugar, honey and sometimes with a few drops of olive oil. A salted version is left to dry in one of their typical alfalfa baskets until it hardens. Sold in the markets, this cheese is usually prepared with goat's milk. Today, butter, cheese and sugar are imported because the locally produced dairy foods are poor and insufficient.

khobz — bread

A few lines from Elias Canetti, one of the great writers of our time, will illustrate all that is sacred, good and eternal about the humble bread.

'In the evenings, after dark, I went to that part of the Djema el Fna where the women sold bread. They squatted on the ground in a long line, their faces so thoroughly veiled that you saw only their eyes. Each had a basket in front of her covered with a cloth, and on the cloth a number of flat, round loaves were laid out for sale. I walked very slowly down the line, looking at the women and their loaves. The smell of the loaves was in my nostrils, and simultaneously I caught the look of their dark eyes. Not one of the women missed me; they all saw me, a foreigner come to buy bread. . . . From time to time each would pick up a loaf of bread in her right hand, toss it a little way into the air, catch it again, tilt it to and fro a few times as if weighing it, give it a couple of audible pats, and then, these caresses completed, put it back on top of the other loaves. In this way the loaf itself, its freshness and weight and smell, as it were, offered themselves for sale. There was something naked and alluring about those loaves; the busy hands of women who were otherwise shrouded completely except for their eyes communicated it to them. "Here, this I can give you of myself; take it in your hand, it comes from mine."

'There were men going past with bold looks in their eyes, and when one saw something that caught his fancy he stopped and accepted a loaf in his right hand. He tossed it a little way into the air, caught it again, tilted it to and fro a few times as if his hand had been a pair of scales, gave the loaf a couple of pats, and then, if he found it too light or disliked it for some other reason, put it back on top of the others. But sometimes he kept it, and you sensed the loaf's pride and the way it gave off a special smell.' The Voices of Marrakech

How can one follow a brilliant description such as that above? But follow I will – if not quite in the same style. Imagine the young teenage girl in her flowing, highly coloured dress walking down the dark, narrow passageways of the kasbah.

She moves gracefully like a swan floating over the coarse earth, balancing on her head a large wooden board filled with smoothly kneaded bread dough. Inside the bakery the master baker, with his young assistants, is busy unloading the dough-rounds and transferring them to a long wooden paddle which he carefully pushes into the dark, burning, cavernous hearth. He quickly pulls back the paddle leaving the bread to cook. The breads bloat, dispersing their aroma, and brown gently. The baker deftly pulls them back. The wooden board is stacked with the warm bread and the young girl returns home zigzagging her way through the throngs in the kasbah.

Most bakeries are small cellars where generations of the same family have plied a living. A master baker is a man of great respect. Early in the morning the young assistant goes round the dark alleys shouting 'The bakery is warm'. Although most families prepare their dough at home they cook them in the local bakery and there are many such edifices, for an old Moroccan saying goes: 'You find five things in the medina – a mosque, a *madrasse* (school), a bakery, a water fountain and a *hamam* (public bath) – at almost every 200 metres.' This was so in the Middle Ages, it is equally so today.

What of the bread?

The most interesting ones are those made with semolina, or a mixture of semolina and flour. Breads are also prepared with barley and millet. In the remote villages one often sees earthenware pots, similar to the Indian *tandoors*, where most of a family's cooking is done. The dough is stuck to the inside of the hot walls of the pot and it slowly bloats and cooks. The bread is then quickly pulled out and eaten warm. This is the *lavash* of the Caucasus, the nan of India and the *mashroudet* of Libya.

hasha

semolina bread

The favourite bread of the Berbers is called *hasha* or *matlou* and is made with semolina. It is a coarse, earthy-flavoured, delicious bread. It is traditionally baked in a tajine (earthenware pot). I suggest you use a baking tray or shallow, round 20-22.5cm (8-9in) cake tin.

15g (1/2oz) fresh yeast or 8g (1/4oz) dried yeast
1 teaspoon sugar
200g (1/2lb) fine semolina
1 teaspoon salt

garnish
Approx 110g (4oz) semolina for coating the bread

Place the yeast and sugar in a small bowl, add 3-4 tablespoons tepid water, stir and leave in a warm place until the mixture begins to froth.

Sieve the semolina and salt into a large bowl, make a well in the centre and pour in the yeast and enough water to make a firm dough. Transfer to a floured working top and knead for 10-15 minutes until you have a soft and elastic dough. Divide the mixture into three and roll into smooth balls. Roll each ball in the semolina until well coated. Sprinkle any remaining semolina over the work top, place the balls of dough on it and cover with a cloth. Leave for about 1-2 hours or until the balls have doubled in size.

Heat the baking tins or trays over a low heat, place the balls of dough, well apart, on the trays, and gently flatten to a 1-2cm (1/2-3/4in) thickness. Prick the top of each several times with a fork. Place in an oven preheated to 350F, 180C, Gas Mark 4 and cook for about 40 minutes or until golden brown. Remove and cool on a wire rack.
Makes 3 loaves

This is the bread that you see people munching either on their way from A to B or, more usually, seated under an olive tree waiting – I know not for what or whom, just patiently waiting. The Meghribi has time to wait . . .

ksra

home-made bread

'The thinnest bread finds itself married to bread' Moroccan saying

In the villages of the High Atlas people have evolved an oven of their own. This is a mud-built, pyramidal-shaped structure about 150cm (5ft) in height with a small opening where wood is burned and where this North African aniseed and sesame seed bread is baked. It is usually made with plain flour, but sometimes (especially in Algeria) equal quantities of flour and semolina are used. The bread has a slight cone shape and is very tasty and aromatic. A similar bread – *Khobz Chir* – is made with barley.

15g (1/2oz) fresh yeast or 8g (1/4oz) dried yeast
1 teaspoon sugar
450g (1lb) fine semolina
450g (1lb) plain flour
1 teaspoon salt
175g (6oz) butter, melted
Rind 1 orange, finely chopped
1 tablespoon green aniseed
2 tablespoons sesame seeds
300ml (1/2 pint) water
2 eggs, beaten

glaze
1 egg yolk, beaten

Place the yeast in a small bowl with the sugar and 3-4 tablespoons warm water. Stir and put in a warm place for about 10 minutes or until the mixture begins to froth.

Sieve the semolina, flour and salt into a large bowl. Make a well in the centre and add the yeast mixture, butter, orange rind, aniseed, sesame seeds and half the water. Mix well and then knead in the beaten eggs and enough of the remaining water to make a soft dough. Add a little more water if necessary. Transfer to a floured working top and continue to knead for about 10 minutes until the dough is smooth and elastic. Divide the dough into three and roll each into a ball. Cover with a cloth and leave for 1-2 hours or until the dough has doubled in size.

Place the balls of dough on lightly greased baking trays and gently flatten until about 2.5cm (1in) thick. Brush the surface of each with the egg yolk. Place in an oven preheated to 350F, 180C, Gas Mark 4 and cook for about 30-40 minutes or until golden. Remove and cool on wire racks. **Makes 3 loaves**

khobz el-aid

festive bread

'To every field of wheat God sends its reaper' Moorish proverb

A particularly popular bread, this is traditionally baked on the first day of the academic year. One small loaf is presented to each pupil on the morrow of his/her school day. It is more of a savoury snack than just a bread as a hard-boiled egg is placed on the centre of the circle of dough and then held in place with thin strips of dough.

15g (1/2oz) fresh yeast or 8g (1/4oz) dried yeast
1 teaspoon sugar
450g (1lb) fine semolina
450g (1lb) plain flour
1 teaspoon salt
110g (4oz) butter, melted
1 egg
1 tablespoon green aniseed, crushed or powdered
300ml (1/2 pint) water
6 hard-boiled eggs
1 egg yolk, beaten
1 tablespoon each of poppy seeds and sesame seeds

Place the yeast and sugar in a small bowl and add 3-4 tablespoons tepid water. Stir and set aside in a warm place for about 10 minutes or until frothy.

Sieve the semolina, flour and salt into a large bowl. Make a well in the centre and add the yeast mixture, butter, egg, aniseed and half the water. Mix well and then slowly knead in enough of the remaining water to make a soft dough. Add a little more water if necessary. Transfer to a working top and knead for at least 10 minutes until the dough is smooth and elastic. Set aside an apple-sized piece of dough to be used for decoration. Divide the rest into six equal lumps and roll into smooth balls. Lightly flour a working top and roll each ball out into a 10-12.5cm (4-5in) round. Cover with clean tea towels and leave for 1 hour to rise.

Take one round and decorate with a pattern or your choice using the prongs of a fork. Brush the surface with egg yolk. Place a hard-boiled egg in the centre of the round. Take the apple-sized lump of dough and roll it out thinly. Cut into 1/2cm (1/4in) wide strips. Place two strips, at right angles to each other, across the egg and press their ends into the edges of the round as illustrated. Coat the strips with egg and sprinkle some of the poppy seeds and sesame seeds all over the loaf. Prepare the remaining loaves in the same way. Place on greased baking sheets and bake in an oven preheated to 350F, 180C, Gas Mark 4 for about 25-30 minutes or until golden. Remove and cool on wire racks. **Makes 6**

kahkis

tunisian savoury bread

'Marry a young woman, even though you will eat bread without yeast'
Moroccan proverb

Kahkis are small dry breads or pretzels. They are of Middle Eastern origin and are really only popular in Tunisia and Libya. They are similar to the classic Egyptian *simit*, Armenian *cheoreg* and Syrian *kaak.* They are ideal for breakfast with coffee and jam and also delicious with cheese. They will keep for a long time in an airtight tin.

This first recipe is a standard one from Tunisia. Compare it with the following one from Libya which is a little more aromatic with the inclusion of cumin and coriander.

15g (1/2oz) fresh yeast or 8g (1/2oz) dried yeast
1 teaspoon sugar
450g (1lb) plain flour
1 teaspoon salt
110g (4oz) butter, melted
300ml (1/2 pint) water

glaze
1 egg beaten

Place the yeast and sugar in a small bowl and add 3-4 tablespoons tepid water. Stir and set aside in a warm place for about 10 minutes or until it begins to froth.

Sieve the flour and salt into a large bowl and make a well in the centre. Add the yeast mixture, melted butter and half the water and mix well. Now knead in enough of the remaining water to form a soft dough. Transfer to a working top and continue to knead for about 10 minutes or until the dough is smooth and elastic. Place in a clean bowl, cover with a cloth and set aside in a warm place for 1-2 hours or until the dough has doubled in size.

Lightly flour a work top and roll out the dough thinly. Cut into oblongs 15 x 10cm (6 x 4in). Roll each one up to form a 10cm (4in) cigarette-shape. Bring the ends together and press one on top of the other to seal. Place on greased baking sheets about 2.5cm (1in) apart. Brush with the beaten egg. Bake in an oven preheated to 350F, 180C, Gas Mark 4 for about 25-30 minutes or until crisp and golden. Remove and cool on a wire rack. **Makes about 40**

kahkis-bil-semsem

sesame sticks

This is similar to the recipe above, but has added spices. The dough is formed into sticks and rolled in sesame seeds.

Dough as above
1/2 teaspoon cumin
1/2 teaspoon coriander
1 egg
50g (2oz) sesame seeds

Prepare the dough as described above, sifting the cumin and coriander into the bowl with the flour. Mix the egg into the dough before adding all the liquid as you may find you do not need so much. Divide the dough into walnut-sized lumps and roll each one out to form a sausage about 1/2cm (1/4in) thick. Cut into 10cm (4in) lengths. Gather up any scraps, roll out and make more sticks.

Roll the sticks in the sesame seeds and place on ungreased baking sheets. Cook in an oven preheated to 350F, 180C, Gas Mark 4 for about 25-30 minutes or until golden. When they are all cooked pile them onto one of the baking trays, turn off the oven and then return the tray of sesame sticks to the oven to dry out. When completely cold store in an airtight container. **Makes about 40**

Superstitions Relating to Bread **It is believed that a negress is imprisoned in the moon because once she defiled a loaf of bread.**

If a person sees a piece of bread lying on the ground, he picks it up, kisses it and places it in a clean and safe place. Some people go as far as to eat a little bit of the same bread, and of course only one person is supposed to portion out the bread at the dining table.

The dish in which bread is kneaded must never be used for any other purpose.

— sauces and pickles —

A very large portion of North African cooking is based on stews – couscous, tajines etc – consequently there are few 'sauces' as we understand them in European cookery. The main sauces can be divided into two categories – 'white' and 'red'. This is particularly so in Algeria and Tunisia and, although they do appear in Morocco and Libya, they are given different names.

marga bayda

This type of sauce has a base of olive oil and *smen* or butter with onions, black pepper, ginger, cinnamon and saffron or turmeric. It is used with couscous dishes and with other meat and vegetable meals.

marga hloua

– sweet sauce –

This sauce has a base of *smen* or butter with saffron, cinnamon and honey or sugar. It is only used with sweet meat dishes such as the sweet tajines.

mhammer

– sauce for roasts –

The base is *smen* or butter with onion, cinnamon sticks and saffron. It is used with roast meats.

plarga hamra

– red sauce –

This sauce has a base of red peppers seasoned with black pepper, cinnamon and salt. It is used with couscous, vegetables and all types of offal and meat.

chte'teha

– hot sauce –

This sauce consists of chilli peppers, garlic, caraway and cumin and is used with fish dishes.

m'chermel

– hot sauce –

This hot sauce is similar to the one above, but incorporates lemon juice or vinegar. It is used with fish and meat dishes.

There are no set rules with these sauces. You can vary both the quantities of the various ingredients as well as the herbs and spices you include. For example you can add parsley, olives, eggs, preserved lemons etc.

There are, however, a few sauces which are 'classics' and which rarely vary. I have included them here, but have discarded two well-known Algerian sauces which are of European (French) origin. These are *Agdat el-Bayd* (sauce mayonnaise) and *Agdat el-Khal* (sauce vinaigrette).

couscous harissa sauce

This sauce is made with harissa (see Glossary). It is perhaps the most widely used and known sauce of Tunisian origin. Harissa can be bought in concentrated form in small tins from most Continental shops, or you can prepare your own following the recipe in the Glossary. Either way you must dilute the harissa with water.

2 tablespoons oil
1 clove garlic, crushed
1 tablespoon harissa
150ml (1/4 pint) water

Heat the oil in a small saucepan, add the garlic and fry for 1 minute. Add the harissa and fry for a further 1-2 minutes. Stir in the water and bring to the boil.

This sauce is enough for 4-6 people as it is very hot and you will probably only need 2-3 tablespoons of it. However if you feel you would like more then simply increase proportions accordingly.

dersa

This similar sauce from Algeria is often used with grills, kababs etc.

2 dried chilli peppers, soaked in tepid water for 1 hour
4 cloves garlic
1/2 teaspoon salt
1/2 teaspoon cumin
120ml (4fl oz) olive oil

Drain the chilli peppers, chop them finely and then crush in a mortar with the garlic, salt and cumin. Place the pulp in a small bowl and mix thoroughly with the oil. You can use this with couscous and tajine dishes as well as many other meat and vegetable dishes.

You can use fresh chillies instead of dried ones and you can substitute the cumin with powdered caraway.

In Morocco some housewives make a mixture of meat broth and chilli peppers mixed with chopped, toasted almonds. This sauce is usually served with Moroccan couscous dishes.

maraga bil-tomatich

tomato sauce

Although a fairly recent arrival in the Meghrib, the tomato has penetrated to the very heart of the culinary culture of the region – as indeed it has virtually throughout the world, barring perhaps those of China and Russia. Interestingly enough Moroccans prefer to use fresh tomatoes while Algerian and Tunisian housewives usually elect to use tomato purée.

There are many tomato-based sauces. I have chosen three to illustrate the wide variety of taste found in the Meghrib. The first one, a standard recipe, is from Libya. Serve with all types of pasta, rice, fried potatoes and other fried vegetables.

675g (1¹/₂lb) tomatoes, blanched and peeled
1 large onion, grated
4 cloves garlic, finely chopped
20g (³/₄oz) butter
1 teaspoon tomato purée diluted in 3 tablespoons water
1 teaspoon salt
¹/₂ teaspoon black pepper
¹/₂ teaspoon dried thyme
5 tablespoons finely chopped parsley
¹/₂ teaspoon powdered bay leaves
1 level teaspoon sugar

Quarter the tomatoes and place in a large saucepan with all the remaining ingredients. Cover the pan and simmer over a low heat for about 20-30 minutes, stirring frequently to prevent sticking. Remove from the heat and leave to cool. Place the mixture in a liquidiser and blend until smooth. Add a few tablespoons of water if necessary. Return to the saucepan and bring to the boil. Serve. **Serves 6**

tomato sauce with meat

This is a Tunisian favourite similar to the one above, but which incorporates minced meat.

1 onion, grated
3 cloves garlic
6 tablespoons finely chopped parsley
3 tablespoons oil
2 large tomatoes, blanched, peeled and chopped

225g (8oz) meat, minced twice
2 tablespoons tomato purée
600ml (1 pint) water
1 teaspoon salt
1/2 teaspoon black pepper
1 teaspoon sweet basil
1 bay leaf
1 level teaspoon sugar

Place the onion, garlic and parsley in a liquidiser and blend until smooth. Add 1-2 tablespoons water if necessary. Transfer this purée to a large saucepan, add the oil and cook for 5 minutes, stirring frequently. Add the chopped tomatoes and simmer for a further 5 minutes.

Add all the remaining ingredients, mix well, cover the pan and cook for 30-40 minutes, stirring occasionally. The meat sauce should be thick and creamy. Serve with pasta and/or cooked vegetables. **Serves 6**

The Tunisians also like to prepare this sauce with boned and flaked fish. Prepare as above, but replace the minced meat with chopped fish flesh.

tomato sauce with harissa

This sauce is a light one which is used throughout the Meghrib, especially with kababs and roast meats.

3 tablespoons oil
1 small onion, finely chopped
1 clove garlic, crushed
2 tablespoons tomato purée
1 teaspoon salt
1/2 teaspoon harissa (see Glossary)
1/2 teaspoon coriander
1/2 teaspoon caraway
600ml (1 pint) water

Heat the oil in a large saucepan, add the onion and garlic and fry until soft. Stir in all the remaining ingredients and bring to the boil. Lower the heat and simmer for about 15 minutes. Some people like to add peas or chopped green peppers or olives to the sauce. **Serves 6**

maraga al-tarkhoun

tarragon sauce

A Tunisian recipe popular throughout the region, which is excellent with fish, but also good with poultry, particularly game, and roasts.

50g (2oz) finely chopped fresh tarragon
25g (1oz) finely chopped parsley
4 tablespoons vinegar
25g (1oz) raisins
2 egg yolks
50g (2oz) butter, melted
1/2 teaspoon salt
1/4 teaspoon black pepper

Place the tarragon, parsley and vinegar in a small saucepan and cook over a low heat for 10 minutes, stirring frequently. Add the raisins, cook for a further 10 minutes and then remove from the heat and reserve.

Place the egg yolks in another saucepan and whisk constantly while you gradually add about three-quarters of the butter. Add the salt, pepper, tarragon mixture and remaining butter and continue to whisk until the sauce has a creamy consistency. Serve immediately.

tabiya

shellfish sauce

This sauce is more of a dressing and is usually served with all kinds of shellfish, grilled prawns or fried fish. It is generously served in all the small seafood restaurants along the Mediterranean coastline of North Africa. It is simply delicious. I have known people who eat this sauce on its own spread on bread.

4 hard-boiled eggs, chopped
110g (4oz) anchovies, finely chopped
110g (4oz) shallots, finely chopped
50g (2oz) fresh chervil, finely chopped
120ml (4fl oz) oil
Juice 1 large lemon
1 teaspoon mustard
1 teaspoon salt
1/2 teaspoon black pepper

Place the chopped eggs in a bowl and mash with a fork until smooth. Add all the remaining ingredients and mix thoroughly. Taste and adjust seasoning if necessary.

chermoula

moroccan marinade/sauce

Chermoula is a much loved marinade/sauce from Morocco. It is equally good with meat (marinate for 1-2 hours before grilling) or fish (30 minutes to 1 hour).

There are several variants of this recipe. The one below is from northern Morocco around the region of Tangier and Ceuta where fish are found in abundance. However, I have been told by those in the know that *chermoula* is 'OK with anything – including camel, gazelle, hedgehog or lizard.' I have tasted camel meat, which was a cross between chicken and goat with a little pork thrown in, but as for the other animal meats I have been told that gazelle tastes a little like rabbit, and about hedgehog and lizard (beloved by the Tuaregs) I know nothing – I have yet to meet my first 'veiled one' from the Sahara.

4 tablespoons oil
75g (3oz) butter
1 onion, sliced into rounds
2 cloves garlic, thinly sliced
50g (2oz) finely chopped parsley
50g (2oz) finely chopped fresh coriander
1 teaspoon black pepper
1/2 teaspoon cinnamon
1/2 teaspoon ginger
1/2 teaspoon saffron diluted in 4 tablespoons water
1/2 teaspoon cumin
1/2 teaspoon thyme
1/2 teaspoon paprika
1 1/2 teaspoons salt
2 bay leaves

Heat the oil and butter in a saucepan and add all the remaining ingredients. Cook over a moderate heat for 12-15 minutes, stirring frequently. Remove from the heat and serve hot or cold. You can now marinate meat or fish in this sauce or you can serve it hot with roasts of your choice.

You can also add to this mixture finely chopped carrots, shallots, celery, 2-3 tablespoons chopped fresh thyme, some powdered cloves or 110g (4oz) raisins. The choice is wide and the sauce is spicy, but mild.

Indeed, spices and herbs have for centuries been associated with medicinal and mystical qualities and potencies. For example the Moor believes that:

coriander causes forgetfulness
mint bears good fortune
fennel steals people's reasoning.

Women associate certain herbs, spices and fruit with love. They believe that at the sight of thyme a man will return to his woman – even against his will – while red pepper will make him forget 100 girls for her. Basil will drive him mad with passion – if he does not see her – while coriander makes him realise he cannot do without her love.

Women employ these plants to capture the love of a man or to return a faithless one.

pickles — torchi

When I asked an elderly woman from Meknez which vegetables and fruits she preserved, she responded 'Olives, peppers, then the others.' When I insisted, politely of course, on knowing what those 'others' were she waved her hands about and expanded with 'Aubergine, onions, beetroot, turnips, carrots, cabbage' – then she stopped, smiled and asked 'Satisfied?' I replied 'Very much, thank you,' and prepared to depart, but suddenly she pulled me by the shirt and added in an apologetic tone, 'I forgot dates, yes, you must remember the dates. *Qtir hlou* (very tasty).'

In the small shops that clutter the kasbabs one finds all the above and many other vegetables pickled and preserved. Certain shops specialise in one or two vegetables. Such an establishment might be one dealing only with olives: olives of different hues, sizes, fresh, stuffed, pickled. The smell and sight are magnificent. Another shop will offer you dates: literally scores of different types in wooden boxes, all glistening with sweetness and emanating a strong reminder of desert and sun.

Olives are the fruit of the Meghrib (see Glossary), followed closely by dates. The fruit and its tree are worshipped by all. There are more proverbs in the Arabic language that exemplify or use the palm tree for a philosophical-moral argument than any other: 'If you are a date-tree, suffer fools to throw stones at you'; 'When the date crop is over everyone mocks at the palm-tree'; and 'In the land of the palm-trees they feed donkeys on dates'.

Maybe so, but not this Libyan recipe for pickled dates. This is worthy of at least a camel!

torchi degli

pickled dates

Dried tamarind can be bought from Indian grocers and some health-food stores. It usually comes in 450g (1lb) packs.

450g (1lb) dried tamarind
900ml (1¹/₂ pints) water
Juice 1 lemon
450g (1lb) dates, stoned and finely chopped
1 clove garlic, crushed
1 teaspoon salt
¹/₄ teaspoon black pepper
¹/₂ teaspoon cinnamon
¹/₄ teaspoon nutmeg

Soak the tamarind in 600ml (1 pint) of the water in a bowl overnight. Strain through muslin and reserve the liquid.

Pour the liquid into a medium saucepan, add the lemon juice and simmer for 5 minutes. Add all the remaining ingredients, mix well, lower the heat and simmer for 10 minutes, stirring frequently. Set aside to cool a little then pour into warm, sterilised jars and seal tightly. Use after 1 week with all kinds of meat and chicken dishes.

felfel masbbar

pickled peppers

After olives, peppers are the most popular vegetable for pickling, cooking or drying. You can find these hot peppers, usually between 5-7.5cm (2-3in) long, in most Indian and continental greengrocers and in many of the larger supermarkets. Try this only if you like your food hot, but other vegetables such as gherkins, small green tomatoes or small onions can be pickled similarly.

I have given several *felfel* recipes since I find this vegetable used at its very best in North Africa. There is a particularly striking resemblance between the food of North Africa and that of Mexico, especially in their use of hot peppers. The relationship, one may argue, stems from Spain, yet Spanish food on the whole is not renowned for its use of felfels.

dja'bout mkhalel

– chilli peppers in vinegar –

This first recipe, from Eastern Morocco, uses small, hot chilli peppers.

900g (2lb) small green chilli peppers
2 tablespoons salt
Malt vinegar

Wash and dry the chillies and, using scissors, trim off all but 1/2cm (1/4in) of each stem. With a large needle or the point of a sharp knife pierce each chilli several times. Pack in one large or two small sterilised jars. Add the salt and fill to the brim with the vinegar. Seal the jar(s) tightly and store in a cool place for 2-3 weeks.

felfel khdar msabbar fe-zait

– green peppers in olive oil –

900g (2lb) green peppers, washed and dried
900ml (1 1/2 pints) vinegar
2 tablespoons salt
Olive oil

Cut the stems off the peppers, deseed and then slice into 2cm (3/4in) thick rounds. Pour the vinegar into a large bowl, add the salt and stir well. Add the pepper rounds and leave to rest overnight. Stir occasionally.

Transfer the rounds to a colander and leave to drain for 1-2 hours. Pack the rounds into sterilized jars, fill to the brim with olive oil and seal tightly. Use after 4-5 days.

felfel mechwi msabbar

– grilled and pickled peppers –

For this recipe you need good, firm green or red peppers with thick flesh.

900g (2lb) green or red peppers
1 tablespoon salt
1 teaspoon black peppercorns
Olive oil

Grill the peppers over charcoal or under a grill, turning several times until the skins are browned and wrinkled. As they are cooked place them in a large saucepan, keeping the lid on to retain their heat. When all the peppers are done you will notice that they have shed their juice. Carefully pour this liquid into another pan.

Taking one pepper at a time remove the skin by first wetting your fingers in the juice, cutting out the stem and seeds and then gently pulling away the outer skin. It should come off easily. Drop the skinned peppers into a colander, sprinkle with the salt and leave to drain for 1-2 hours.

Now arrange the peppers in small sterilised jars, scattering in a few peppercorns at random, filling them to within 5cm (2in) of the brims. Pour pepper liquid into jars and if necessary add enough oil to completely cover the peppers. Seal tightly. Stand the jars on a grid or something similar in a large saucepan and add enough cold water to come three-quarters of the way up the jars. Bring to a quick boil and then simmer for about 1 hour. Switch off the heat and leave the jars in the pan to cool. When cold remove jars, dry and stone.

torchi bil-khodra

mixed vegetable preserve

This recipe is typical. The vegetables used can be varied and very often turnips, green tomatoes, shredded cabbage leaves and small aubergines are used.

900g (2lb) green peppers, washed, stemmed, seeded and halved lengthways
3 green chilli peppers, halved lengthways
2 small cucumbers, with a few incisions in each, and halved
1 fennel bulb, quartered
2 carrots, peeled, quartered lengthways and halved
2 sticks celery, cut into 7.5cm (3in) pieces
110g (4oz) young French beans, topped and tailed
12-15 green olives, crushed in a mortar
Salt
About 1.2 l (2 pints) water, boiled and cooled
About 1.8 l (3 pints) vinegar

Place all the prepared vegetables in a large bowl, sprinkle with 1 tablespoon salt and cover with cold water. Leave to soak overnight. Drain in a colander and then pack into two large sterilised jars. Sprinkle 1 tablespoon salt into each jar. Pour half the boiled and cooled water into each jar and then fill to the brim with the vinegar. Seal tightly.

Store for at least 2-3 weeks, and rinse the vegetables under cold running water before serving.

badendjel mragad fe-khal

aubergines in oil

'With slowness the aubergine is eaten' – the growing of the aubergine requires unusual attention – Moroccan expression

For this recipe you need small aubergines not more than 7.5-10cm (3-4in) in length. These are often to be found in Indian and Middle Eastern groceries.

Sometimes 110g (4oz) ground, green shelled walnuts are added to the mixture. Blanched, ground almonds are equally suitable.

900g (2lb) small aubergines, washed and stalks removed (do not peel)
1 clove garlic, finely chopped
1/2 teaspoon chilli pepper
1 teaspoon salt
1 tablespoon powdered caraway
About 450ml (3/4 pint) water, boiled and cooled
600ml (1 pint) vinegar
2 tablespoons salt

Make an incision about 2.5cm (1in) long down each aubergine. Place the aubergines in a large saucepan half filled with boiling water and simmer for 12 minutes. Drain. Mix the garlic, chilli pepper, salt and caraway together in a small bowl and push a little of the mixture into each incision.

Arrange the aubergines in a large sterilised jar. Mix the water, vinegar and salt together and pour over the aubergines. Seal tightly and leave for at least 2-3 weeks in a warm place before serving. Rinse under cold water just before serving.

lim mragad

lemon preserve

Limes and lemons are preserved in a most unusual manner as this recipe from Algeria shows. It is equally popular in Morocco where it is better known as *Msir* or *Hamid Msyiar*. Very simple to prepare, these lemons often appear in tajine dishes. They give an extraordinarily refreshing taste to the dish in question.

The quantities given here can be increased, but do use small jars as once a jar has been opened the fruit will not last for very long. Always refrigerate the jars after they have been opened.

900g (2lb) firm, juicy lemons, washed and dried
5-6 tablespoons salt
About 600ml (1 pint) water, boiled and cooled

Stand each lemon upright and slice them through and down to form quarters, but do not cut right through – the quarters should remain attached at the base. Salt the insides generously and then reshape the lemons by pressing them gently into their original form.

Pack the lemons tightly in small sterilised jars and fill to the brim with the water. Seal tightly and store in a dry place for 3-4 weeks.

limoun keshara

– preserved lemon rind –

The lemon rinds are placed in a colander, sprinkled with salt and left overnight. In the morning they are stored in sterilised jars and sealed for 5-6 weeks, by which time they have turned a brownish colour. Before using soak for 2-3 hours in cold water changing it at least once. Some people like to add olive oil to the jars.

For 900g (2lb) lemons use 110g (4oz) salt and about 450ml (3/4 pint) oil. For use see relevant recipes.

— sweets, pastries and desserts —

'A lucky year is that in which the fruits of the earth are without worms.'

A basket of fresh fruit filled with oranges of many kinds, cherries, tangerines, dates of many colours and shapes, grapefruit, grapes, figs, apricots, pomegranates, etc etc.

A basket of fresh fruit is God's gift to man. It is the colour, music and the wealth of the very soil.

A basket of fresh fruit is the finish to a copious meal.

A basket of fresh fruit is what most Meghribians are served for their dessert, for North African cuisine is rather limited in pastries and desserts. Most 'traditional' pastries are either of Middle Eastern or Spanish origin, while many of the sweets sold in the pâtisseries are of French extraction. Indeed, one can wander from cake shop to cake shop in search of authentic Meghribi pastries to no avail. The confectioners only make and sell French-inspired sweets. It is only in the medinas and homes that one finds the rich, honey-soaked cakes and pastries which are filled with almonds or dates and sprinkled with rose-flower water.

Cakes and pastries were traditionally prepared for special occasions such as births, weddings, anniversaries, saints' days, pilgrimages etc. Some are still associated solely with one particular celebration while others have, over the years, become everyday fare.

kesksou bil rommane

couscous with pomegranates

This first recipe, the simplest dessert, is made with 'left-over' couscous grains and pomegranates. You can't get any simpler than that!

175g (6oz) couscous, steamed (see page 134)
2-3 large pomegranates, halved
110g (4oz) icing sugar
2 tablespoons olive oil
2 tablespoons orange blossom water

Remove the seeds from the halved pomegranates and place in a large bowl. Add all the remaining ingredients and mix well. Refrigerate for at least 2 hours before serving.
You can also add 50g (2oz) raisins, 50g (2oz) chopped nuts and 1/2 teaspoon cinnamon to give this sweet more 'body' and interest. **Serves 6**

sellou

ramadan sweet

A more elaborate, yet essentially simple, dessert is this Moroccan *sellou* which is traditionally served during the month of Ramadan, to celebrate a child's birth or at weddings. The sweet is piled up like a cone and decorated with almonds.

It is rumoured amongst the palm trees that *sellou* has manifold miraculous qualities. It eases the break of the Ramadan fast, strengthens and invigorates children, cures maladies and enriches a new mother's milk!

225g (8oz) plain flour, sifted
110g (4oz) sesame seeds
75ml (2 1/2fl oz) oil
50g (2oz) blanched almonds
2 teaspoons cinnamon
1/2 teaspoon aniseed
1 grain mastic (gum arabic), crushed with a little sugar
25g (1oz) butter
75g (3oz) honey

50g (2oz) caster sugar
Whole almonds or hazelnuts

Place the flour in a large saucepan and cook over a low heat, stirring constantly for 15-20 minutes or until it is lightly browned. Transfer to a large bowl.

Put the sesame seeds in a small pan and cook over a low heat, stirring constantly until they are golden. Remove from the heat. Heat the oil in a small pan, add the almonds and fry until golden. Remove with a slotted spoon and place in a blender. Reserve the oil. Add the sesame seeds to the almonds and blend to a powder. Add this to the flour together with the cinnamon, aniseed and powdered mastic and mix well.

Melt the butter and honey in a small pan, pour into the flour mixture and add the reserved oil. Mix with a wooden spoon until all the liquid has been absorbed. Transfer this mixture to a serving plate and pile it into a cone shape. Sprinkle generously with the sugar and decorate with the nuts. Serve with tea or coffee. **Serves 4-6**

farka

couscous gâteau

A Tunisian recipe where the steamed couscous is moistened with syrup, mixed with dates and nuts and shaped into a cake. Serve warm or cold.

225g (8oz) couscous
90ml (3fl oz) oil
175g (6oz) sugar
300ml (½ pint) water
110g (4oz) fresh or dried dates, stoned
50g (2oz) walnuts
25g (1oz) pine kernels
25g (1oz) blanched almonds, roasted
25g (1oz) hazelnuts, roasted
25g (1oz) pistachios
1 teaspoon cinnamon

garnish
25g (1oz) granulated sugar

Spread the couscous out on a large plate, sprinkle with a little warm water and work lightly between your fingers so that each grain is separated, moistened and beginning to swell. Leave for 10 minutes. Pour half the oil over the couscous and again work it lightly between your fingers.

Meanwhile half fill the bottom of a couscousier, or a large saucepan over which a colander will fit snugly, with water and bring to the boil. When the couscous is ready pour it into the top part of the couscousier. If using a colander first line it with fine muslin or a tea towel because the holes may be too large. Cover and steam the couscous for 45 minutes, stirring occasionally.

Meanwhile prepare the syrup by placing the sugar and water in a small pan, bringing to the boil and simmering for 15 minutes. Remove from the heat.

Reserve 6 dates for decoration and chop the remainder finely. Reserve a few nuts for decoration, then place the rest in a blender and grind.

When the couscous is ready turn it out on a large baking sheet and pour the syrup over it. Stir it well and leave for about 15 minutes, stirring every few minutes to help it absorb the syrup. Rub between your fingers to break up any lumps and return to the top of the couscousier or the colander. Check that there is enough water in the bottom pan and then steam for 30 minutes.

Place the chopped dates on the baking tray and pour the couscous over them. When cool enough to handle pour the rest of the oil over the couscous, add the ground nuts and half the cinnamon and mix well with your fingers breaking up any lumps. Transfer the mixture to a large serving dish and shape into a cake. Halve the reserved dates and decorate together with the remaining nuts. Sprinkle with the remaining cinnamon and the sugar. **Serves 6**

basbousa-bil-zabadi

libyan semolina cake

'Li andu smid, kul yom id' – For him who has semolina, every day is a feast.

This dessert from Libya is similar to countless others from Egypt and the Middle East where desserts with semolina, or a mixture of flour and semolina, are often called *halawats* ('sweet' in Arabic). These sweets come with a variety of nuts, fruits, sometimes with cheese or cream.

Serve cold with tea or coffee.

75g (3oz) blanched almonds
225g (8oz) unsalted butter
150ml (1/4 pint) yogurt
110g (4oz) sugar
175g (6oz) fine semolina
1 teaspoon baking powder
1 teaspoon vanilla essence

syrup

225g (8oz) sugar
150ml (1/4 pint) water
2 tablespoons lemon juice

garnish
About 14 blanched almonds, toasted

First prepare the syrup by placing the sugar, water and lemon juice in a saucepan and bringing to the boil. Lower the heat and simmer for 10 minutes or until the syrup forms a slightly sticky film on a spoon. Set aside to cool. Toast the almonds under the grill until golden and then chop finely.

Melt the butter in a saucepan. Pour the yogurt into a large bowl and add half the melted butter, the sugar, semolina, baking powder, vanilla essence and chopped almonds. Mix thoroughly until well blended.

Grease a round baking tin about 20cm (8in) in diameter, pour in the mixture and smooth over with the back of a spoon. Bake in an oven preheated to 400F, 200C, Gas Mark 6 for 20 minutes. Remove from the oven, cut into 5cm (2in) lozenge shapes and press one toasted almond into the centre of each lozenge. Return to the oven and bake for a further 15 minutes or until the surface is golden brown. Remove from the oven and pour the cold syrup evenly over the surface. Return to the oven for a further 3-4 minutes.

Warm the remaining butter, remove the *basbousa* from the oven and pour the butter evenly over the surface. Leave to cool. You can serve with cream if you wish.
Makes 12-14 pieces

m'hencha

almond pastry

Let us now turn to the next important ingredient in the preparation of many North African sweets – almonds. The region is rich with these. There are two varieties – sweet and bitter. North Africa is a major exporter of this fruit and it is also much used in her cooking, notably in her pastries. One such dish is *M'hencha* which, translated, means 'the serpent'. This sweet is made with *ouarka* pastry (see Glossary) which is filled with almonds, coiled around like a serpent and generously sprinkled with icing sugar. This is a classic from Fez.

As for *M'hencha*, she (the serpent is female!) is magic to look at and to taste. You can use commercial filo pastry instead of *ouarka* if you wish. It can be bought from most Middle Eastern and continental shops.

12 sheets filo pastry trimmed to about 30 x 20cm (12 x 8in)
1 egg yolk

filling
225g (8oz) ground almonds
175g (6oz) icing sugar
2 tablespoons orange blossom water
50g (2oz) unsalted butter, melted
2 egg yolks, beaten
2 teaspoons cinnamon

garnish
2-3 tablespoons icing sugar
1 teaspoon ginger

Place the almonds, sugar, orange blossom water and butter in a saucepan and mix to a paste. Cook over a low heat for 10-15 minutes or until the sugar dissolves. Remove from the heat, add one of the egg yolks and the cinnamon and mix thoroughly.

Stack the filo sheets on top of each other on the work surface and cover with a cloth. Remove one sheet and place on the work surface with one of the longer sides nearest you. Brush all over with some of the remaining egg yolk and lay another filo sheet on top of it. Take one sixth of the almond paste and arrange it in a ridge 3.5cm (11/2 in) in from the edge nearest you and reaching right to the two shorter ends. Fold the 3.5cm (11/2in) of pastry over the filling and then roll up in the rest of the pastry. Brush the top edge with egg to stick it down. Repeat with remaining filo and filling. Brush a round baking tray about 22.5-25cm (9-10in) in diameter with a little melted butter. Take one roll and very carefully curl it around itself to form a coil. Do this gently or the filling will burst out. Place this coil in the middle of the tray. Take another roll, place one end of it next to the outside end of the coil on the tray and coil this roll around the first one. Continue using the rolls to extend the coil, sticking the ends of each roll together with a little egg yolk. When all the rolls are on the tray brush all over with the remaining egg yolk.

Bake in an oven preheated to 375F, 190C, Gas Mark 5 for about 30 minutes or until golden. Remove from the oven and leave to cool. Lift onto a serving plate, sift the icing sugar evenly over the top and decorate with the cinnamon. **Serves about 8**

bastela ktefa

moroccan pancakes

A real classic of the Moroccan cuisine, *bastelas* are paper-thin, crispy pancakes, golden in colour and fragrant with orange blossom water. They are traditionally stacked in a pile with the various layers separated by a finely chopped almond mixture or a milk and sugar mixture. This sweet makes a majestic finish to a sumptuous meal.

If you wish you can substitute the milk mixture with a cream filling and the recipe for it follows the one below.

In recent years this dessert has been much popularised throughout the Arab world as well as in Israel where many Moroccan Jews have settled.

The various stages for preparing this sweet can be done in advance and assembled just before serving.

**24 sheets *ouarka* pastry (see Glossary and double the quantities) or
24 sheets filo pastry**

milk mixture
**1.2 l (2 pints) milk
110g (4oz) sugar
3 level tablespoons rice flour
120ml (4fl oz) orange blossom water
25g (1oz) butter**

almond mixture
**Oil for frying
175g (6oz) blanched almonds
75g (3oz) sugar**

First prepare the milk mixture by placing the milk and sugar in a saucepan and bringing slowly to the boil, stirring constantly until the sugar dissolves. Meanwhile place the rice flour in a small bowl, add a few tablespoons of the milk and mix to a liquid paste. Stir into the boiling milk, add the orange blossom water and butter, lower the heat and simmer for about 5 minutes, stirring constantly until the mixture thickens. Remove from the heat and set aside to cool.

Heat a little oil in a small pan, add the almonds and fry until golden. Remove with a slotted spoon and drain on kitchen paper. Chop the almonds finely and mix in a small bowl with the sugar.

When you have prepared all the *ouarka* sheets use a 22.5cm (9in) round plate as a pattern to trim off the uneven edges of each sheet. Stack these 22.5cm (9in) round sheets of pastry on top of each other and cover with a tea towel. (Stack, cut and cover the filo sheets similarly.) Heat some oil in a large frying pan and then, one by one, fry the sheets of dough until golden, turning once. Remove with a slotted spoon and drain on kitchen paper. Pile on top of each other on a baking sheet and keep warm in a low oven until ready to serve.

To assemble the sweet place two sheets of *bastela* on top of each other in a shallow serving dish. Sprinkle with a little of the almond mixture. Add another sheet of pastry and spoon a little of the milk mixture over it. Add another sheet and sprinkle with almonds. Continue these layers of pastry, milk and almonds until all the pastry is used up. Pour the remaining milk mixture over the top and serve immediately. **Serves 6**

bastela min krema

pancakes with cream

This sweet is even more spectacular than the one above, being decorated with poached egg whites and caramelised sugar.

24 sheets *ouarka* pastry (see Glossary and double the quantities) or
24 sheets filo pastry

cream mixture
3 eggs, separated
1.2 l (2 pints) milk
1 tablespoon vanilla essence
175g (6oz) caster sugar
1 tablespoon flour

almond mixture
Oil for frying
175g (6oz) blanched almonds
110g (4oz) sugar

garnish
2 tablespoons caramelised sugar or just slightly melted honey

First prepare the cream filling. In a bowl whisk the egg whites until stiff. Place the milk and vanilla in a saucepan and bring to the boil. Remove from the heat. Take spoonfuls of the egg white and drop them into the milk. Cook for 1-2 minutes, carefully remove with a slotted spoon and reserve.

In another bowl whisk the egg yolks and sugar until white. Gradually whisk in the flour and continue to beat for 2-3 minutes. Slowly stir some of the hot milk into this mixture until runny and then stir it into the milk pan. Return the pan to the heat and simmer for 3-4 minutes, stirring constantly. Remove from the heat and leave to cool.

The mixture should be light and almost liquidy. If it thickens when cold stir a little cold milk into it. Set aside.

Heat a little oil in a pan, add the blanched almonds and fry until golden. Remove with a slotted spoon and drain. Chop finely and mix in a small bowl with the sugar. Prepare and layer the pastry as described in the recipe above, substituting the cream for the milk. When you have used the last sheet of pastry, and poured any remaining cream over it, arrange the poached egg whites on top and dribble the caramelised sugar or liquid honey over them. Serve immediately. **Serves 6-8**

kab-el-ghazel

gazelle horns

Continuing on the theme of almonds this recipe, another classic of Berber origin popular in Morocco and Algeria, is dedicated to the horns of the favourite Arab animal – the gazelle, a symbol of grace, beauty and gentleness. It is also one of the few pastries that can be found in most pâtisseries.

225g (8oz) plain flour
2 tablespoons melted butter
3 tablespoons orange blossom water

filling
225g (8oz) ground almonds
175g (6oz) icing sugar, sifted
1 teaspoon cinnamon
2-4 tablespoons orange blossom water

First prepare the filling by mixing the almonds, icing sugar and cinnamon together in a bowl. Add enough of the orange blossom water to bind the mixture together. Knead until smooth. Divide into 16 balls. Roll each ball into a sausage about 5cm (2in) long which is thicker in the middle and tapers at both ends. Set aside.

Sift the flour for the pastry into a mixing bowl, make a well in the centre and add the melted butter and orange blossom water. Gradually fold the flour in and then, little by little, add just enough cold water to form a dough. Place on a work surface and knead for at least 20 minutes until the dough is very smooth and elastic. Divide into 2 balls. Take one ball of dough and roll it out into a strip about 10cm (4in) wide and at least 75cm (30in) long. You will find that you will be able to stretch the pastry by wrapping first one end of the pastry and then the other over the rolling pin and pulling gently.

Arrange 8 of the almond sausages on the pastry in a line about 3.5cm (1¹/₂in) in from the long edge nearest you, leaving about 5cm (2in) between each sausage. Fold the pastry over the sausages to enclose them completely. Cut down between each sausage. Taking 1 pastry at a time press the edges together to seal in the filling. Trim the pastry edge to a semi-circle, but do not cut too close to the filling or the edges will be forced open during cooking and the filling will ooze out. Crimp the edges with the prongs of a fork. Now pinch the pastry up to form a steep ridge and gently curve the ends around to form a crescent shape. Repeat with the remaining pastries. Repeat with remaining ball of dough and almond filling.

Place on greased baking sheets and cook in an oven preheated to 350F, 180C, Gas Mark 4 for 20-30 minutes or until a pale golden colour. Cool on wire racks and store in an airtight tin when cold. **Makes 16**

kab-el-ghazel mfenned

Prepare the pastries as above and when they are cooked soak them in orange blossom water and then roll in icing sugar until they are completely coated and are snow-white in colour.

ghoriba louze

almond pastries

Originally of Middle Eastern origin (*ghorayebah,* lover's pastries), these sweets are made with flour or semolina, almonds and butter. The pastries vary in size and shape, some are ball-shaped, others flat and still others patterned. Sometimes they are stuffed with dates or other fruits.

Sometimes the name *ghoriba* is given to pastries which are also called *magroud.* These are lozenges made with semolina and almonds. I have included several of these pastries as they are very typical of the region. They keep well – if you can refrain from eating them! This first recipe is from Algeria.

1 small egg
150g (5oz) icing sugar, sifted
Finely grated rind of 1 lemon
1 teaspoon vanilla essence
1/4 teaspoon cinnamon
225g (8oz) ground almonds
Plain flour

garnish
Icing sugar

Place the egg and icing sugar in a large bowl and whisk until the mixture is white. Add the lemon rind, vanilla essence and cinnamon and mix well. Now stir in the ground almonds. Gather the mixture up in a ball and knead for a few minutes until soft and workable. If you find it a little sticky add just enough plain flour to bind.

Lightly oil your palms and shape the mixture into balls slightly larger than a walnut. Pass each ball from one palm to the other gently flattening it into a round 6-7.5cm (2½-3in) in diameter. Put on greased baking trays about 2.5cm (1in) apart. Sprinkle each round generously with icing sugar and bake in an oven preheated to 350F, 180C, Gas Mark 4 for 15-20 minutes or until golden. Remove and set aside to cool. Store in an airtight tin when cold. **Makes 12-14**

ghoriba mughrabi

moroccan pastry balls

225g (8oz) unsalted butter, melted and white sediment discarded
110g (4oz) icing sugar, sifted
350g (12oz) fine semolina (or plain flour)

garnish
Icing sugar

Pour the melted butter into a large bowl and add the icing sugar and semolina. Knead together until it forms a ball. Set aside for 2-3 hours.

Knead vigorously until the mixture becomes soft. Take a walnut-sized lump and pass it from one palm to the other until it becomes very soft. Place on a buttered baking tray. Continue until you have used up all the mixture.

Bake in an oven preheated to 350F, 180C, Gas Mark 4 for 10-15 minutes or until golden. Remove and leave to cool. When cold cover generously with icing sugar and store in an airtight tin. **Makes about 30**

helilat el-louze

crescent-shaped pastries

'Everyone rakes the embers to his own cake' Libyan saying

These small, crescent-shaped pastries are from Algeria. They are excellent with tea or coffee and will keep for a long time in an airtight tin.

110g (4oz) butter
110g (4oz) caster sugar
Zest of 1 lemon
110g (3oz) ground almonds
1 large or 2 small eggs
225g (8oz) plain flour

garnish
50g (2oz) vanilla sugar or caster sugar

Place the butter and sugar in a large bowl and beat until smooth, pale and creamy. Add the lemon zest, ground almonds and egg(s) and stir until well blended. Sift in the flour and knead with your hands to form a smooth ball of dough. Take walnut-sized lumps, roll into 7.5cm (3in) long sausages and curve into crescent shapes.

Place on greased baking sheets and brush with egg yolk. Bake in an oven preheated to 350F, 180C, Gas Mark 4 for 15 minutes or until very lightly golden. Remove from the oven and sprinkle with sugar. Bake for a further 10 minutes or until golden. Cool on wire racks. **Makes 25-30**

magroud el-assel

honey pastries

A speciality from Tlemcen (Algeria). These pastries are filled with almonds or dates. I have given recipes for both.

450g (1lb) medium or fine semolina
110g (4oz) unsalted butter or half butter and half olive oil
1 teaspoon salt
1/2 teaspoon saffron diluted in 2 tablespoons water
2 tablespoons orange blossom water
90-120ml (3-4fl oz) water

almond filling
225g (8oz) ground almonds
110g (4oz) caster sugar
1/2 teaspoon cinnamon
2 tablespoons orange blossom water

to cook
1 egg yolk, beaten
Oil for frying

to serve
350g (12oz) honey, melted

First prepare the filling by mixing all the ingredients together in a bowl. Set aside.

Place the semolina in a large bowl, add the butter (or butter and oil mixture), salt and saffron and rub in until all the semolina grains are coated with fat. Add the orange blossom water and, little by little, the water and knead until the mixture is smooth and holds together. Divide the pastry into 4 balls. Lightly flour a work surface and roll one of the balls out into a sausage about 22.5cm (9in) long and 2.5cm (1in) in diameter.

Flatten the sausage slightly until about 7.5cm (3in) wide. Arrange one-quarter of the almond filling in a ridge along the centre of the dough. Bring the two long edges together and pinch firmly to close. Roll until smooth and then gently flatten until 3.5cm (1¹/2in) thick. With a sharp knife cut diagonally into 3.5cm (1¹/2in) pieces. Brush the ends where the filling shows with the egg yolk. Repeat with remaining dough and filling.

Heat some oil in a large saucepan, add a few of the pastries and fry for about 10 minutes, turning once, until golden. Remove with a slotted spoon and drain on kitchen paper while you fry the remaining pastries in the same way.

Melt the honey in a saucepan, add a few pastries at a time, turn in the honey and remove to a plate with a slotted spoon. Return each one to the honey once more and then arrange on a serving plate. The pastries are often sprinkled with coarsely chopped almonds or pistachio nuts. **Makes 24**

maġroud qsentina

– constantine-style stuffed lozenges –

Here the *magroud* are stuffed with dates.

Dough as above

date filling
350g (12oz) stoned dates
2 tablespoons water
4 tablespoons oil
2 teaspoons cinnamon
1 tablespoon grated orange rind
Pinch ground cloves

Place all the filling ingredients in a liquidiser and blend to a purée. Transfer to a bowl and prepare the *magroud* as described above.

An alternative way of cooking these pastries is to place them on greased baking sheets and cook in an oven preheated to 300F, 100C, Gas Mark 4 for about 20-25 minutes or until golden.

Libyans like to sprinkle these honey-soaked pastries with sesame seeds.

bradj

semolina cakes filled with dates

From Algeria, land of the fierce Tuareg horsemen, about whom a folk song says:
'Kou Kaa sits among the women
like a grape vine shoot among tamarisks,
Kou Kaa sits among the women
like a date palm rising among iraks.'
The Unwritten Song

450g (1lb) medium or fine semolina
175g (6oz) unsalted butter, melted
2 tablespoons orange blossom water
About 120ml (4fl oz) water

filling
225g (8oz) stoned dates
1/2 teaspoon cinnamon
Pinch powdered cloves

First prepare the filling by chopping the dates and placing in a small saucepan with the cinnamon and cloves. Add a few tablespoons of water and cook over a low heat, mashing constantly with a wooden spoon until the mixture resembles a purée and the water has evaporated. Shape into a ball and set aside to cool.

Place the semolina in a large bowl, make a well in the centre and pour in the melted butter. Rub in with your fingers until all the semolina grains are coated with fat. Add the orange blossom water and enough of the water to make the mixture hold together. Knead until the dough is smooth. Divide into two equal balls. Take one ball and place on a work surface. Place the ball of dates on top and then cover with the second ball of dough. Now gently flatten until you have a round flat cake about 1cm (1/2in) thick. Cut into 2.5cm (1in) squares or lozenges.

These pastries are traditionally cooked in a tajine over a low heat. You can use a large frying pan instead. First brush the pan with a little butter and then arrange as many pastries as possible in it. Cover and fry over a low heat for about 20 minutes, turning once until both sides are golden. Remove and place on a wire rack to cool while you fry any remaining pastries in the same way adding a little more butter if necessary. **Makes about 30 pieces**

ghoriba dial jeljlane

sesame seed cakes

A Moroccan recipe which is very tasty, especially if you like sesame seeds.

225g (8oz) sesame seeds
110g (4oz) plain flour, sifted
175g (6oz) caster sugar
1 tablespoon baking powder

Zest of 1 lemon
3 eggs
2 teaspoons vanilla essence
50g (2oz) icing sugar

Place the sesame seeds in a saucepan and cook over a medium heat, stirring constantly until golden. Set aside to cool. Place the flour in another pan and cook in the same way. Place the flour in a large bowl.

Place the sesame seeds in a blender and reduce to a powder. Add to the flour and stir in the sugar, baking powder and lemon zest. Make a well in the centre and add the eggs and vanilla. Mix well and then knead for about 10 minutes or until you have a smooth dough. Oil your palms and then divide the dough into walnut-sized balls.

Spread the icing sugar out on a large plate. Taking one ball at a time press it into the icing sugar and flatten to 1cm (1/2in) thick. Arrange on greased baking sheets, about 1cm (1/2in) apart, with the sugar side up. Bake in an oven preheated to 350F, 180C, Gas Mark 4 for about 15 minutes or until lightly golden. Remove and cool on wire racks. Serve with tea or coffee. **Makes 18–20**

briouat

almond pastries in honey

'The almond tree lies, but the apricot speaks the truth' – Alluding to the fact that almond trees sometimes blossom in summer without giving any fruit
Moorish saying

This is a Moroccan speciality which is made with *ouarka* pastry (see Glossary). However you can use commercial filo pastry instead. There are two fillings, but the first is by far the most popular.

7-8 sheets filo pastry
25g (1oz) butter, melted
450g (1lb) honey

almond filling
450ml (3/4 pint) oil
225g (8oz) blanched almonds
175g (6oz) icing sugar
1 teaspoon cinnamon
1 large or 2 small eggs
3 tablespoons orange blossom water

First prepare the filling by heating 150ml (1/4 pint) of the oil in a saucepan. Add the almonds and fry until golden. Remove with a slotted spoon and drain on kitchen paper.

When cool place the almonds in a blender and grind. Reheat the oil, add the ground almonds, icing sugar and cinnamon and mix well. Remove from the heat, add the egg(s) and blend thoroughly. Stir in the orange blossom water and set aside to cool.

Place the sheets of filo on top of each other and cut into oblongs about 15 x 10cm (6 x 4in). Stack on top of each other and cover with a cloth to prevent them drying out. When the filling is cold take one rectangle of filo and lay it out with one of the short sides nearest you. Take 1 heaped teaspoon of the filling and place it on the filo near the end closest to you. Spread it out with the back of the spoon. Fold in the end nearest you and then fold over the two long sides. Brush a little melted butter over the other short end and then fold the filling over. The end result should be a flat parcel shape. Continue with remaining pastry and filling.

Place the remaining 300ml (½ pint) oil in a large saucepan and heat. Place the honey in another pan and bring just to the boil. Turn off the heat. Drop a few of the *briouats* into the hot oil and fry for about 1 minute, turning once, until golden. Remove with a slotted spoon and drop into the honey. Leave for 2-3 minutes then remove with a slotted spoon and place on a serving dish. Continue to fry the *briouats* and soak them in the honey. Every now and then return the honey to the heat. Do not boil for too long or it will become too thick. Allow the pastries to cool and then serve. **Makes about 36**

rice filling

225g (8oz) long-grain rice, rinsed thoroughly, or ground rice
6 tablespoons milk
110g (4oz) sugar
25g (1oz) butter
2 tablespoons orange blossom water

If using long-grain rice boil it in water for 15-20 minutes or until tender and then drain. Cool and squeeze tightly to extract any moisture. Place the cooked rice or ground rice in a saucepan with the milk, sugar and butter and cook over a low heat until the mixture forms a homogeneous mass. Stir in the orange blossom water and set aside to cool. Proceed as with the recipe above. With this filling do not dip in honey, but sprinkle with icing sugar and cinnamon instead.

halouet hab elmalouch

cherries in almond paste

Tunisians have a particular gift for presenting their pastries and desserts. I well recall my first encounter with the magical world of Tunisian pastries in downtown Paris, the twilight district of Belville, several years ago. We (my wife and I) were visiting a relative's shop when I noticed the nearby display counter of a small, dark pâtisserie where rows and rows of pastries glittered and sparkled. It was pure magic! Never had I seen such unashamed abundance of colour – green, pink, snow-white, deep dark chocolate, golden etc *ad infinitum*; all vying with each other.

We resolved to take some back with us to England. On the last day of our tour I drove to the little shop in Belville, and bought two of each kind of pastry, one to eat on the way, the other to dissect and analyse.

But this first encounter of mine with Tunisian pastries ended in tragedy. The weather that summer was far too good to be true. It was a record-breaking heat that accompanied us from Paris to London. My wife and I tried hard to save the decomposing sweets boiling in the boot of our car. We ate them as fast as possible, but to no avail. Back home the boxes were partially empty and what was left of the pastries was in a sad, crumbling state of discoloration and disintegration. I was unable to analyse them, but my palate and stomach assured me nevertheless that they were excellent!

One of those sweets that I recall is this recipe for glacé cherries coated in an almond paste. It is an attractive little sweet that children and grown-ups will love. It is ideal with coffee after a meal.

225g (8oz) ground almonds
175g (6oz) icing sugar
1 egg white
Few drops of red colouring
225g (8oz) whole glacé cherries

garnish
Apple stalks (saved over several days if you can) or slivered almonds
25g (1oz) icing sugar

Place the ground almonds, icing sugar and egg white in a bowl and mix well. Add a few drops of red food colouring and knead until you have a soft, deep pink paste. Take a marble-sized lump, flatten it a little and then mould it around a cherry. Place on a well buttered baking sheet. Continue until you have used up all the paste and cherries. Place an apple stalk or slivered almond in the top of each ball to resemble a stem.

Place the baking sheet in an oven preheated to 250F, 130C, Gas Mark 1/2 and bake for 15 minutes. Remove from the oven and sprinkle with the icing sugar. When cold place in small 'sweet' paper cases. **Makes about 35**

halwa ditzmar

date slices

Another similar sweet is made with dates – the fruit of the desert.
This recipe is from Libya, but it appears in most North African sweet tins.
Use fresh fruit for it if you can.

450g (1lb) dates, stoned
450g (1lb) figs, peeled and mashed
225g (8oz) walnuts, coarsely chopped
50g (2oz) coarsely grated chocolate (optional)
1/2 teaspoon aniseed
3 tablespoons honey

Place all the ingredients in a large bowl and mix well. Pack the mixture firmly into a 15 x 15cm (6 x 6in) cake tin, cover and store. To serve cut into small squares and serve with tea or coffee. Will keep for about 1 week. **Makes 20-30 pieces**

fustukh mahchi

stuffed walnuts

'Among the walnuts only the empty ones speak' – Those who boast and are arrogant make most noise.

Another of those magical Tunisian sweets.

225g (8oz) ground almonds
1 egg yolk
1 tablespoon orange blossom water
About 275g (10oz) halved walnuts

syrup
225g (8oz) sugar
150ml (1/4 pint) water
Juice 1/2 lemon

garnish
50g (2oz) granulated sugar

First prepare the syrup by placing the sugar, water and lemon juice in a saucepan and bringing to the boil. Lower the heat, simmer for 5 minutes and remove from the heat.

Place the ground almonds, egg yolk and orange blossom water in a bowl. Adding 1 tablespoon of the syrup at a time, knead until you have a firm paste. Take 1 teaspoon of the paste and roll into a ball. Place between 2 walnut halves and press together. Continue until you have used up all the paste.

Return the syrup to the heat and simmer until it forms a sticky film on a spoon. Remove. Spread the sugar over a plate. A few at a time, drop the stuffed walnuts into the syrup, turn until well coated and then lift out with a fork and roll in the sugar. Place on a large plate and leave to dry for 24 hours. Arrange in small paper cases and serve. **Makes about 40**

snobar mahchi

– stuffed pine kernels –

This is a variation of the above.

110g (4oz) ground almonds
225g (8oz) pine kernels
1 egg yolk

syrup
175g (6oz) sugar
90ml (3fl oz) water
Juice 1/2 lemon

First prepare the syrup by placing the sugar, water and lemon juice in a saucepan and bringing to the boil. Lower the heat, simmer for 5 minutes and remove.

Place the almonds in a bowl. Coarsely chop half the pine kernels and add to the almonds together with the egg yolk. Adding 1 tablespoon of the syrup at a time knead the mixture to a smooth firm paste. Roll the paste into small walnut-sized balls. Spread the remaining pine kernels out on a plate.

Return the syrup to the heat and simmer until it forms a sticky film on a spoon. Drop the balls into the syrup and turn to coat. Lift them out with a fork and roll in the pine kernels. Place n a plate and leave to dry for 24 hours. Serve in small paper cases.
Makes 20-24

seferjal

quince with honey

Although fruits are usually eaten raw there are a few cooked fruit desserts of interest. Such a one is this recipe from Algeria. It is essentially a paste of quinces flavoured with honey, spices and nuts. It makes a delicious spread and is ideal for breakfast with bread and a glass of mint tea.

You can also prepare apples and hard pears in the same way.

900g (2lb) quinces
6 tablespoons honey (or more, to taste)
1 teaspoon cinnamon
1/4 teaspoon ground nutmeg
2 tablespoons ground almonds
1 teaspoon oil

garnish
1 tablespoon finely chopped walnuts or pistachios

Half fill a large saucepan with water and bring to the boil. Quarter the quinces without peeling or coring them and drop them into the water. Simmer for 5-10 minutes or until the fruit is tender. Remove the pieces with a slotted spoon and set aside to cool. Place in a sieve set over a bowl and rub through with a wooden spoon. Add the remaining ingredients to the pulp and mix well. Transfer to a serving plate, sprinkle with the chopped nuts and set aside to cool. **Makes about 450g (1lb)**

tuffah bil assel

apples with honey

'If you find a meal of fruit at the gate of the orchard don't proceed'
Moroccan proverb

In this recipe, for apples stuffed with cream and honey, quinces or pears could be used instead. The recipe is from Libya, but has definite northern Mediterranean influences – notably Italian. It is a fine dessert.

600ml (1 pint) water
225g (8oz) sugar
Few drops red food colouring
6 large cooking apples, peeled and cored

garnish
300ml (1/2 pint) double cream, whipped, or clotted cream
6 cherries, fresh or glacé

Place the water and sugar in a large saucepan and bring slowly to the boil, stirring constantly until the sugar has dissolved. Add 3-4 drops red food colouring and stir well. Arrange the apples in the liquid and cook over a low heat for 15-20 minutes or until tender – the amount of time will vary depending on size of apples. Do not overcook. Baste the apples frequently with the syrup while cooking so that they become an attractive pinkish-red colour. Lift from the pan with a slotted spoon, place in a serving dish and set aside to cool.

When cold fill the centre of each apple with cream and top with a cherry. Refrigerate until ready to serve. Meanwhile simmer the pan juices for a further 15 minutes or until they thicken. Just before serving heat this syrup and pour over the apples. Serve immediately. **Serves 6**

haloua rhifa

wedding honey cake

This extremely sweet dessert, a speciality of Fez in Morocco, is always served at weddings and often at other socially important occasions such as births and circumcisions. Always prepared in large quantities, the recipe is for 10-12 people. It is eaten with small spoons.

You can buy mastic (gum arabic) from many Indian and Middle Eastern grocers.

450g (1lb) plain flour
1 teaspoon salt
Oil for frying
1.5kg (3lb) honey
5 tablespoons orange blossom water
1 teaspoon powdered mastic
75g (3oz) butter, melted

Sift the flour and salt into a large bowl and make a well in the centre. Little by little add enough tepid water to make a soft dough. Transfer to a work surface and knead for at least 20-25 minutes until you get a very elastic and pliable dough. Rub your palms with oil and roll the dough between them until well coated with the oil. Divide the dough into small balls about the size of a small apple. Heat some oil in a large frying pan. Lightly flour a work top, take a ball of dough and roll out very thinly. Carefully transfer to the hot oil and fry for a few minutes, turning once until evenly golden. Remove, drain and reserve. When all the dough is cooked in the same way crush these sheets of dough into a bowl.

In a large saucepan bring half the honey to the boil and stir in the crushed dough, orange blossom water and powdered mastic. Simmer for 2-3 minutes and then pour the mixture into a large shallow pan. Set aside for 24 hours.

Next day bring the rest of the honey to the boil in a small pan and pour over the cool paste, stirring constantly. Pour mixture into a sieve to drain off any excess oil. Pile the *haloua* into a cone shape on a large plate and top with the butter. **Serves 10-12**

About weddings and marriages, there is a story that clearly reflects the power of poetry in the daily affairs of the Berber tribes of the High Atlas. Though almost completely illiterate the peasants had a great respect for men of letters and especially so for storytellers, poets and letter writers.

Children were married at a very early age and often within the same clan or family to 'keep the money in the family'. Zineb was thus married to her cousin who unfortunately soon left her, departing to another village. After a time Zineb's mother went to see the well-known poet-philosopher Ali-on-Yousef, asking for help. Next morning Ali went to see the young man, called him over and spoke:

'Poet of the Ail-Jennad,
I sing of men of distinction.
Young Zineb
White as a fine linen
Is desired by all
Including the mighty chiefs.

She has paid me one douro
Fed me with the finest spices.
Her vows still belong to you
In the name of Allah, reciprocate,
For men of noble race
Prefer death to disgrace.'

Poèmes Kabyles Anciens

These last two lines of Ali's have become part of the psyche of Meghribi society. As for the young man; he returned to his Zineb. Such was once the power of poetry! Perhaps our marriage guidance counsellors, as well as men of the church, should bring a little more poetry into everyone's lives.

feqas

crispy moroccan biscuits

There are several versions of these small titbits. I have given the recipe for the traditional plain feqa as well as for one with raisins and almonds.

15g (1/2oz) fresh yeast or 8g (1/4oz) dried yeast
1 teaspoon sugar
350g (12oz) plain flour
1 teaspoon salt
110g (4oz) icing sugar, sifted
50g (2oz) butter, melted
4 tablespoons orange blossom water
1 tablespoon aniseed
1 tablespoon sesame seeds, grilled until golden
1/2 teaspoon powdered mastic

Place the yeast and sugar in a small bowl with 4-5 tablespoons tepid water and set in a warm place until it begins to froth. Sift half the flour into a large bowl and add the salt and the yeast mixture. Gradually add enough water to make a soft dough. Transfer to a floured work surface and knead for 10-15 minutes. Place in a large clean bowl, cover with a tea towel and set aside in a warm place for 2-3 hours.

Sift in the remaining flour and add the rest of the ingredients. Knead for a further 10 minutes. Break off apple-sized lumps and roll into sticks about 20cm (8in) long and 1-2cm (1/2-3/4in) in diameter. Place well apart on greased baking sheets and set aside in a warm place for a further 2-3 hours. Prick with a fork in several places and bake in an oven preheated to 350F, 180C, Gas Mark 4 for 7-9 minutes until half baked. Do not let them brown. Remove from the oven and leave to rest for 5-6 hours. Some people like to leave them overnight. Cut into 2.5cm (1in) pieces, place on a large baking sheet and continue to bake in an oven preheated to 350F, 180C, Gas Mark 4 until golden. Remove, cool and store in an airtight container. **Makes about 80-100**

feqa'min zbib

raisin and almond biscuits

'He became a raisin before he was a grape' – Said of a student who pretends to be a scribe.

110g (4oz) icing sugar
2 eggs
2 tablespoons melted butter
2 tablespoons oil
110g (4oz) ground almonds
1 teaspoon vanilla essence
110g (4oz) raisins
350g (12oz) plain flour, sifted

Sift the icing sugar into a large bowl, add the eggs and whisk until creamy and pale. Add the melted butter and oil and whisk for a further 2-3 minutes. Add the almonds, vanilla and raisins and mix well. Gradually stir in the flour, gather up the mixture and knead for a few minutes until smooth. Divide the dough into five balls and place on a lightly floured work surface. Lightly flour your palms, take one ball and roll it into a sausage about 15-20cm (6-8in) long and 2.5-3.5cm (1-1¹/₂in) thick. Repeat with remaining balls.

Place on a lightly greased baking tray and bake in an oven preheated to 350F, 180C, Gas Mark 4 for 12-15 minutes. Remove from the oven before the surface changes colour. Set aside until completely cold. When completely cold cut the sausages into thin rounds about ¹/₂-1cm (¹/₄-¹/₂in) thick. Spread the pieces over 2 large baking sheets and cook in an oven preheated to 350F, 180C, Gas Mark 4 for a further 15-20 minutes or until golden, turning once. Remove and, when completely cold, store in an airtight tin. **Makes 80-100 pieces**

gioush

sesame-honey fritters

Rich, honey-soaked sweets from Morocco. They are a dark golden brown in colour, plaited and coated in sesame seeds. These kinds of pastries are known throughout North Africa. They are rather heavy and sticky, but very tasty.

225g (8oz) plain flour
Pinch salt
15g (1/2oz) fresh yeast or 8g (1/4oz) dried yeast
1 teaspoon sugar
110g (4oz) sesame seeds
50g (2oz) butter, melted
120ml (4fl oz) oil
4 tablespoons wine vinegar
1/2 teaspoon saffron
1 tablespoon orange blossom water
1 egg yolk
Oil for frying

syrup
450g (1lb) honey

garnish
25g (1oz) sesame seeds

The night before sift 110g (4oz) of the flour and the salt into a bowl. Place the yeast, sugar and 3 tablespoons of warm water into a small bowl, stir and leave in a warm place for about 10 minutes or until the mixture begins to froth. Pour into the sifted flour and gradually add about 120ml (4fl oz) tepid water to form a soft dough. Knead vigorously for 10-15 minutes. Shape into a ball, place in a clean bowl, cover with a damp cloth and leave in a warm place overnight.

The next day spread 110g (4oz) sesame seeds over a large baking tray and cook in the oven or under the grill turning several times until evenly browned. When the sesame seeds have cooled a little, place in a blender and grind until fine.

Sift the remaining flour into a large bowl, add the ground sesame seeds, the melted butter and the oil. Heat the wine vinegar in a small saucepan, remove and stir in the saffron and orange blossom water.

Place the yeast dough on a lightly floured work surface and punch down. Make a well in the centre, add the vinegar-saffron mixture and knead well. Add the egg yolk and knead for a further 2 minutes. Now add the sesame dough and knead one into the other for about 10 minutes.

Sprinkle the work surface and a large baking tray with flour. Break off a walnut-sized lump of dough and roll into a ball. Now roll it into a pencil-thin strip about 25cm (10in) long. Break off one-third of the strip and press one end of it into the centre of the remaining length. Now plait the three lengths together, press the ends together, and place on the baking tray. Repeat until you have used up all the dough. Cover the *gioush* with a cloth and leave to rest for 20 minutes.

Heat enough oil in a large saucepan to deep fry and add 2-3 *gioush*. Fry gently for 10-15 minutes until brown and crisp. Turn gently halfway through the cooking time. Meanwhile heat the honey in a saucepan wide enough to take the *gioush*. When cooked lift them out with a slotted spoon, drain and place in the honey. Leave to steep for 2-3 minutes, turning once. Keep the honey over a very low heat while the *gioush* are in it, but remove from the heat at other times or else it will become too thick and toffee-like. Remove from the syrup, place on a tray and sprinkle generously with sesame seeds. Cook the remaining *gioush* in the same way. Serve cold. **Makes 16-20**

haloua dial jeljlane

This sweet is made with a mixture of sesame seeds, almonds, mastic and honey. Simple to prepare, these sweets are very rich with a distinctive sesame seed flavour.

450g (1lb) sesame seeds
225g (8oz) blanched almonds, coarsely crushed
675g (1¹/₂lb) honey
¹/₂ teaspoon powdered mastic

Toast the sesame seeds and almonds as described in the recipe for *Ghoriba dial Jeljlane* (page 264.

Bring the honey to the boil in a medium saucepan and simmer for a few minutes. When you can dip a spoon into it and the honey trickles down in threads then it is time to stir in the mastic, sesame seeds and almonds. Stir well, simmer for 5 minutes and remove from the heat. Pour into a well-oiled, shallow tin and set aside to cool. Cut into squares or lozenges.

sfenaj

raisin doughnuts

Throughout Morocco and Algeria, in small, starkly-lit shops, you can see men seated behind a large cauldron of boiling oil into which they drop round doughs made of flour or fine semolina. They are then retrieved and usually thrown into an equally large pan of syrup or honey. These are doughnuts, the progenitors of the many varieties now available throughout the world. The very first doughnuts were prepared by the ancient Egyptians and I am sure that the Meghribi version is equally as old.

I have included three recipes. This first is from Morocco and Algeria, the second – Yo-yo – is from Tunisia and the third is from Libya. They are all simple, light and tasty and well worth trying. Often eaten for breakfast or with afternoon tea, but children will love them at any time.

15g (1/2oz) fresh yeast or 8g (1/4oz) dried yeast
1 teaspoon sugar
300ml (1/2pt) tepid water
450g (1lb) plain flour
Pinch salt
50g (2oz) raisins
Oil for frying

garnish
Icing sugar or syrup

Place the yeast and sugar in a small bowl with a little of the tepid water, stir and put in a warm place until it begins to froth.

Sift the flour and salt into a large bowl and stir in the raisins. Make a well in the middle and pour in the yeast mixture. Now gradually mix in enough of the water to make a soft dough. Gather into a ball and knead on a lightly floured work surface for at least 10 minutes until soft and elastic. Put in a clean bowl, cover with a tea towel and set aside in a warm place for about 2 hours or until the dough has doubled in size.

Heat enough oil in a large saucepan to deep-fry. Lightly flour your hands and then divide the dough into 16 lumps. Taking one at a time roll it into a ball, flatten it a little and make a hole through the centre with your index finger. Cook a few at a time in the oil over a medium heat for 8-10 minutes, turning once, or until golden. Do not fry too quickly or the insides will not be thoroughly cooked. Remove with a slotted spoon and drain on kitchen paper.

These doughnuts are served either dredged with icing sugar or coated in syrup or Cherbet (see Glossary for its preparation). Serve warm or cold. **Makes 16**

yo-yo

This is the Tunisian version of this sweet and it has, of course, to include eggs which are undoubtedly one of the national 'foods' of the land. Indeed government circles were so worried about the vast use (or misuse) of eggs that President Bourgiba himself had to go on television in 1977 to warn people against the obsessive consumption of eggs.

The clever combination of orange and honey gives off a wonderful aroma and makes a really delicious doughnut.

2 eggs
3 tablespoons oil
3 tablespoons fresh orange juice
1 tablespoon finely grated orange rind
350g (12oz) sugar
225g (8oz) plain flour
2 teaspoons bicarbonate of soda
300ml (1/2 pint) water
2 teaspoons lemon juice
110g (4oz) honey
Oil for frying

Place the eggs, oil, orange juice and rind in a large bowl with 50g (2oz) of the sugar and whisk until well blended. Gradually sift in the flour and bicarbonate of soda and beat until the mixture is smooth. Set aside while you prepare the syrup.

Place the water in a saucepan with the remaining sugar and the lemon juice and bring to the boil. Simmer for 5-7 minutes. Add the honey, stir until it dissolves and then simmer for a further 5 minutes. Set aside while you prepare the doughnuts.

Heat sufficient oil in a large pan to deep-fry. Lightly flour your palms and shape the dough into 5cm (2in) balls. Taking one at a time pass between your palms to flatten slightly and make a hole through the centre with your index finger. Drop two or three doughnuts at a time into the oil and cook gently for 7-10 minutes, turning once until golden and cooked through. Remove with a slotted spoon and drain on kitchen paper. Drop into the warm syrup and leave to soak up as much syrup as possible. Arrange on a large plate and serve warm. **Makes about 12**

lugmat-el-quadi

– libyan-style doughnuts –

The Quadi (Muslim judge) has such a sweet tongue that folk named these small, roundish syrup-soaked doughnuts in his honour – it sometimes pays to be a waffler!

These doughnuts are known throughout North Africa and the Middle East. They originated way back in the ninth and tenth centuries in Baghdad where poets sang the praises of such delights while chefs rivalled each other in creating more and more exotic versions. This recipe is very good, easy to prepare, and your guests will be enchanted.

15g (¹/₂oz) fresh yeast or 8g (¹/₄oz) dried yeast
1 teaspoon sugar
150ml (¹/₄ pint) tepid water
225g (8oz) plain flour
Pinch salt
150ml (¹/₄ pint) milk
Oil for frying

syrup or cherbet
See Glossary

garnish
¹/₂ teaspoon cinnamon

First prepare the syrup according to instructions in the Glossary. Place the yeast and sugar in a small bowl and dissolve in a little of the tepid water. Set aside in a warm place for about 10 minutes or until the mixture begins to froth.

Sift the flour and salt into a large bowl and make a well in the centre. Pour the rest of the water and the milk into the yeast mixture and beat thoroughly. Gradually add this liquid mixture to the flour and gradually beat the flour in until the dough is soft and smooth, but not quite a liquid. Cover and leave to rise in a warm place for an hour. Beat the dough at least once more and leave to rest again. The final dough should be a well fermented, sponge-like mixture.

Heat enough oil in a large saucepan to deep-fry. When the dough is ready, wet a teaspoon, take a teaspoonful of the mixture and drop it into the oil. An alternative method is to take up some of the dough in one hand and gently squeeze it up between thumb and forefinger to form small walnut-sized balls. Fry a few at a time over a medium heat, turning occasionally until golden, crisp and cooked through. Remove with a slotted spoon and drain on kitchen paper. Dip immediately into the cold syrup and lift out with a slotted spoon. When they are all ready arrange them in a pyramid on a large plate. Sprinkle with the cinnamon and serve while still warm. **Makes 20-24**

dableh

rosette-shaped doughnuts

These doughnuts are much simpler fare than those above. The dough is cut into thin strips, coiled up and fried in hot oil. The sweets are then dipped in syrup and garnished with sesame seeds – delicious!

This recipe is from southern Libya and the doughnuts are traditionally served during the nights of Ramadan, as indeed are the Moroccan version called *Chebbakiya*.

450g (1lb) plain flour
Pinch salt
2 teaspoons baking powder
120ml (4fl oz) oil
2 eggs
150ml (1/4 pint) water
Oil for frying

syrup or cherbet
See Glossary

garnish
50g (2oz) sesame seeds

Prepare the syrup according to instructions in the Glossary.

Sift the flour, salt and baking powder into a large bowl. Make a well in the centre and add the oil and eggs. Now gradually add enough of the water to form a soft dough. Transfer to a lightly floured work surface and knead for at least 10 minutes until smooth and pliable. Cover with a tea towel and leave to rest for 30 minutes.

Divide the dough into two balls. Lightly flour the work surface, take one ball and roll it out into a thin rectangle. Sprinkle the surface with a little flour and leave for 10 minutes while you roll out the other ball of dough. Fold the first rectangle in half bringing the two short ends together. Fold over again and again until the strip of dough is too thin to fold over. Cut this roll of dough crossways into 1/2cm (1/4in) thick slices. Taking one slice at a time undo it and then coil it up loosely. Repeat with the other sheet of dough.

Heat enough oil in a large saucepan to deep fry. Fry a few at a time in the oil, turning once until golden. Do not worry if the end unravels slightly because it helps the inside coils to cook. Remove with a slotted spoon, drain on kitchen paper and dip into the syrup. Remove with a slotted spoon, arrange on a large plate and sprinkle generously with the sesame seeds. **Makes about 50**

jabane

moroccan nougat

This nougat is of very ancient origin. It is traditionally served during the Mimouna festivities which are held on the last night of the Jewish feast of Passover and is followed by trips to the countryside or the seashore.

There was – and I hope still is – a charming tradition in Morocco when the first leavened breads after the Passover were offered to the Jews by their Muslim neighbours. Usually a large tray would be decorated with, as well as the bread, fish, milk, butter, mint tea and flowers. It was then taken to the Jewish homes with an uproarious accompaniment of '*You-You*' and the traditional '*Terbel*' – may you have a long life – was exchanged.

Jabane always appears on the Mimouna table and there are many varieties of this nougat. The finest and, I hasten to add, the most expensive are found in the small shops of Fez. They come made with honey, almonds, strawberries, mixed nuts etc. The Spanish *turrones* originate from this humble sweet of Morocco.

450g (1lb) sugar
300ml (1/2 pint) water
1 level teaspoon powdered mastic
2 egg whites
110g (4oz) blanched almonds, roasted in a hot oven for 5-7 minutes

Place the sugar in a large saucepan with the water and bring to the boil, stirring constantly until the sugar dissolves. Stir in the mastic and continue to simmer until the syrup thickens into threads, but remove from the heat before it begins to change colour. Leave until lukewarm.

Meanwhile beat the egg whites until stiff and then gently pour the lukewarm syrup onto them. Beat with a wooden spoon for at least 20 minutes and then stir in the almonds. Pour this white mixture into a well-oiled tin or dish and set aside to cool and harden. Cut into small squares or lozenges.

— drinks —

'Bring wine!' I said;
But she that sped
Bore wine and beautiful roses.
Now from her lips
Sweet wine I sip,
And from her cheeks red, red roses.

Ibn Zaidun of Cordoba

The poet in the splendour of Cordoba or Seville may have sung of wine and roses in the spirit of Omar Khayyam, Haffiz or Saidi of Persia, the progenitors of all that was 'original' in Islamic poetry of the times, but (and this is a reluctant 'but') he drank cool, gurgling spring water once the muse had departed.

The Moors were never accustomed to imbibing intoxicating drinks. Firstly there was no such tradition amongst them and secondly the prophet forbade their use. The Koran stated:

'Believers, wine and games of chance, idols and diving arrows are abominations devised by Satan. Avoid them so that you may prosper. Satan seeks to stir up enmity and hatred among you by means of wine and gambling and to keep you from the remembrance of Allah and from your prayers. Will you not abstain from them?'

Wine, simply, was the product of colonisation. The French, Spanish and Italians in turn created vineyards and a North African viniculture industry that flourished till the day the *colons* packed their bags and went home.

The North African does not drink. The vineyards are shrinking in acreage. The EU has implemented restrictions, forbidding non-Common Market wines from easy access to member countries, and the once prosperous Algerian wine industry is now in the doldrums. However, there are still some excellent wines produced all over the Meghrib (barring Libya). Algeria in particular is still a major force with new markets such as the former USSR importing her produce.

The North African is a sober person. The only drunks found tottering in the bars and streets of any city will inevitably be westerners – celebrating Bacchus and the relative cheapness of his produce.

❧

chay

tea

The drink of North Africa is tea – mint tea! For millennia the Meghribi used to drink an infusion of mint and absinthe or wormwood (medicinally used since the days of the Pharaohs, but now illegal because it affects the nervous system). Tea was unknown. Then, in 1854, during the Crimean War when several European and Baltic lands were closed to British goods, the indefatigable English traders looked around for new markets. Many trading posts such as Tangier, Mogador and Constantine had their warehouses filled to capacity with the finest quality teas from India, China and Ceylon. It is not known who it was who first suggested mixing tea with mint leaves, but the idea caught on and spread until today mint tea has become the symbolic beverage of North Africa – soaked in mysticism and socio-religious mannerisms.

The tea should be green. Very good quality green tea is often prepared without mint – none of your teabags please! The mint varies both in taste and appearance from region to region, but the mint *Mentha vinais* is the most sought after. That from the regions of Meknes and Zerbou is claimed to be of the finest quality with firm stalks and dark green, highly flavoured leaves. The mint should always be fresh.

Indeed one of the most charming scenes that a tourist encounters upon his/her first arrival in the Meghrib is the sight of men or children (but hardly ever women) walking through the streets with large bunches of fresh mint under their arms – just like the Frenchmen with their baguettes.

The meal is over, the guests are discussing the merits of such and such a dish, the affairs of state and of man in general. The table has been cleared. 'Praised be the Lord for his generosity' whispers an old man stroking his greyish beard. '*Hamdoulah*' (thanks to the lord) echo all.

The tea-drinking rite commences. The host sits in front of the tea table – in its humblest form a small wooden tray 60cm (2ft) in diameter, set on three legs; in wealthy homes elaborately decorated samovars, large teapots and cups. Yet the ritual is always the same. The host first rinses the teapot with boiling water. He then proceeds to put 2 or 3 teaspoonfuls of green tea in each teapot (there are usually 2), adds a little water and then throws it all away. He next adds sugar to taste, but often a little too sweet for western tastes and then fills the teapots with boiling water. This is the first stage of tea-making and one that is much appreciated by 'tea experts'.

The tea is left to breathe for 2-3 minutes, then the host stirs it with a spoon, tastes it, half fills a cup for each guest and offers it. While the guests drink their tea the host commences the second stage of tea-making – the addition of mint. He puts in a handful of the finest quality fresh mint leaves, having first crushed them in the palms of his hands and then adds a teaspoon of green tea and sugar. The teapots are refilled with boiling water, covered and the tea left to breathe for a few minutes. The host then stirs the pots with a spoon, gently crushing the mint which should always remain at the bottom of the pot, tastes and then refills his guests' cups. The usual procedure is for a guest to drink 3 cups of tea.

Wherever one travels in the Meghrib, from the humblest house to government offices, mint tea is ritually served. It is indeed the 'coffee' of the orient. The barber, shoemaker, carpet dealer etc will put you at ease with a glass of sweetened mint tea. Whether a bargain is struck or not, mint tea is given with a smile and genuine sincerity i.e. no strings attached.

In the recipe below I have given proportions for 6 people.

2 tablespoons green China tea
6 tablespoons sugar (adjust to taste)
1 large handful of mint leaves (stalks removed)
6 cups boiling water

One after the other place all the ingredients in a large teapot, pouring the boiling water in last from a height of 30-45cm (1-1¹/₂ft).

Add, if available, orange blossoms (petals only) or 1-2 tablespoons orange blossom water – these give that extra flavour to the tea. If you don't have these try chopping a little orange peel into small pieces and adding to the pot.

Mix the tea well then fill a glass and pour it back into the pot. Now pour the tea into glasses or cups, serve hot and thank the Lord!

In Libya mint tea is not as universally drunk as in the rest of the Meghrib. Libyans prefer plain 'black' tea.

In the Touat region of south-west Algeria mint tea is prepared in two pots, one containing only sugar and mint leaves, the other the tea and boiling water. The cups are filled half and half from these two pots. Inevitably roasted peanuts are served with this *Tzay Touat*. Peanuts are of course a basic ingredient in the cuisine of Central Africa.

In some homes in winter, when mint is difficult to find, other herbs are added to the tea. Of these the most popular is still absinthe although verbena, marjoram, sweet basil and orange flowers are used. In Libya cardamom and cloves are often used in winter time for medicinal purposes.

qahwah

coffee

Coffee arrived in the Meghrib, not as one would naturally assume, with the Arabs, but with the Ottomans. Undoubtedly a few Berbers who had travelled to Arabia on pilgrimage would have drunk this 'black mud', but it was during the occupation of their lands by the Ottoman Turks from the seventeenth century onwards that 'Turkish' coffee was first introduced. Turkish coffee, better known as 'Moor's' coffee in Tunisia or *Qahwah Albayt* or *Qahwah el jazoua* in Algeria, is not all that popular outside the cities except perhaps in Libya where Ottoman-Egyptian influences are at their strongest.

In the Meghrib generally if one asks for coffee one is offered French *café au lait*. Indeed in most cities the latter appears to have taken over the mantle of 'national beverage' from mint tea. Café au lait of course is coffee with milk – a lot of milk or, to put it another way, milk with a little coffee.

The North Africans when making coffee flavour it with a few drops of orange blossom water or a pinch of cinnamon. Below is their recipe for qahwah. The quantities are per person. Increase them accordingly. The amount of sugar depends on taste. The usual quantity is 1 teaspoon per person, but the North Africans often increase this to 2 – they do have a very sweet tooth!

There are two points to note. When buying the beans ask for 'Turkish' coffee beans. There are so many varieties of coffee available today that one has to be emphatic. The coffee is traditionally prepared in a *jazoua*. This is a small, long-handled metal pot (copper or brass) that is narrower at the top. You can buy these *jazouas*, in varying sizes, in most Indian stores as well as large department stores and shops specialising in kitchen equipment.

1 teaspoon sugar
1 coffee cup of water
1 teaspoon coffee

Mix the sugar and water together in the *jazoua* and bring to the boil, stirring, until the sugar has dissolved. Add the coffee, stir well and bring to the boil again. As the coffee froths up remove the *jazoua* from the heat and let the froth subside. Return the *jazoua* to the heat again until the froth reaches the brim and then remove once again. Repeat this process twice more. Remove from the heat and pour into a coffee cup. Do not add more sugar and never stir, for the sediments must not be disturbed.

In Morocco this type of coffee is often prepared without the sugar which is only added at the end.

If you wish you can add 1 or 2 drops of orange blossom water, either just before or just after removing from the heat for the last time. You can also add a pinch of cinnamon along with the coffee.

In parts of eastern Libya and amongst the Bedouins the coffee is often flavoured with cardamom (1/2 a seed per cup) and 1/4-1/2 teaspoon of powdered saffron per cup. The sugar is omitted. This coffee, known as *Qahwah Badawiya* or *Qahwah-al-hilo* has a slightly bitter flavour and is drunk a few sips at a time.

'Let the once-dead earth be a sign to them. We gave it life, and from it produced grain for their sustenance. We planted it with the palm and the vine and watered it with gushing springs, so that men might feed on its fruit. It was not their hands that made all this. Should they not give thanks?' The Koran

Naturally, the Prophet (blessed be his name) was generalising, for under no

circumstances can one say that Allah has been generous to his people. From the Atlantic to the Arabian Gulf, the people of peace (Islam) live under the most torrid desert or semi-desert conditions with very few of the above mentioned benefits (except for the palm) at their convenience.

Water is the scarcest commodity in the Meghrib. It is at its most plentiful in Morocco, its least in Libya. Hence water, springs and rivers have been worshipped for centuries. The Romans went to a great deal of trouble to bring water to their towns, but the Bedouin often has to perform his ablutions with sand instead of water.

The inventive James Richardson (in *Travels*) devised a plan whereby he saved (solely for his gratification) enough water to survive his difficult journey. This is what he did.

'Now for the stratagem. Apprehending this waste of water, I got twelve pint bottles filled with water at Tripoli, which were packed away as wine and spirits, neither Mohammad or Said [his servants] suspecting the contrary. Accordingly I quietly despatched my couple of bottles of aqua pura per day, as the London lady drinkers are said to take their sly drops from the far corner of the cupboard, without the least suspicion of my fellow travellers. I overheard, once, Mohammad speaking of me say "By God! these Christians, what lots of rum they drink; that's the reason, Said, the sun does not kill him – he'll never die. These Christians, Said, are the same as the daemons; they know everything, but God will punish them at last – if not, there's no God, or Prophet of God".'

Water sellers, juggling their ware, still do the rounds and for a small sum one can drink fresh natural spring water in the heat of the summer. Theirs is a dying trade, for the commercially packed plastic bottles offering either plain or sparkling mineral waters and all brands of locally produced 'soft' drinks have arrived.

Ice-making factories still churn out huge blocks of ice which are ceremonially sawed, covered in hessian bags and carried home to be cut into smaller pieces and added to water or home-made fruit drinks to ease the passing of a summer's day. In the narrow alleys of the kasbahs, indeed, on the corner of most main streets an 'orange juice man' stands patiently waiting for trade. His is a small home-made cart stacked with oranges, a fruit-squeezing machine, a dozen glasses and a bowl of water – for washing the glasses. Business is brisk. He cuts an orange in half, squeezes its juice into a glass and offers it to his customer who drinks, pays and departs. '*Shukran*' (Thank you). The flies, hovering above, every now and then make a swift dive, take a quick lick and fly back. Those more brave linger on the edges of the glasses, others foolishly take a swim, regardless of the consequences. In the heat of the summer drowning is perhaps the best way to go – for a fly!

The most popular fruit juice is orange but others, especially lemon and pomegranate, are also much sought after. I am well aware that most of my readers are versed in the preparation of home-made fruit juice so I will dispense with the simple ones where the fruit is squeezed and drunk straight. However, I would like to say a few words about some others which are prepared in the Meghrib.

lemonade

Add a lot of water to freshly squeezed lemon juice. Add sugar to taste and stir until dissolved. Add a few drops of orange blossom water and some ice and serve.

acir el qaress

If you wish to be a little more ambitious try this Algerian speciality, which makes enough for 6-8 glasses.

6 lemons
1 grapefruit
150g (5oz) sugar
2 x 1 litre (approx 1½ pints) bottles mineral water

Cut the lemons and grapefruit in half and squeeze out their juice. Pour into a large bowl. Add the sugar and mix thoroughly. Pass the mixture through a fine sieve into a serving bowl and serve with ice cubes and diluted with the mineral water. You can also prepare orangeade in this way.

acir tchina

12 oranges
1 lemon
1 grapefruit
8 tablespoons sugar
2 x 1 litre (about 1½ pints) bottles mineral water

Reserve 1 orange. Halve the remaining fruits and squeeze out the juice. Continue as with the recipe above. Peel the reserved orange, cut it into thin rounds and add to the orange mixture. Serve as above. **Makes 6-8 large glasses**

grape juice

If you have your own vine or can find grapes cheap enough try this drink. Use about 5kg (10lb) grapes and remove large stalks. Crush the grapes and pass through a sieve. Collect the juice in a bowl, add the juice of 1 small lemon and flavour with 1-2 tablespoons orange blossom water, 1/2 teaspoon cinnamon and 2-3 tablespoons sugar.

pomegranate juice

When pomegranates are available in the shops – they usually appear around Christmas time – don't ask yourself 'what do I do with these?' This is one recipe you should try. The colour alone is enchanting, never mind the taste.

Use about 5kg (10lb) pomegranates. Halve the fruit, remove the seeds and put in a liquidiser with a little water. Blend to a pulp. Pass this pulp through a fine sieve and collect in a bowl. Stir in the juice of 1 large ripe lemon, 3-4 tablespoons sugar (or more to taste) and 1 tablespoon orange blossom water. Stir well. Serve with ice, it is very nice!

And when you and your loved ones are seated in the comfort of your abode drinking this delectable red juice of pomegranate seeds think (for a moment at least) of the poor, love-torn Berber who sang this sad, sorrowful song:

'Oh my Yarma!
I followed the stream
To the pomegranate spring
To assuage my desire,

Its master was watching
From inside the house,
He shouted to me "Drop it! drop it!
Help! stop thief!"

God preserve me from such ignominy!
What! I, a thief?
I did not eat enough to satisfy me.
I did not carry any away on my back.
I only picked one
To assuage my desire.'

'The Unwritten Song,' Berber Folk song from Kabylis, Algeria

hlib bel louz

milk of almonds

A beautiful drink made from the milk of almonds. It is one of the most popular drinks in the Arab world and is usually drunk during religious festivals. There are many variations and I have given two, one from Libya and Egypt and the other from Morocco.

225g (1/2lb) ground almonds
900ml (11/2 pints) water
675g (11/2lb) sugar
2 tablespoons orange blossom water or rosewater

Put the ground almonds into a muslin cloth or bag and fasten securely. Place the water in a large bowl, add the bag of almonds and leave for about 1-11/2 hours rubbing and squeezing it occasionally to release the almond milk and turn the water milky. Finally squeeze the bag tightly to extract every last drop of the almond milk.

Pour the almond milk into a large saucepan, add the sugar and bring slowly to the boil, stirring constantly until the sugar dissolves. Just before removing from the heat stir in the orange blossom water or rosewater. Pour into a jug and leave to cool. Refrigerate until needed. Serve, diluted to taste, with ice-cold water or ice cubes.

moroccan variation

225g (1/2lb) ground almonds
900ml (11/2 pints) water
2.5 l (4 pints) milk
275g (10oz) caster sugar
3 tablespoons orange blossom water

Follow the recipe above mixing the water and milk together before soaking the bag of ground almonds. Only heat the almond milk enough to dissolve the sugar – do not boil. Serve as above.

sahleb

resin drink

This drink is made with *sahleb – Satyricum hircinum* – which is a resin sold in hard form. It is very expensive and rather difficult to trace, but well worth the effort – as any Middle Easterner will agree.

Popular in Egypt and Libya, it makes a wonderful winter's drink.

600ml (1 pint) milk
1 teaspoon ground sahleb
2 teaspoons finely chopped pistachios or a mixture of almonds and walnuts
Pinch of ground cinnamon

Heat the milk in a saucepan, add the sahleb and stir constantly until the mixture comes to the boil. Lower the heat and simmer for 10-15 minutes, stirring frequently. Pour into small dessert cups, sprinkle with the nuts and cinnamon and serve. **Serves 4**

hlib bil assel

milk and honey drink

A favourite with mountain folk, it is tasty and refreshing.

900ml (1¹/2 pints) milk
4 teaspoons honey
1 tablespoon caster sugar
Juice 1 lemon
About 110g (4oz) finely chopped strawberries or stoned cherries

Place the milk, honey and sugar in a large bowl and whisk vigorously for 5-10 minutes. Stir in the lemon juice and chopped fruit. Refrigerate until ready to serve, in tall glasses with ice. **Serves 6**

rouwayneh

libyan millet and fenugreek drink

A most unusual drink made with millet, fenugreek, fennel, wheat and cumin seeds.
It is normally prepared in very large quantities and it is believed to have many
medicinal properties, particularly for stomach ache.

I find that this drink is definitely an acquired taste, but Libyans swear by it!

50g (2oz) millet
50g (2oz) chickpeas
15g (1/2oz) fennel seeds
15g (1/2oz) cumin seeds
15g (1/2oz) whole allspice
50g (2oz) whole wheat
50g (2oz) fenugreek

Put all the ingredients, with the exception of the fenugreek, on a large baking sheet
and place in an oven preheated to 350F, 180C, Gas Mark 4 for about 20 minutes or
until they begin to change colour. Remove from the oven, mix in the fenugreek and
leave to cool.

Reduce this mixture to a powder (a coffee grinder is excellent for this task!), then
store in a tightly sealed jar.

To serve, mix 1 level tablespoon of the powder in a glass with 1 tablespoon of sugar
and cold water. Some people like to strain this mixture through fine muslin into another
glass to get rid of the coarser sediments. **Makes 24-30 glasses**

— glossary —

azem mujafaff

– dry bones –

Beef or sheep's bones with a little meat still clinging to them are washed, rubbed all over with cooking salt and left to rest overnight in a dry place. They are then put out to dry under the sun for 5-6 days. These bones are used in such dishes as tajines and couscous. Make sure the bones are really dry. Will keep for 4-5 weeks.

baharat

– mixed spices –

This is similar to allspice (*bahar*), but includes cumin, coriander, black pepper and paprika. To prepare mix together 1 tablespoon of each. Store in a small jar and use as required.

cherbet

– syrup –

Traditionally syrup was prepared with honey, but today it is often replaced by a sugar syrup, although in certain regions of Morocco and Libya honey is still predominantly used. The syrup comes in two densities – very thin and runny, and very thick like honey or treacle.

Syrup used in North Africa is usually flavoured with orange blossom water. This contrasts with the predominant use of rosewater in the Middle East. The amount of flavouring is entirely a matter of personal taste, but generally speaking the further east one travels through the Meghrib the less scented is the syrup.

900ml (1¹/₂ pints) water
450g (1lb) sugar
Juice 1 lemon
90ml (3fl oz) orange blossom water

Place the water, sugar and lemon juice in a saucepan and bring to the boil, stirring constantly until the sugar dissolves. Lower the heat and simmer for 5-10 minutes for a thin syrup or 20-25 minutes for a thick syrup. A few minutes before the end of the cooking time add the orange blossom water and stir well. Remove from the heat and leave to cool. This syrup will store well and can be re-used.

harissa

– hot sauce –

This is the national spice of Tunisia, although it does appear in both the Algerian and Libyan cuisines. The Tunisian cuisine is highly seasoned and harissa is used in almost every dish – except desserts!

In the countryside children are often fed with a slice of bread spread with a thin layer of harissa diluted with a little olive oil and tomato purée. This is very like the Middle East of my childhood when a slice of bread was rubbed with garlic and a little salt. Only the rich in my town could afford the tomato purée!

You can make your own harissa with the recipe below. However small tins of Tunisian harissa can be purchased from most Indian and Middle Eastern stores. Ask for 'harissa sauce for couscous'.

225g (8oz) dried hot chilli peppers
4 cloves garlic, peeled
3-4 tablespoons water
1 tablespoon coriander
1 teaspoon ground caraway
1 tablespoon salt

Cut the peppers in half and remove seeds and stalks. Place the peppers in a large bowl of water and leave to soak for 30 minutes. Drain and place in a liquidiser with the garlic and water and blend to a purée. Scrape into a bowl and mix the coriander, caraway and salt in thoroughly. Store in a covered jar and use as instructed with relevant dishes.

hilba

– fenugreek paste –

This Libyan paste is made with fenugreek (*Trigonella foenum-graecum*) and coriander. It is popular throughout Egypt and the Arabian peninsula, particularly in the Yemen where it is not only used extensively in all kinds of dishes, but is often used as a spread on bread or as a dip.

You should be able to buy fenugreek seeds from Indian grocery stores. Some of the large commercial spice companies also produce them.

2 teaspoons fenugreek seeds
180ml (6fl oz) cold water
3 cloves garlic
75g (3oz) fresh coriander leaves, chopped
1 level teaspoon salt
1 tablespoon lemon juice
2 small hot chillies, seeded

Place the fenugreek and water in a cup and leave to soak for 24 hours. Drain off the water and transfer the seeds to a liquidiser. Add all the remaining ingredients and blend to a smooth purée. Spoon into a jar, seal and store in the refrigerator. Use as specified in relevant recipes.

khli

– dried meat –

This highly specialised dried meat is the pride and joy of the Moroccan cuisine. Berber by origin, its roots go back to time immemorial. Usually made in vast quantities *khli* is particularly beloved by the people of Fez and Marrakech. It is also popular in Algeria and Libya where it is better known as *khadid*.

The recipe below is for 5kg (11lb) of meat only. You can make more or less accordingly. It is time consuming to prepare and has three distinct preparation steps – marination, drying and cooking.

marinade
50g (2oz) cooking salt
40g (1¹/₂oz) ground coriander
8g (¹/₄oz) cumin
1 clove garlic, crushed
¹/₂ tablespoon vinegar
1 tablespoon oil

drying
5kg (11lb) beef

cooking
900g (2lb) beef fat
2.5 l (4 pints) water
2 l (3¹/₃ pints) groundnut oil
250ml (8fl oz) olive oil

First prepare the marinade, called *chermoula*, by mixing all the ingredients together in a large bowl. Set aside.

For convenience sake ask your butcher to cut the beef into long 3-4cm(1-1¹/₂in) thick strips. Wash them under cold running water and drain. Add these strips to the marinade and mix well making sure that each one is well coated. Cover and leave overnight. The next day mix again and then leave for a further 5-6 hours.

Now put the strips of meat out to dry. (Reserve any remaining marinade.) In North Africa it would be in the courtyard, but in Britain it will probably have to be in the kitchen or larder. In fact in this land of abundance – of cats, dogs and rain, the larder is perhaps the safest, though not necessarily the ideal, place. Thread string through the ends of the strips and suspend from a clothes-line with pegs. Leave to dry for 8-10 days or longer until thoroughly dry. To check try this simple method. Cut a little of the meat with a sharp knife. If there is no trace of moisture inside then the meat is ready.

To cook cut the fat into 1cm (1/2in) cubes, rinse in a colander and drain. Place in a large saucepan, cover with the water and bring to the boil. Lower the heat, cover the pan and simmer for 10 minutes. Add the remaining ingredients, the dried meat and whatever remains of the marinade. Return to the boil and cook over a moderate heat, stirring occasionally until the water has completely evaporated. To check that the *khli* is done break a piece with your fingers.

Pour the fat into a large container and place the meat in a large bowl – traditionally a *gsaa*. When cold transfer the meat to large earthenware jars or large preserving jars. Pour the still liquid fat over the meat until completely covered. Leave for 2-3 hours or until completely cold. Seal tightly to make the jars airtight and store. Use as directed in relevant recipes.

Khli is traditionally prepared once a year in enormous quantities – often 100-150kg (220-330lb) at a time. Once prepared the meat can be kept for up to 2 years. Nothing of course is wasted by the canny folk from the hills and as there are often smaller pieces of meat and marinade left in the bottom of the pan these are reheated, removed, cooled and stored separately. This is called agrisse and is used in the preparation of several dishes e.g. *Rghaif el Ferrani*.

mergues

– spicy sausage –

These are hot, spicy sausages popular throughout North Africa, but are best in Tunisia. They are very versatile, and can be grilled, baked, cooked in omelettes etc. In recent years they have appeared in France, brought when the *pieds-noirs* (French North Africans) returned from Algeria en masse. Although they are now sold by French butchers, the best are still to be found in the small Tunisian café-restaurants that have sprung up all over French cities.

Another sausage, *saucisse de foie*, is made with liver – usually calf but sometimes chicken. It is grey in colour and is less spicy than the classic Mergues.

900g (2lb) lean lamb or beef
175g (6oz) beef fat
4 cloves garlic
1/2 teaspoon cinnamon
1/2 teaspoon chilli pepper
2 teaspoons harissa (see page 292)
1 tablespoon powdered fennel seeds
150ml (1/4 pint) oil
1 teaspoon ground coriander
1 tablespoon salt
1 teaspoon black pepper
About 1m (40in) sheep or beef intestines, cleaned

Mince the meat, fat and garlic together and transfer to a large bowl. Add the remaining ingredients (except the intestines) and knead for several minutes until smooth and well blended.

Meanwhile soak the intestines in cold water for 3 hours, which makes them easier to handle. To put the mixture into the intestines you need a plastic funnel with a nozzle width of about 2.5cm (1in).

Fit one end of the intestine over the nozzle and gently work the whole of the intestine onto the nozzle. Force the meat down through the funnel into the intestine. As the intestine fills up it will slip off the nozzle. When the whole intestine is full run it lightly through one hand to distribute the meat evenly. Set aside. Continue until you have used up all the meat.

To make into sausages, fold one intestine in half and then tie or knot at 15cm (6in) intervals. Leave to hang over the sink for 4-5 hours before using. Store in the refrigerator for a few days or freeze until required.

olives

A basic ingredient that appears throughout the cuisines. I am well aware that in Britain and Europe we find olives already preserved or stuffed, but I have nevertheless included these simple olive preservation methods more for interest than for every day practical use.

There are of course several types of olives, but the main choice is between violet, green and black.

Below are some simplified methods for their preservation. The Meghribi housewives use much larger quantities, but I have satisfied myself with a sample of 5kg (about 11lb) for each type of olive.

– green olives –

5kg (11lb) green olives

Break the olives with a stone and wash in a colander under cold running water for 3-4 minutes. Transfer them to a large jar or preserving bottles and cover with cold water. For the following 3 days change the water twice a day or until the olives are no longer bitter – you may have to continue changing water for a further 1-2 days. When the olives are mellow fill the bottles up to the brim with fresh water and cover.

– black olives –

5kg (11lb) black olives, damaged or over-ripe ones discarded
1.1kg (2¹/₂lb) salt
Groundnut oil

Clean and wash olives in a colander under cold running water for 3-4 minutes. Now mix in the salt, set the colander in a large bowl and leave to drain. It is advisable to weigh the olives down with 2 or 3 large stones or bricks – this helps a black liquid to exude.

Five days later spread the olives out on a large plastic cloth and leave in the sun! You may now say 'what sun?' Let us hope that all this will be happening when there is a little sun available – if not then continue this procedure in a warm corner of your kitchen. Let the olives rest for 2 days then return them to the colander with stones on top for another 5 days. Repeat this procedure 3 more times.

Now spread the olives once more under the sun – we are now really tempting providence! – or in your warm kitchen, for 3 days. Rub in some groundnut oil until they are all well coated. The olives are now ready. Pack them tightly into jars and cover.

– violet olives –

5kg (11lb) violet olives
15kg (33lb) bitter oranges (elrang is the local type)
1.2kg (2¹/₂lb) salt

Violet olives are those coloured between green and black, when they are just before full ripeness. With a sharp knife make an incision from top to bottom of each olive as far in as the stone. Wash in a colander under cold running water for 2-3 minutes. Transfer to jars or bottles, fill with cold water, seal and store for 4 weeks. Change the water, add fresh water, cover, seal and leave for a further 12 days.

At the end of this period buy the bitter oranges. Wash, peel and quarter them and mix with the salt. Rub through a sieve and collect the juice. Empty the water from the bottles and replace it with the bitter orange juice. Fill to the brim. Seal the bottles and keep for at least 5-6 days before use.

If the orange juice is not enough top up with water.

There is the charming story of the old Berber who, realising that his end was nigh, went to his garden and spoke to it. 'Look after my children after I am dead.'

The garden said, 'No! Gardens live in the present with those who daily labour with us.'

The old Berber went to his fields and pleaded, 'Look after my children when I am gone.'

The fields replied, 'No! We cannot foretell the future. We know not the ways of nature and we need human help.'

Finally the old man went to his olive grove. 'When I am dead, look after my children.' 'Very well,' whispered the leaves and branches, 'we will, even if your children never come to look after us. We will always give them our goodness.'

ouarka or malsougua or dioul

– paper-thin dough –

These are different names for the same paper-thin pastry dough which is used to make *bastela*, *breiks* and pancakes. Traditionally they are prepared on charcoal-heated ovens called *tbsil dial ouarka*, but a little home ingenuity – a heavy-based frying pan or copper crêpe pan – will give satisfactory results.

Although you can substitute this pastry with commercial filo I suggest you attempt these thin transparent sheets at least once.

The recipe below is for twelve sheets – increase or decrease quantities according to relevant recipes.

Tunisians use only semolina as a base, but Moroccans and Algerians also include sifted flour.

175g (6oz) fine semolina
175g (6oz) plain flour, sifted
1/4 teaspoon salt
600ml (1 pint) water
7 tablespoons olive oil

If you have a small moveable charcoal grill or a primus stove the preparation of these sheets of pastry will be much simplified. If not then I suggest you improvise. Fill a large deep saucepan, about 25cm (10in) in diameter, three-quarters full with water. Invert a large, heavy-based frying pan over it and bring the water to the boil over a moderate heat.

Meanwhile prepare the batter by placing the semolina and flour in a large bowl. Add the salt and half the water and knead for several minutes. Now little by little add the remaining water, stirring continuously until it has all been absorbed. Continue kneading for at least another 10 minutes, lifting the batter and beating it against the sides of the bowl. The batter should be just liquid enough to find its own level. Cover the batter with 1.5mm (1/16in) water and leave for about 1 hour.

To cook, brush the surface of the hot inverted pan with a little of the oil. Now wipe the surface with a clean cloth or paper towel so that there is only a light film of oil left on the surface. Lightly wet your hands with cold water and scoop up a handful of the batter. Tap the hot pan with the dough by lowering and raising your hand regularly – the dough will be deftly caught as it touches the hot surface and will leave a fine layer each time. Take care not to burn your fingertips. When the pan is covered with the batter remove the dough by lifting it with a palette knife and place it on a clean cloth, shiny side up – so that the sheets don't stick to each other. Lightly re-oil the pan between preparing each sheet. Repeat with remaining batter and stack the cooked sheets on top of each other. Wrap in a clean cloth to prevent them drying and then proceed with relevant recipe.

If you are not going to use them immediately then brush the edge of each sheet of dough with a little oil, wrap in a cloth and then in foil. They will keep like this for 2-3 days.

If there are any large holes in the pastry return it to the pan and dab some more batter to fill the gap. And if any pastry is torn do not throw it away, but set aside. It can be used in *bastela* recipes or to strengthen *breik* recipes.

ras-el-hanout

– 'Head of the shop' spice –

A mixture of spices and herbs. This is the spice of the feast of Aid el Kebir, of Mrouziya and many wintery dishes. It is used with most poultry and game dishes. It was also widely used as a medicine against colds etc.

Nowadays, outside Meghribi villages, *ras-el-hanout* can be bought ready-made in all *souk-el-attarines* (spice markets) of North Africa.

There were well over twenty-five spices and herbs involved in the preparation of this spice, but today only those that are readily available are used. Here, for your edification, I have listed the more important ones. If you mix approximately 1 tablespoon of each you can achieve a very good substitute.

Rosebud (*Boutons de roses*) – imported from Persia by the Arabs

Belladonna berries

Cinnamon

Chinese cinnamon (*dar el Sini ed dûn*)

Cardamom

Cloves

Kebala (*cubèbe*) – a grey perfumed pepper also known as West African black pepper

Turmeric

Wall bromegrass (*Tharrâ*), from Sudan – a very aromatic rhizome, the fruit of the ash tree, and reputed to have aphrodisiac qualities

The roots of the lesser galangal (*Galanga officinalis*)

Ginger

German iris

Common lavender (*khuzama*) – the flowers

Bsibsa (Java almond) – the shell or husk that covers the almond and also the nut

Gouza Sahraouia (*Maniguette*) – grains of the Zingiberaceae family, from the Ivory coast

Black cumin

Jamaican hot peppers

Palma christi (castor oil plant)

Dar Felfell – the fruit of the 'long Malayan' pepper

Black pepper

reuchta

The name *reuchta* (meaning 'thread') is of Persian origin and has passed into the Arabic language.

There are two main varieties of this pasta: *reuchta jda* (very thin noodles) and *noissara* (1 cm or 1/2in thick, square noodles).

225g (8oz) plain flour
1/2 teaspoon salt
1 large egg, beaten
Water

Sift the flour and salt into a large bowl and make a well in the centre. Add the egg and 2 tablespoons of water and knead until you have a stiff dough. Add a little more water if necessary. Transfer to a floured work surface and knead for about 10 minutes.

Divide the dough into two balls. Taking one at a time, roll each portion out as thinly as possible. To prevent the dough sticking sprinkle with cornflour occasionally. When they are both rolled out leave them for 45 minutes.

Fold each sheet in half, fold in half again and again and so on until it is impossible to fold over anymore. Cut crossways into 1/2cm (1/4in) wide strips. Unroll the coils of dough, lay out on a cloth and leave to dry for 45-60 minutes or until completely dry. Store in jars.

To cook, bring some lightly salted water to the boil in a large saucepan, add the noodles and simmer for 5-6 minutes. The exact time will depend on thickness of noodles. Drain and use as required.

rghaif

This is a very versatile dough which can be wrapped around savoury or sweet fillings or fried as pancakes and served either sprinkled with sugar and cinnamon or dipped in honey.

An Algerian version uses fine semolina instead of the flour, as in M'Hadjeb.

450g (1lb) flour
2 teaspoons salt
15g (1/2oz) fresh yeast or 8g (1/4oz) dried yeast, diluted in
3 tablespoons warm water
300ml (1/2 pint) tepid water
3 tablespoons oil

Sift the flour and salt into a large bowl and make a well in the middle. Add the diluted yeast and, little by little, the water. Knead briskly until a dough is formed. Transfer to a work top and knead for at least 20 minutes until very pliable and elastic. Coat your hands with a little of the oil and roll the ball of dough between them until well greased. Divide the dough into smaller balls – their size depends on the recipe you are following. Make sure your hands are always oily.

smen

– clarified butter –

Smen is the same as the Middle Eastern *samna* and similar to *ghee* which is extensively used in Indian cooking. It is better known as clarified butter.

Today throughout North Africa and the Middle East, it is less and less used, except in the countryside where peasants still prepare their own *smen*.

Replace it with unsalted butter. The recipe below is included for reference.

1kg (2lb 4oz) salted butter

Melt the butter in a pan over a low heat, stirring regularly. With a slotted spoon skim off the residue while boiling. When the butter has melted pour it into a jar through fine muslin. Leave to cool, then cover and store. *Smen* can be kept for up to a year.

It is the best to use when making sweets and desserts since it will be lighter and clearer than commercial butter. Of course you can always use ghee which is easily available in all Indian and other large grocery stores.

— map of north africa —

SPAIN

MEDITERRANEAN SEA

Bône
(Annaba)

Algiers

Constantine   Tunis

Tangier   Tetuan   Oran   Sous

ATLANTIC OCEAN   Tlemcen   Kairawan   Kerkennah
                                                                              Islands
Rabat   Meknez   Sfax (Safagis)
Casablanca   Djerba
         Fez   TUNISIA
MOROCCO   Tripoli
         ATLAS MOUNTAINS
Marrakech   ALGERIA

                                                              Ghadames

                                                                        LIBYA

                                SAHARA

                                                        Ghat

bibliography

Africa – A Geographical Study, A. B. Mountjoy and C. Embleton, London 1965

A History of Africa, J. P. Fage, Hutchinson & Co., London 1978

A History of the Maghrib, J. A. Abun-Nasr, Cambridge University Press, 1971

Algeria and Sahara, Valerie and Jon Stevens, Constable, London 1977

A Manual of Hadith, Maulana Muhammad Ali, Curzon Press, 1944

Au Anthology of Moorish Poetry, transl. A. J. Arberry, Cambridge University Press, 1953

Auto Nomad in Barbary, Wilson MacArthur, Cassell, London 1950

By Bus to the Sahara, Gordon West, The Travel Book Club, London 1948

Cambridge History of Islam (Vols 1 & 2), ed. P. M. Holt, Cambridge, 1970

Chants du Maghreb, Abdelmajid Ramada, Fedala (Maroc), 1958

Description de l'Afrique, Johannes Leo Africanus, transl. A. Epaulard (2 vols), Paris 1956

Description du Maghreb et de l'Europe au III–X siècles, Hadj-Sadok Mohammad, Carbonel, Algiers 1949

Holy Bible, King James version

In the Lap of Atlas, Richard Hughes, Chatto & Windus, London 1979

Islam, Muhammad Zafrulla Khan, Routledge & Kegan Paul, London 1962

Jardins de Marrakech, Abdelhanine Sebbata, Seppea, Marrakech, Morocco

Kitab-al-Ibar, Book 1, Abd-ar-Rahman Abu Zayd Ibn Khaldun

L'Afrique Romaine, Eugene Albertini, Algiers 1949

La Peste (the Plague), Albert Camus, transl. Stuart Gilbert. Hamish Hamilton, London 1947

La Poésie Arabe maghre'bine d'Expression Populaire, Arabic and French text by M. Delhaflaoui, François Maspero, Paris 1980

Larousse Gastronomique, ed. N. Froud and C. Turgeon, Hamlyn, London 1961

Marriage Ceremonies in Morocco, R. Westermarck, Macmillan & Co., London 1914

North African Journey, Bernard Newman, Robert Hale, London 1955

North West Africa, Wilfrid Knapp, Oxford University Press, 1977

Notes on the Bedouins and Wahabis, J. L. Burckhardt, ed. Duseley, London 1831

Paraboles et Contes d'Afrique du Nord, J. Scelles-Millie, G. P. Maisonneuve et Larose, Paris 1982

Poèmes Kabyles Anciens, Mouloud Mammeri, François Maspere, Paris 1980

Tales of Mystic Meaning, transl. and ed. R. A. Nicholson, Chapman & Hall, London 1931

The Arab Revival, Francesco Gabrieli, transl. L. F. Edwards, Thames & Hudson, London 1961

The Eastern Key (Kitab Al-Afadah wa'l-Itibar), Abd Al-Latif al-Baghdadi, transl. R. H. Zand and J. A. I. E. Videan, George Allen & Unwin Ltd, London 1965

The Golden Trade of the Moors, E. W. Bovill, Oxford University Press, London 1968

The Histories, Herodotus, transl. A. J. Arberry, Cambridge University Press, 1953

The Koran, transl. N. J. Dawood, Penguin, London 1956

The Life of Belisarius, Lord Mahon, London 1848

The Magaddimah, Abd-ar-Rahman Abu Zayd Ibn Khaldun, transl. F. Rosenthal (3 vols), Bollingen, New York 1958

The Unwritten Song, W. R. Trask (Vol 1), Jonathan Cape, London 1969

The Voices of Marrakech, Elias Canetti, transl. J. A. Underwood, Marion Boyars, London 1978

Traditions et Coutumes des Communautés Musulmanes et Juives, Eddif International, Paris 1981

Travels in the Great Desert of Sahara, 1845-1846, James Richardson, Richard Bentley (2 vols), London 1848

Travels in Syria and the Holy Land, J. L. Burckhardt, ed. Lt Col W. Leake, London 1822

Tunisia, Anthony Sylvester, The Bodley Head, London 1969

Wit and Wisdom in Morocco, E. Westermarck, George Routledge & Son Ltd, London 1955

index